SAVITZ

Criminal Violence

Criminal Violence

National Patterns and
Behavior

Lynn A. Curtis

Lexington Books
D.C. Heath and Company
Lexington, Massachusetts
Toronto   London

Library of Congress Cataloging in Publication Data

Curtis, Lynn A.
  Criminal violence.

  Bibliography: p.
  Includes indexes.
    1. Crime and criminals—United States. 2. Violence—United States.
  3. Victims of crime—United States. I. Title.
  HV6791.C87   364'.973   74-15535
  ISBN 0-669-96024-1

Published simultaneously in Canada.

Printed in the United States of America.

International Standard Book Number: 0-669-96024-1

Library of Congress Catalog Card Number: 74-15535

To My Parents

Contents

List of Figures

List of Tables

Foreword

The study of violence is not new. Nor is the examination of crimes of violence. But when the National Commission on the Causes and Prevention of Violence (1968-69), under the chairmanship of Milton Eisenhower, sought to study in detail the major crimes of homicide, rape, assault, and robbery, James Short and I, who were serving as codirectors of research, realized that much new research was needed. Consequently, we enlisted the talents of Lynn Curtis to join the staff of Melvin Tumin and Donald Mulvihill of the Task Force on Crimes of Violence. I was aware of his varied background of training in the United States and in England, and aware that he had enormous energy and devotion to scholarship, but I was unprepared for the extent of Curtis's prodigious work and his continued insight and capacity to develop new areas of research.

Offender-victim relationships were first discussed systematically by Mendelsohn and von Hentig. I tried to add some empirical display to their theoretical concepts in a study of criminal homicide. Edward Green on robbery, Menachim Amir on rape, André Normandeau on robbery, and Stanley Turner on the ecology of juvenile delinquents and their victims added more victim-offender studies. This work by Lynn Curtis covers a greater variety of crimes of violence, describes a large seventeen-city survey that covers the whole country, and gives details in a comprehensive style not previously presented.

The statistical analyses are solid and sound. They reach beyond the work done by the National Violence Commission and offer descriptive material that scholars and practitioners should find useful for future research and policy planning. The author has virtually exhausted the cross-references of the data available to him, has presented a discussion more lively than the usual table talk of much sociological research, and deserves the wide dissemination of his study which I trust this publication will provide.

Social research and public policy have only recently become keenly aware of the criminal victim and victim-offender relationships. The victim surveys conducted by the Law Enforcement Assistance Administration and the Bureau of the Census, public concern with victims of rape, and legislative moves to provide victim compensation in crimes of violence are a few indexes of this awareness. The work presented here provides important data to be considered in discussions of any of these topics.

The author cites and considers most other research and descriptive studies that have any relationship to the original material in this study. He also makes cross-cultural and international comparisons, which he has handled with caution and respect for the many qualifying conditions that make such comparisons difficult.

The mark of painstaking search and research is clearly present. If the reader carefully reads through the abundant materials offered in this volume, he will not become overwhelmed; instead he will increasingly appreciate the richness of this work as a source document, as a reference compendium, and as a statistical analysis that can form a firm base for a developing theory.

Marvin E. Wolfgang

Philadelphia
November 1974

Preface

Criminal Violence presents the results of a 1967 national survey of criminal homicide, aggravated assault, forcible rape, and robbery. The objectives are to provide a unifying source of base-line data on major violent crime, to determine the extent to which the four criminal behavior systems merge, and to analyze the most clearcut national and regional patterns for the same variables used in comparable American and foreign studies.

Supervision of the national survey was one activity of the author as Assistant Director of the Task Force on Individual Acts of Violence of the National Commission on the Causes and Prevention of Violence. Although some of the data tables, such as race of offender by race of victim, received considerable national publicity and have since come into the common knowledge of experts, there was only time for a very preliminary discussion of the survey in the *Crimes of Violence* Task Force Report of the Commission. The survey data were then more completely analyzed as a doctoral dissertation at the University of Pennsylvania. The present volume is a revision and elaboration undertaken at the Bureau of Social Science Research.

The national survey covered seventeen cities. In the sample, police reports were photocopied and sent to the Violence Commission in Washington, D.C. under the guidance of professionals in each city. These people, already burdened with the responsibilities of highly demanding positions, contributed their expertise and time without pay. Without them and their assistants, the survey would not have been possible. In Atlanta were Dr. John T. Doby, Chairman, Department of Sociology and Anthropology, Emory University and Mrs. Maryann Albrecht; in Boston, Professor Stephan Schafer, Department of Sociology and Anthropology, Northeastern University; in Chicago, Mr. Charles N. Cooper, Cook County Office of Economic Opportunity; in Cleveland, Dr. Charles McCaghy, Department of Sociology, Case Western Reserve University; in Dallas, Dr. Sidney J. Miller, Department of Sociology, Southern Methodist University; in Denver, Professor Gresham M. Sykes, Director, Administration of Justice Program, University of Denver College of Law; in Detroit, Dr. Eliot Luby, Lafayette Clinic; in Los Angeles, Dr. Gilbert Geis, Department of Sociology, California State College at Los Angeles; in Miami, Mr. Victor H. Mealy, Director, Head Start Social Service, Dade County Public Schools; in Minneapolis, Dr. John Clark, Department of Sociology, University of Minnesota; in New Orleans, Dr. Robert E. Tournier, Department of Sociology, Tulane University; in New York, Dr. John Martin, Department of Sociology, Fordham University; in Philadelphia, Dr. Thorsten Sellin, Professor Emeritus, University of Pennsylvania and Co-Director, Center for Studies in Criminology and Criminal Law, University of Pennsylvania and Dr. Frank Cannavale, Department of Sociology and Center for Studies in Criminology and Criminal Law, University of Pennsylvania; in St. Louis, Dr. Nelson Heller, Resource Allocation Unit, St. Louis Metropolitan Police Department; in San Francisco, Mr. Thomas J. Sweeney, Assistant Executive Director San Francisco Committee on Crime and Mr. William B. Smith; in Seattle, Dr. Clarence Schrag, Department of Sociology, University of Washington and Mr. Jack Craig.

Just as important was the excellent cooperation received from the police in each city for an endeavor that was often troublesome and time-consuming. The following Police Chiefs and department staff members were involved (although many of them, as many of the social science professionals, have since moved on to other places or positions): in Atlanta, Superintendent Fred Beerman, Assistant Superintendent Charles W. Blackwell, and Assistant Superintendent Clinton Chaffin; in Boston, Commissioner Edmund McNamara; in Chicago, Superintendent James B. Conlisk, Chief Otto Kreuzer of the Detective Division, Deputy Chief Michael Spiotto of the Detective Division, Director Carl Miller of the Records Division, and Mr. Bart Ranier of the Data Processing Division; in Cleveland, Chief Patrick Gerity, Patrolman Charles L. Greiner, Systems Analyst, Detective Inspector James M. Limber, Lt. Howard A. Blackwell, and Lt. Joseph F. Mongel; in Dallas, Chief Carl Batchelor and Sgt. Charles Elwonger, who directed the staff of the Research and Development Section; in Denver, Chief G.L. Seaton; in Detroit, Commissioner Johannes F. Spreen and Inspector Jack Shoemaker, Commanding Officer, Record Bureau; in Los Angeles, Chief Thomas Reddin and Douglas McFadgen of the Records and Identification Division; in Miami, Chief Walter E. Headley and Capt. K.E. Fox; in Minneapolis, Superintendent Calvin Hawkinson; in New Orleans, Superintendent Joseph I. Giarrusso; in New York, Commissioner Howard Leary, Chief Inspector Sanford D. Garelik, and Capt. James Meehan; in Philadelphia, Commissioner Frank L. Rizzo; in St. Louis, Chief Curtis Brostron; in San Francisco, Chief Thomas J. Cahill and Director Dennis Smith, Bureau of Identification; in Seattle, Chief Frank Ramon and Lt. Roy Skagen; in Washington, D.C., Chief John B. Layton, Assistant Chief Charles K. Wright of the Technical Services Division, Inspector William D. Foran of the Criminal Investigation Division, Lt. Patrick L. Burke and Sgt. Bernard F. Kelly of the Homicide Squad, Detective Sergeant Frank Rinaldo, Detective Sergeant Embrey Minor, and Detective Edward Guggenheim of the Sex Squad, Capt. Ralph L. Stines of the Robbery Squad, Capt. Clark W. Hamm and Detective Mathew J. Vinciguerra of C.I.D. East and Sgt. Louis A. Fantacci of C.I.D. West.

During the Violence Commission, James Short, Co-Director of Research, provided that blend of insight and kindness for which he is so well known. Donald Mulvihill, Co-Director of the Task Force, boss and colleague during the good times and bad, fire ant attorney, and dear friend, has helped in so many fruitful ways. He is that rare Irishman, one with a harem. As the other Co-Director of the Task Force, Melvin Tumin lent advice on the design of the survey. James Campbell, General Council on the Violence Commission but a better political scientist and sociologist than most, has always been encouraging and intellectually stimulating. With competence and grace, Elizabeth Kutzke served as assistant director of the survey through the data collection and initial analysis. Robert Tigner was assistant director for the spatial investigation and did a fine job. (If only he hadn't always won at tennis.) After the Violence Commission ran out of cash, a grant from the Center for Studies in Criminology and Criminal Law at the University of Pennsylvania saved the day and paid for the computer generated maps in the areal study. Richard Abbott guided well the vast amount of computer work. Professionally innovative but personally constant, he was, in spite of his modesty, the smarts of the Assist. Frank Devolder, Chief Automated Data Management Services Division, and John Perdue, Chief, Systems and Programming Section, General Services Administration worked with us in developing the survey coding sheets.

To N.I.M.H., Saleem Shah, and George Weber, grateful appreciation for dissertation traineeship support. During that phase, Phillip Sagi forced combat with all the nagging methodological and substantive problems that one would prefer to rationalize as not being there. Sarah Boggs skillfully unwound the complexities of ecological analysis.

At the First International Symposium on Victimology, Israel Drapkin supplied many hard-to-get papers that contributed to new ideas. His hospitality and charm in Jerusalem will be remembered by many of us. Director of the Bureau of Social Science Research, Robert Bower approved professional activity time for the revision, let all the typing flow through the pool and was tolerant of the author's fits of deviance. Albert Biderman sifted the manuscript with that crabby but humane non-linear intellect, yielding all manner of helpful fallout.

Antonette Simplicio orchestrated the typing at BSSR and secretly really does enjoy all our screamings at one another. The work of Edward Smith, Deborah Besman, Amy Goodman, Prem Khurana, Jean Malenab, Diane Meyers, Delores Mitchell, Gail Rothberg, Balbir Singh, Catherine Valentour, and Judith White was most appreciated. The first draft (the dissertation) was done for free on an old Smith Corona. It was an outrageous amount of work, and the typist had to be either mad or Mother. My love to Mother.

The most is owed to Marvin Wolfgang, professional mentor, financial underwriter, personal stabilizer, a wise and vigorous man who always comes through.

Acknowledgments

Permission to use copyrighted material has been given by Art Buchwald, *Connection* magazine, the Dallas Morning News, *The Thunderbolt*, and the Universal Press Syndicate. The material from R. Guy, "Black Perspectives on Harlem's State of Mind" is reprinted by permission of the *New York Times,* © 1972. The excerpt from J. McIntyre, "Public Attitudes Toward Crime and Law Enforcement" is reprinted from Vol. 374 of the *Annals of the American Academy of Political and Social Science,* © 1967. The quotation from M. Arnold, "The Silent Murders," is reprinted by permission from the *National Observer,* © Dow Jones and Company, Inc., 1971. The material from R. LeVine, "Gussi Sex Offenses: A Study in Social Control," is reproduced by permission of the American Anthropological Association from the *American Anthropologist* Vol. 61, No. 6, 1959 and is not for further reproduction. Excerpts from W. Connor, "Criminal Homicide, U.S.S.R./U.S.A.: Reflections on Soviet Data in a Comparative Framework," is reprinted by special permission of the *Journal of Criminal Law and Criminology,* © 1973 by Northwestern University School of Law, Vol. 64, No. 1. The quotation from F. Zimring, "The Medium is the Message: Firearm Caliber as a Determinant of Death from Assault" is reproduced with permission of the *Journal of Legal Studies,* Vol. 1, No. 1, © 1972, The University of Chicago.

1

The National Survey

... At 3:15 p.m., the reporting officer arrived on the scene and found a circular five-inch hole in the screen made by a shot gun blast. The victim was found lying on his back on the bedroom floor. The pattern made by the shot on the living room wall indicated that the subject was hit in the hallway approximately twelve and one-half feet from the screen. A witness said the victim had complained to the suspect about talking too loud in front of his apartment. The victim then drew a gun, pointed it at the suspect's head, and pulled the trigger three times, without the gun going off. The suspect ran toward the project across the street, and the victim fired one shot at him. The suspect then came back with a shot gun, fired through the victim's door, and fled the scene.

... *The victim was interviewed at the hospital. She related that she had been cut by her husband, who had picked a fight with her and then slashed her on the left side of the stomach without reason or provocation. She had just come home from work and found her husband in an intoxicated condition. Following the quarrel, the husband allegedly picked up a kitchen butcher-type knife and slashed her. The offender was also interviewed. After advising him of his constitutional rights, the reporting officer decided that the offender was under the influence of alcohol to the point where interviewing him would be useless. The offender did admit cutting his wife, however. His version was that both he and his wife had been drinking and that he had cut his wife with the aforementioned knife, following the argument that she had instigated.*

... The victim left her apartment at approximately 7 p.m. She arrived at the cafe between 8:30 and 9, decided that she was not hungry, and left without ordering anything. She had started walking westbound on Third Street when the suspects came by in a car. Suspect 1 got out of the car and took her by the arm, asked her where she was going, and then told her that she was to accompany them. At this time, suspect 2 also got out and both suspects walked the victim to the car. The victim made no outcry and did not resist their efforts to force her into the vehicle. They drove up and down side streets and at an unknown location stopped and picked up suspects 3 and 4. The driver then proceeded to an apartment. The victim recalled that there was a front room, a bedroom, and a small room like a den that had no furniture in it. It was in this small room that suspect 1 took her, forced her to the floor and removed her panties. Suspect 1 then had an act of intercourse with the victim. As each suspect completed an act of intercourse with the victim, the next suspect in turn entered the room and sexually assaulted the victim. Each suspect had intercourse with the victim twice. The suspects then left the apartment with the victim, drove her to the corner of Eighth and Main, and told her to get out.

... *Upon arrival the officers were informed by the victim that he had been on the street corner waiting for a public service bus. He was approached by six*

Negro males who were walking north on Center Street. The youths surrounded him—four of the boys stood behind him, one to his right and one directly in front of him. The youth directly in front ordered him to remove his black leather coat. Prior to this action, the boy standing in front asked one of the boys standing behind, "Is that him?" Someone behind said, "Yes." The boy in front then pretended that the coat rightfully was his property. The boy on his right took a pocket knife from his clothing and pointed it at the victim's stomach. The victim's coat and wrist watch were removed, with the knife still pointed at his stomach. As the boys started to walk south on Center Street, one of them asked, "Do you have any money?" The victim answered in the negative and the youths continued walking south.

Objectives

As a concept, "crime" is unwieldy. Many believe that the key to building a realistic general theory of deviance lies in first understanding component microsystems. One product of such thinking has been the emergence of a considerable literature that examines the circumstances of a specific crime along with the characteristics of and relationships between the victims and offenders involved. Building on Von Hentig,[1] Wolfgang set much of the present-day tone of these inquiries with his 1958 *Patterns in Criminal Homicide* based on Philadelphia police data.[2]

Among the other single-city American empirical studies of major violent crime (homicide, assault, rape, and robbery[3]) that have closely paralleled Wolfgang's methodology, as well as his format and content, are the works of Pokorny on Houston homicide,[4] Voss and Hepburn on Chicago homicide,[5] Pittman and Handy on St. Louis assault,[6] Amir on Philadelphia rape[7] and Normandeau on Philadelphia robbery.[8] Although not always as closely structured to Wolfgang nor as interested in covering the same variables, a number of other contributions on violent crime have presented comparable information in certain areas as well as analyses that are kindred in spirit. A partial list of relevant contributions includes the work by the Washington, D.C. Crime Commission on all four major violent crimes,[9] Zimring on Chicago homicide and assault,[10] Burnham on New York homicide,[11] Wilt and Bannon on Detroit homicide,[12] Reiss on Chicago assault, rape, and robbery,[13] Nelson and Amir on Berkeley rape,[14] Chappell and Singer on New York rape,[15] Agopian et al. on Oakland rape,[16] Hayman et al. on Washington, D.C. rape,[17] McDonald on Denver rape,[18] Giancinti on Denver rape,[19] the Seattle Law and Justice Planning Office on Seattle rape,[20] Conklin on Boston robbery,[21] and Feeney and Weir on Oakland robbery.[22]

Early in the life of the National Commission on the Causes and Prevention of Violence, it was decided to embark on a Wolfgang-type analysis but for a big city sample that for the first time carried across national dimensions and all four major violent crimes. *Criminal Violence*, which presents the results of this study, has several objectives:

First, provide a unifying source of base-line data on major violent crime that can be compared to the single-city studies. In no small part, this book is designed as a reference, comparing the national survey results to the American studies cited above as well as to foreign work. Systematic comparisons are built into the tables, cited in the text, and detailed for referral in the extensive footnotes.

Second, determine the extent to which the four criminal behavior systems merge and the degree of their uniqueness. Comparisons among the major violent crimes will further help consolidate past work and give insights on how to differentiate the kind of policy responses discussed at the end of the study.

Third, describe the most clearcut national and regional patterns for the same variables used in the single-city studies, with an eye to their policy and theoretical implications. The information available from police reports is not etiological. It does not describe causal processes. Rather, it lends itself to a descriptive, exploratory, factual profile of crime. This is the kind of analysis to which the study limits itself, as did Wolfgang's *Patterns in Criminal Homicide*; neither study claims to the critical reader that it will do more. From a policy viewpoint, the importance of such work was brought out by the 1967 President's Commission on Law Enforcement and Administration of Justice. The Commission underscored the need for comprehensive factual reconstructions as social indicators of criminal events. "This type of information must be secured more systematically if greater understanding of the different conditions under which crimes occur is to be achieved."[2 3] The final chapter in *Criminal Violence* assesses some of the direct policy implications. In addition, the data are useful from a theoretical perspective. They build an empirical framework around which speculations, interpretive concepts, causal explanations and, ultimately, a theoretical understanding of criminal violence can be shaped. It is not the purpose of this volume to engage in theorizing. However, the companion volume published with *Criminal Violence*, titled *Violence, Race and Culture*, begins with the national survey findings and uses them as a dimension in the development of one possible interpretation of criminal violence.

Description of the National Survey

The definition of each of the four crimes examined in the national survey is based on that established by the FBI and required of police departments in reporting crime for the annual *Uniform Crime Reports*.

Strictly speaking, *criminal homicide* in the United States includes murder (commonly in the first and second degrees), non-negligent (or voluntary) manslaughter, and negligent (or involuntary) manslaughter. Most negligent manslaughters involve automobiles, however, and thus point to significantly different situations than murder and non-negligent manslaughter. Therefore, information on only the first two sub-categories was collected from police in the national sample. Accordingly, references to the FBI data on "criminal homicide" in the annual *Uniform Crime Reports* are based on murder and non-negligent manslaughter.

Aggravated assault is considered assault with intent to kill or for the purpose of inflicting severe bodily injury—by shooting, cutting, stabbing, maiming, poisoning, scalding, the use of acids, the use of explosives or by other means. In the *UCR*, the category excludes the "less serious" forms of assault, assault and battery, and "fighting."

Forcible rape is composed of rape by force, assault to rape, and attempted rape, but excludes statutory offenses (those where no force is used and the victim is under the age of consent).

Robbery includes stealing or taking anything of value from a person, either by force or by creating fear. Strong-arm robbery, stick-ups, armed robbery, assault to rob, and attempt to rob are all acts included as "robbery" in the *UCR*. Because robbery is such a broad category, however, it has been separated into armed and unarmed components throughout this study.

The survey was limited to the following large urban areas because of the heavy concentration of serious violence in them:[24] Atlanta, Boston, Chicago, Cleveland, Dallas, Denver, Detroit, Los Angeles, Miami, Minneapolis, New Orleans, New York, Philadelphia, St. Louis, San Francisco, Seattle, and Washington, D.C. A 10 percent sample of police offense and—when suspects were apprehended—arrest reports for the year 1967 was collected for each of the 4 crimes in each of the 17 cities. (Although the descriptor "offenders" will be used for convenience, it should be remembered that all such data based on police records refer only to *suspected* offenders.) To assure a reasonably large sample, a lower bound of 50 reports for any city-crime type was requested. If less than 50 reports were filed, all were sent. To avoid an unmanageable amount of coding and data processing for some crime types in several cities of megalopolis stature, an upper bound of 200 was employed. The relative importance of each city in terms of its crime incidence vis-à-vis the rest was then statistically reinstated via the weighting system explained in Appendix B, where the study's methodology is detailed.

The narratives opening Chapter 1, edited from reports in the sample, suggest the texture of the police records and some of the information that they make available. Criticism of such data is well known. Only a fraction of all crime committed is reported, and there are many differences in recording objectivity and crime classification among departments.[25]

The variability among cities in reporting is nicely illustrated by Chappell et al., who examined the forcible rape reports from two of the cities in the national sample. The Boston reports were terse, formal, laconic, and vague about what happened. They were pressed into a seemingly preordained formula. But the Los Angeles reports were richer in detail and tended "to be in the nature of Dostoevskian endeavors, with a goodly amount of Mickey Spillane added in. . . . Bras, capris, and other garments are often ripped asunder . . . and the attack is apparently carried on with a fair bit of gusto." It was also "patently obvious that what each department regards as the kind of case to be classified as forcible rape and forwarded to the *Uniform Crime Reports* for tabulation as such is far from equivalent."[26]

In defense of police reports, Wolfgang argued in 1958 that they "provide a more comprehensive and valid description of crime, the victim, and the offender than any other source of data."[27] On balance, this may well be still true. Victimization surveys—the most recent, sophisticated, and exhaustive being the Census Bureau-LEAA National Crime Panel Survey—are probing the "dark figure" of unreported crime and collecting a wealth of data from victims. But these vitally needed social indicators must still resolve many methodological problems[28] and offer very limited insights on offenders.

With an awareness of the limitations of the data and an interest in validating evidence whenever it is available, the following chapters concentrate on those variables obtainable from the police reports that past research promises will yield the most insight into violent crime. Chapter 2 examines race of offender by race of victim; sex by sex; and age by age. Chapter 3 considers interpersonal relationships; Chapter 4, offender motive; Chapter 5, victim precipitation; Chapter 6, injury and weapon used; and Chapter 7, spatial and distance patterns. The concluding chapter summarizes the results and presents implications for future research and policy. Appendix A outlines national survey data on three more variables that were judged to have lesser importance—location, temporal patterns, and multiple offenders. Appendix B lists several other variables originally coded for use in the national survey but later not pursued for a variety of reasons.

The police offense and arrest reports collected for the national survey describe situations that may or may not involve multiple victims and offenders. There is usually just one of each in homicide, but multiples, especially of offenders, increasingly appear in the other crimes. How should they be accounted for in describing the patterns of interest? Statements can be made about victims and offenders separately: "Half of all mates killed were female and most robbers were male." Multiples can be avoided by talking about the case: "One-third of the homicide cases occurred in the home." Or, the "interaction" between each offender and each individual victimized can be used as the basic unit of analysis. If, for example, a report includes two offenders and one victim, there is just one case, but two victim-offender combinations or interactions.

Although previous comparable studies have all been based on cases and victims and offenders treated separately, it was decided here to use the base that seemed most appropriate for each variable. More often than not, interactions were selected.[29] As a partial test of the possible biases introduced by this approach, the interaction-based data on interpersonal relationships in Chapter 3 are compared to case-based data and the case-based data on location in Appendix A are compared to interaction data.

Interactions where the offender was apprehended and cases "cleared by arrest" (where at least one suspect was taken into custody) have been given emphasis because they contain the most information. With minor exceptions, all the tables presenting national survey data are based on clearances. Yet, the sample was taken across *all* police reports of each type in each city regardless of whether or not an arrest was made.[30] Non-cleared frequencies for most variables are therefore contrasted in the text to cleared percentages.[31] This has rarely been done systematically, if at all, in previous research.

The number of arrests compared to non-arrests gathered in the survey reflects differential clearance rates. Homicides are balanced towards clearances, robberies towards non-clearances, and assaults and rapes are intermediate. Table 1-1 shows the number of cleared and uncleared interactions and cases after the weighting system was applied. The analysis is based on 3,789 cleared and 5,854 uncleared interactions. The case counts are 2,966 clearances and 3,657 non-clearances.

The police data are too crude to allow for analysis more refined than the simple frequency distributions that Wolfgang also used. One exception is the correlational analysis and computer isoline mapping of Chapter 7. Chi-square tests of significance[32] were originally run for some variables, and other measures of association were considered. But, similarly, it soon became apparent that little precision could be gained from the coarse police data beyond the patterns most obtrusive in an examination of the percentages in the tables. The word "significant" is therefore not used in a statistical sense, except for the correlations of Chapter 7 and when citing studies that do employ tests.

The national survey data are in the form of percentage distributions based on

Table 1-1

Statistical Number of Cleared and Uncleared Interactions and Cases after Application of the Respective Weighting Systems, 17 American Cities

Statistical Numbers[a] / Crime Types	Cleared		Uncleared	
	Interaction Base	Case Base	Interaction Base	Case Base
Criminal Homicide	668	608	192	164
Aggravated Assault	1493	1238	1413	1167
Forcible Rape	617	522	797	537
Armed Robbery	509	310	2075	1089
Unarmed Robbery	502	288	1377	700
TOTAL[b]	3789	2966	5854	3657

[a]Note that these are not the true numbers received from the 17 police departments cooperating in the survey, but the "statistical numbers" resulting from application of the weighting system to the true numbers. See Appendix B.

[b]The N's on some tables in the following chapters depart from these totals for the reasons given in Appendix B.

a sample of reports; they are not rates of violent crime incidence per 100,000 population.[33] If the survey data were in the form of rates, then the probability of victimization could be discussed. For example, in analyzing interpersonal relationships, we could make a statement like "a victim is more likely to be robbed by a stranger than by a friend." What can be directly asserted with the present frequency distributions is *when* a victim is robbed, the likelihood is greatest that the offender will be a stranger" and so forth.

However, rates will be discussed at appropriate times. From the beginning, the reader must keep in perspective the trends in reported violent crime rates over the period that includes the 1967 data on hand. The year 1967 falls in the middle of the decade showing the greatest sustained rise in reported major violent crime since official FBI figures were first published in 1933. Whereas riots and other civil disorders slacked off by the end of the sixties, reported serious personal violence continued to rise into the seventies. From 1963 through 1972, the reported increases in offense rates in cities with populations of 250,000 or more have been up 149 percent in criminal homicide, 101 percent in aggravated assault, 171 percent in forcible rape, and 263 percent in robbery.[34] These trends are shown in Figures 1-1 and 1-2.

Regional and International Comparisons

For the most part, the tables in *Criminal Violence* present—one variable at a time—the aggregated data from all 17 cities in the national survey. Many cross tabulations were also run. Salient findings are reviewed in the text, but the great volume of these tables prohibited publishing them.[35] Occasionally, the analysis justifies breaking out data from individual cities. In addition, the cleared survey data have been aggregated into regional clusters. Boston, New York, Philadelphia, and Washington, D.C. were grouped into the Northeast; Atlanta, Dallas, Miami, and New Orleans into the South; Chicago, Cleveland, Detroit, Minneapolis, and St. Louis into the North Central region; and Denver, Los Angeles, San Francisco, and Seattle into the West.

Just as the "national" figures profile big-city patterns rather than reflect a probability sample across the urban-rural continuum, so each of these "regions" is really just a "regional city," describing only the influence of its respective urban components. One cannot automatically assume that the patterns of these assembled urban islands are stratified throughout the regions with which they are associated; nor are the cities within a given region necessarily similar. Thus, Dallas may well deviate from the Deep South cities of Atlanta and New Orleans in the "southern" aggregate—and Miami perhaps even more so. The survey weighting system (Appendix B) assures that the influence of any one city for any crime reflects the relative incidence of that crime in that city. Consequently, the data from and reporting idiosyncracies associated with cities having a very

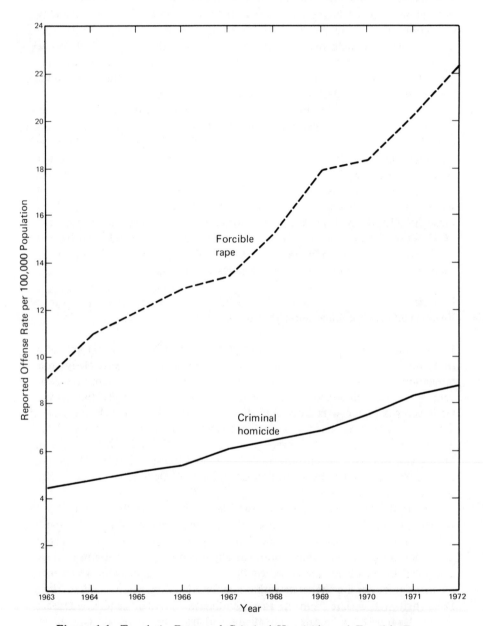

Figure 1-1. Trends in Reported Criminal Homicide and Forcible Rape Offense Rates Nationally, 1963-1972. Source: FBI *Uniform Crime Reports.*

high crime incidence dominate their regional aggregates even more than is the case with the national composite. The "western" results, for example, basically address urban California. In addition, low sample sizes must be confronted more often in the regional findings than the national aggregate, and any biases present in a specific city-crime type are less likely to be washed out in a pool of only 4 or 5 rather than 17 cities.

The regional data are marginal because of these constraints, and, again, the supporting tables are not cost-effective to reproduce.[36] However, regional comparisons within the same research design have never been made for most of the patterns under investigation, and knowledge about how crime and other social phenomena vary regionally is meager. Certain regional observations and speculations therefore have been included with the hope that future work can build on our inroads towards an analysis that avoids ethnocentric conclusions and unicultural, idiosyncratic interpretations.

The aggregate U.S. findings are also compared to data from foreign countries. The difficulties raised in the likening of regions are even more severe. International comparisons of crime are notoriously difficult to make because of non-standardized legal definitions, variations in statistical collection and reporting, and different cultural prescriptions for what is and is not deviant.[37] Unlike the case for the regional aggregates, the comparative data here are not within our research design. The span in years among various studies is a further complication: we face a space-*time* continuum.

The rationale for nonetheless proceeding along the hazardous road of cross-cultural comparisons, if only in a cautious way, is the promise of deeper insight into American patterns because of the perspective. Bohannon hoped to set a precedent for comparative work in his pathbreaking 1960 book *African Suicide and Homicide*. But he admits disappointment over the pace of scholarship that followed. In 1969 he still had to observe:

What is needed, and what we (or anybody else) cannot at the moment supply, is a large-scale cross-cultural study of the relationship between the victim and the aggressor in large numbers of societies, together with those societies' definitions and evaluations of violence and their stated or implied values for judging the violent acts.[38]

The kind of in-depth anthropological profiles that would live up to Bohannon's standards are beyond the scope of *Criminal Violence*. But we will integrate some of the criminological contributions by students of other countries, many of whom seek to control for, or at least explain, the legal, statistical, and cultural pitfalls associated with the analysis. The confounding impediments to cross-cultural analysis are also somewhat mitigated by the fact that the four crimes of interest occupy a universe of seriousness generally recognized by statutes throughout the world.

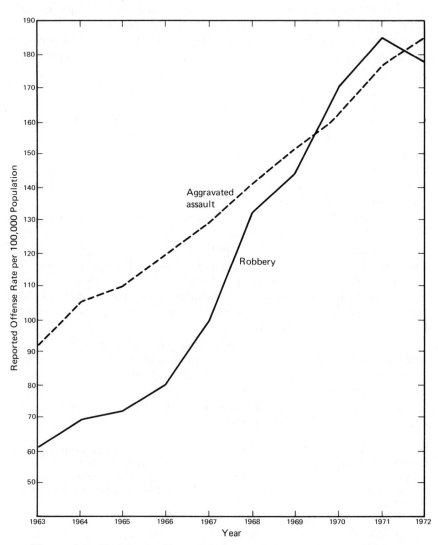

Figure 1-2. Trends in Reported Aggravated Assault and Robbery Offense Rates Nationally, 1963-1972. Source: FBI *Uniform Crime Reports.*

No claims are made to an exhaustive review of foreign empirical work, but much of the recent and significant does surface. The richest literature is on homicide. The most comparable investigations available include work on all four major violent crimes in Montreal;[39] homicide in England and Wales,[40] Scotland,[41] Denmark,[42] Florence,[43] Poland,[44] the USSR,[45] Israel,[46] various parts of Africa,[47] Delhi,[48] the tribes of Central India,[49] the Maria tribe of East Central India,[50] and the Southern Province of Ceylon;[51] assault in London;[52] rape in England and Wales[53] and Denmark;[54] and robbery in London.[55] A number of other studies of foreign countries, relatively less useful here, are also cited.[56]

None of the sources covers all of the national survey variables. The treatment of comparable items in these studies runs from simple, and, at times, ad hoc expositions of undigested facts to more reflective attempts at explaining patterns in cross-cultural perspective. Importantly, our own attempts at unified explanations and preliminary hypotheses of international scope are limited by these inconsistencies. When enough countries are represented, as is the case only for homicide, rough contrasts can be made by continent; by urban, rural and country-wide population densities; by the "West" versus the "non-West"; and, in an economic and technical sense, by "more advanced" versus "less advanced" populations.[57] The integrative tables that have been constructed cope with the reality that almost every study uses different classifications and gives different meanings to the same descriptive terms (especially for interpersonal relationships and motives). The tables accordingly submitted to an iterative process by which the original categories applicable to the United States were modified as each successive foreign investigation was added. Even so, some data had to be "forced" into categories that were not completely sensitive to the original ones. A certain degree of misclassification undoubtedly resulted.[58]

Notes and References

1. Von Hentig (1948).

2. Wolfgang (1958) examined 588 Philadelphia homicides occurring between 1948 and 1952.

3. These are the crimes considered violent in the FBI "Index" of serious crime. For parsimony of expression the phrases "criminal violence," "serious violence," and "major violent crime" will be used to refer to these acts.

4. Pokorny (1965) studied 438 homicides committed between 15 March 1958 and 31 December 1961.

5. Voss and Hepburn (1968) looked at 395 Chicago killings for 1965.

6. Pittman and Handy (1964) examined 241 St. Louis aggravated assaults committed in 1961.

7. Amir (1965) studied 646 forcible rapes occurring in Philadelphia between 1958 and 1960. This dissertation was published in 1971 (University of Chicago Press), but most citations are to the original University of Pennsylvania manuscript.

8. Normandeau (1968) examined 1722 Philadelphia robberies occurring between 1960 and 1966.

9. The report of the President's Commission on Crime in the District of

Columbia (1966, cited as the D.C. Crime Commission) undertook a survey that included, among other crimes, 172 homicides, 131 aggravated assaults, 151 forcible rapes and 297 robberies committed in Washington over various sample periods in the mid-sixties.

10. Zimring (1968; 1972) examined criminal homicides and aggravated assaults reported in Chicago during 1965, 1966, and 1967.

11. Burnham (1973) studied 100 cleared New York City homicides committed in 1971.

12. Wilt and Bannon (1974) studied 693 homicides reported to the Detroit Police in 1972. Clearances and non-clearances were included. All reports of first and second degree murder, non-negligent manslaughter, negligent manslaughter (excluding traffic deaths), and excusable and justified homicide were studied.

13. Reiss (1967) studied assault, rape, and robbery, among other crimes, occurring in Chicago in 1965 and 1966.

14. Nelson and Amir examined 33 hitchhike rapes and 131 non-hitchhike rapes reported in Berkeley between 1968 and 1970.

15. Chappell and Singer (1973) studied 704 complaints of forcible rape, or attempted rape, made to the New York City Police between February 1970 and 31 January 1972. This was a 1 in 10 random sample of forcible rapes and a 1 in 3 random sample of attempts.

16. Agopian et al. (1972) analyzed 192 forcible rapes reported to the Oakland Police during 1971.

17. Hayman et al. (1971) studied 1,243 rapes where the victim reported to the hospital for treatment (about half of all reported rape) in the District of Columbia from July 1969 to December 1970.

18. MacDonald (1971) analyzed "two hundred consecutive victims" of forcible rape reported in Denver between 1968 and 1969.

19. Giancinti (1973) studied all forcible and attempted rapes (excluding statutory rape) reported in Denver from 1 July 1970 to 30 June 1972. Included were 915 cases, cleared and uncleared.

20. The Seattle Law and Justice Planning Office covered 266, or 96 percent, of all rapes reported in Seattle in 1973, clearances and non-clearances.

21. Conklin (1972) studied all robberies recorded by the Boston police in the first 6 months of 1964 and 1968. He also interviewed samples of 67 offenders and 90 victims. Important information on robbery precipitation, weapons used, injury of victims, and offender typologies is presented.

22. Feeney and Weir (1973) examined samples of robbery and pursesnatch police reports from Oakland in 1964 and 1969. Samples of 113 incarcerated robbers and 160 victims were also included. The list given in the text is not meant to be comprehensive, but it does include much of the frequently cited and comparable recent work on one or more of the major violent crimes. Many police departments now tabulate some of the variables of interest here, but no survey has been made of the police. The annual *Uniform Crime Reports* cover a

few of the topics for the nation as a whole, and these findings are included here. (The *UCR* for any one calendar year come out the following summer. In an attempt to reduce reference problems, however, citations here to the FBI *UCR* refer to the year of the data, not the year of G.P.O. publication.)

23. President's Commission on Law Enforcement, Assessment Task Force (1967, p. 77).

24. See the FBI *Uniform Crime Reports* for any year.

25. For detailed discussion of police reporting problems, see Wolfgang (1963) and Mulvihill and Tumin with Curtis (1969).

26. Chappell et al. (1972, pp. 855-6).

27. Wolfgang (1958, p. 13).

28. See, for example, Biderman (1967), Biderman and Reiss (1967), and Biderman (1973).

29. The considerations of race, sex, age and interpersonal relationships, motive, victim precipitation, injury, and weapon used all address face-offs between each offender and his or her particular victim(s). An interaction base was accordingly deemed most sensitive to the information demands. The discussions of location, temporal patterns, and multiple offenders have a contextual objective that is above particular transactions. The informational need addressed the event as a whole. The more encompassing case was therefore selected. The areal chapter plots victim, offender, and crime locations separately and computes distances between these sets of points.

30. There were some city exceptions. See Appendix B.

31. See Curtis (1972) for all the original tables on non-clearances.

32. For an introductory treatment of the Chi-square statistic, see Blalock (1960, p. 15).

33. This follows the relative emphasis on frequency distributions in Wolfgang (1958) and most of the replications for other crimes.

34. These figures were computed from the 1963 and 1972 *Uniform Crime Reports.*

35. The interested reader is referred to the original dissertation; see Curtis (1972).

36. See Curtis (1972) for the regional tables.

37. For a discussion of these problems, see Mulvihill and Tumin with Curtis (1969, c. 2).

38. Bohannon (1969).

39. Tardiff (1966) took a 100 percent sample of homicide (N = 48), assault (N = 119), rape (N = 113) and a 10 percent sample of robbery (N = 202) in Montreal for 1964. Cleared and uncleared cases were combined. The "homicides" included murder, attempted murder, and manslaughter.

40. Gibson and Klein (1969). This is a Home Office Report on Murder. It played an important role in the recent Parliamentary debates on capital punishment. All murders in England and Wales between 1957 and 1968 were

covered. Gibson and Klein separately analyzed "abnormal" and "normal" murder. About one-third of the killings in England and Wales were classified as "abnormal"—cases where the offender was found insane or which involved murder followed by suicide. The "normal" murders were more comparable to the American homicides studied in the survey, so only the data from this classification were included here. The Home Office Report usually included both cleared and uncleared events, but in some instances (for example, interpersonal relationships) only cleared cases were tabulated.

41. Gibson and Klein (1969) also analyzed murder in Scotland from 1957 to 1968. Less data were presented than for England and Wales, but the same format was used. The figures incorporated here were for "normal" murders only, sometimes included uncleared cases and sometimes only clearances and generally focused on a span of several years because of the low number of murders in Scotland during any one year.

42. Svalastoga (1956) examined 172 homicides in Denmark between 1934-1939 and 1946-1951. All the cleared cases with one offender and with a known interpersonal relationship were used. Involuntary homicides were not included.

43. Simondi (1970) studied the court records of 80 cases of first degree attempted or completed murders plus infanticides committed in Florence, Italy between 1951 and 1963. He used the entire universe. Manslaughters were excluded. There were 94 offenders and 86 victims.

44. Holyst (1967) and Holyst (1969) are based on criminal homicides as defined by Article 225 of the Polish Criminal Code of 1932. Included are killings from the entire country over the years 1955 to 1961, with varying N's because of differential availability of information.

45. Connor (1973) summarized several researches in the Soviet Union: Gertsenzon's study, conducted in the late 1960s, of 100 randomly selected cases of "deliberate homicide under aggravating circumstances" in the city of Moscow; Vlasov and Kocharov's 1963 study of an undetermined number of homicides in Briansk, Vladimir and Kalinin oblasti (provinces); Podbegailo's study of similar offenses, occurring in Rostov oblast during 1961-62; and an apparently nation-wide survey of homicides by the All Union Scientific Research Institute of Criminalistics of the USSR Prokuratura, undertaken in the early 1960s.

46. Landau and Drapkin (1968) examined cleared cases of criminal homicide in Israel between 1950 and 1964, except for killings by infiltrators from the neighboring Arab countries. There were 279 offenders and 311 victims. Data were gathered from special police homicide files, the Central Criminal Register and reports of prison social workers. Comparisons among Western Jews, Oriental Jews, and non-Jews (almost all Arabs) were made throughout the study.

47. The major study is Bohannon, ed. (1960). Seven rural African tribes in Nigeria, Kenya, and Uganda were studied by different anthropologists. Bohannon analyzed two of the tribes. Different periods of time between the 1930s and

1950s were covered in the essays. The records used differed in quality from one country to another, although each area was under the influence of British law and administration. Data on the same variable (for example, interpersonal relationships) were usually not available for all tribes. Each author included all available cases over the time period studied, but there were some variations in the acts included for each of the tribes: Alur (cleared homicides and attempts), Bunyoro (cleared and uncleared homicides and attempts, excluding accidents and events that were not premeditated—for example, brawls), Gisu (cleared and uncleared homicides), Luo (cleared and uncleared homicides), Luyia (cleared homicides with convictions), Soga (cleared homicides with convictions, excluding accidents), Tiv (cleared and uncleared cases, excluding accidents). The great majority of the events studied were culpable, involving homicide that was branded wrong in the society where it occurred.

A later work, by Mushanga (1970), presents all 336 homicide cases coming to three district courts in Western Uganda (Kigezi, Ankole, and Toro) from 1955 to 1966, plus 148 cases "for comparative purposes" tried by one high court judge between 1965 and 1968. There were 484 cases, 569 offenders and 501 victims in all. Only the totals are used here.

48. Rao (1968) focused on all (52) murders reported in Delhi in 1963, cleared and uncleared. In some instances all 46 murders in 1962 and all 48 murders in 1964 were added.

49. Driver (1961) examined all (144) murder convictions between 1946 and 1956 on the official records of two courts of sessions having jurisdiction over 4,000,000 people in Central India. The locus of crime was mainly rural.

50. Elwin (1943) covered all (100) murder convictions on court record between 1921 and 1941 of the aboriginal Bison-horn Maria tribe in rural East-Central India.

51. Jayewardene and Ranasinghe (1963) studied all (88) homicide cases, cleared and uncleared, occurring in the Southern Province of Ceylon in 1960. The data were collected from the police and the courts. In recent years the Southern Province, which includes both urban areas (mainly along the coast) and rural places, has had a reputation for criminality in general and crimes of violence in particular. The homicides studied were not uniquely correlated to either the urban or rural locales.

52. McClintock (1963a) considered all crimes of violence in London for 1950 (N = 1,150), 1957 (N = 1,919) and the first half of 1960 (N = 2,536). For the variables relevant here, however, the data were usually from 1950 and 1957. Cleared and uncleared cases were included. In England, "crimes of violence" basically include sex offenses, homicides, and the British equivalent of aggravated assault ("malicious wounding"). The data were presented in a form such that homicide couldn't be separated out. At times, it was possible to separate out the sexual offenses. When disaggregation was not possible, the data were still useful as proxies to aggravated assault, because the overwhelming percentage of the "crimes of violence" consisted of "malicious woundings."

53. Radzinowicz (1957) began his study in 1950 and carried it out over 14 districts in England and Wales. It included both agricultural and industrial communities but emphasis was on the urban areas, especially London. All (2,178) offenders involved or alleged to have been involved in indictable sexual offenses and all (914) offenders against whom proceedings were brought for non-indictable sexual offenses over the study period were incorporated. Thus, only cleared cases were studied. "Sexual offenders" included both male and female victims. The tabulations and references here, however, separate out just those crimes against females. Most were "indecent assault on females," and only a small percentage, rape proper. Unfortunately, rape could not be broken out, so we will really only be able to refer to English "sexual offenses against females." These data may therefore present a biased picture of English rapes. The investigation was included, however, because of the dearth of international studies on rape.

54. Svalastoga (1962) appraised 141 cleared cases of rape and attempted rape that came before the court in Denmark between 1946 and 1958. This represented almost all clearances brought before the court during the 1956 to 1958 period and a 50 percent non-random sample for the preceding years. The sample mainly reflected rape in provincial cities and rural areas.

55. McClintock and Gibson (1961) covered all (287) reported robberies in London for 1950, all (462) for 1957 and all (333) for the first half of 1960. The data for the variables of interest here, however, were usually from 1950 and 1957. Cleared and uncleared cases were included, although most of the reliable data on offender characteristics were for convicted persons. The sources of information were found scattered in a great variety of documents: crime reports, statements taken by the police, correspondence files, crime complaint books, charge sheets, court registers, court calendars, medical reports, probation officers' reports, and the criminal record files. Wherever it was thought desirable, the information was amplified by interviews with the police officers and probation officers concerned in particular cases.

56. These include Avison (1973), Falk (1952), Freed (1973), Frenkel (1930), Gilles (1965), LeVine (1959), McClintock (1963b), MacDonald (1911), Palmer (1973), Straus and Straus (1953), Ting and Tan (1969), Van Bemmelan (1960), Von Hentig (1940, 1948), Verkko (1951), West (1968), Williams (1962), and Yen (1929).

57. Given the studies available, the "West" refers to North America, Western Europe and American or European Jews in Israel. The "non-West" refers to the Soviet Union and her satellites, Africa, Asia, and the Oriental Jews and Arabs in Israel. "More advanced" countries in an economic and technical sense here will be considered to cover North America, Western Europe, the Soviet Union and her satellites, and the urban areas of Africa and Asia. The heading also includes Western and Oriental Jews in Israel. The "less advanced" populations for which there are data are found in rural Africa, rural Asia, and among the Arabs in Israel.

58. Scholarly perseverance might demand a detailed outline of where in any integrative table the data from any particular foreign study were placed. The need would be to show where each bit of data fell in the study's original classification scheme, how it was transferred, and where it was placed in the synthesized tables here. In the absence of such an exhaustive and, perhaps, excessively anal exercise, cautionary notes highlight potential problems of misclassification as they arise.

Source: *The Thunderbolt*, Newspaper of the National States'
Rights Party, Marietta, Georgia, October 1969.

Race of Offender by Race of Victim

The United States

The consensus definition of "race" by an international panel of geneticists and anthropologists convened by the United Nations specifies "a group or population characterized by some concentrations, relative as to frequency and distribution, of hereditary particles (genes) or physical characteristics, which appear, fluctuate, and often disappear in the course of time by reason of geographic and/or cultural isolation."[1]

Race, of course, also has a sociocultural meaning. The International Encyclopedia of the Social Sciences states:

Social races are composed of subjectively significant groups, unrestricted by age and sex criteria, in which membership is sociocentric (i.e., appears the same to all egos), is established at birth, endures for life, and confers special behavioral obligations or privileges. Social races differ from other stratified groups (such as classes with low rates of outmobility) in their methods of maintaining membership and group identity.[2]

It is the sociocultural perception of race that we deal with in the police report data of the national survey. The FBI *Uniform Crime Reporting Handbook*, which serves as a guide to local police filling out reports, simply instructs officers to classify offenders and victims as white, Negro, Indian, Chinese, Japanese, and "all other." The classification is made according to the judgement of the reporting police officer and reflects his or her perception of the physical appearances of persons in each category, plus information that may be secured on ethnic origin. The procedure follows the Bureau of Census approach in past years of requiring that the census taker determine race.[3]

Although more precise methods would be desirable, the police classifications do allow for a profile of interracial versus interracial crime by blacks and whites, the two racial groups in the United States from which most offenders and victims are drawn. Table 2-1 is based only on those clearances in the national survey where the persons involved were black or white.[4] Roughly two-thirds of the homicide, assault, and rape clearances were among blacks, while most of the rest were all-white. Non-clearances were also run.[5] The outcome was about the same, except that black-white (the offender will always be indicated first) uncleared frequencies were higher than their cleared counterparts. To some extent, this may have been because the offenders in non-clearances were more often strangers, who were more difficult for police to apprehend than nonstrangers. Thirty eight percent of the armed robbery clearances were all-black and 47 percent black-on-white; non-clearances broke down similarly. The proportions remained about the same for unarmed robbery clearances, but fully 61 percent of the uncleared interactions were black-on-white.

Table 2-1

Race of Offender by Race of Victim, Major Violent Crimes, 17 American Cities, 1967, Clearances (Percent)

Race of Offender-Victim	Crime				
	Criminal Homicide	Aggravated Assault	Forcible Rape	Armed Robbery	Unarmed Robbery
Black-Black	65.7	65.9	59.6	38.4	37.1
White-White	24.0	23.9	29.6	13.2	17.9
Black-White	6.5	8.4	10.5	46.7	43.9
White-Black	3.8	1.8	0.3	1.7	1.1
Total %	100.0	100.0	100.0	100.0	100.0
(N)	(571)	(871)	(465)	(269)	(251)

Base: Interactions.

Note: Only those clearances where race of both offender and victim was known are included. Non-whites other than blacks are not included. In robbery, clearances where the victim was an "institution" are not included.

Among the more interesting regional findings, the western aggregate in the sample—dominated by Los Angeles and San Francisco—had the highest proportion of black-white rapes (17 percent, compared to 8 percent in the Northeast, 8 percent in the South and 9 percent in the North Central aggregate).[6] Some of the explanation is likely to be demographic—for example, there are proportionately more white women and fewer black women for black men to rape in Los Angeles and San Francisco than in many other cities in the survey.[7] *Violence, Race and Culture*, the companion volume to this research, also addresses possible black power and social distance interpretations.

The studies in Philadelphia, Washington, D.C., Chicago, Detroit, St. Louis, Houston, and New Orleans generally supported the national survey findings for cleared homicide and assault, but there were higher interracial figures in San Francisco.[8]

The black-white frequency was lower in the Philadelphia and Chicago rape studies with data prior to the national survey, but higher than the 17-city aggregate of clearances in studies after 1967 done in Washington, D.C., Kansas City, New Orleans, Denver, Seattle, San Francisco, Berkeley, and Oakland. In fact, the black-white percentage was the single highest in Seattle, San Francisco, and Berkeley (whereas the all-black pattern predominated elsewhere).[9] These results tend to support the higher black-white western figures in the national survey.

The robbery studies in Philadelphia, Washington, D.C. and Chicago with data prior to the 1967 survey had higher all-black and lower black-on-white proportions. But, as in rape, investigations with later data (in Philadelphia and

San Francisco) had higher black-white percentages than the national aggregate for clearances.[10]

Racial Bias. It can be argued that the police records used for these investigations as well as in the national survey have produced racial figures that are highly suspect and biased against blacks.

Arrest information may produce different results than in events where the offender was not apprehended (especially in robbery, where the 1967 national clearance rate was only 30 percent, compared to 88 percent in homicide, 69 percent in assault, and 61 percent in rape[11]), but the survey controls for the difficulty by comparing clearances to non-clearances.

The more serious dilemma is that the estimated real incidence of 3 out of the 4 crimes is considerably higher than the reported incidence. In his national victimization study, Ennis estimated that the real rate of assault is twice the nationally reported rate; the true rape rate, almost four times as high; and the true robbery rate, 50 percent greater than the police rate (with the homicide "gap" apparently small).[12] More recently, the LEAA Crime Panel in 8 cities estimated assault as 1.5 times greater than reported, with rape and robbery twice as great.[13]

Consequently, the real offender-by-victim racial dynamics may be different from the reported ones. In particular, it can be contended that American police have given new meaning to Claude Rains' classic order at the end of *Casablanca*—by rounding up blacks as the usual suspects. Yet available evidence from reputable scholars—for example, Black, Skolnick, Tiffany, McIntyre, and Rotenberg,[14]—does not necessarily underscore the assertion of racial discrimination by police in making arrests and sometimes dismisses the significance of the issue.

Consider the victims. In terms of the frequency with which they were related to Ennis, the most important reasons for their not reporting included the victim's beliefs that the police couldn't do anything, the episode was a private rather than a criminal matter, the real offender might not be caught, the police wouldn't want to be bothered, the offender shouldn't be incriminated, the time involved was not worth it, and the offender might seek revenge.[15] The LEAA Crime Panel Survey has come up with similar findings.[16] Can these disclosures be combined with general knowledge on assault, rape, and robbery to prove a reporting bias against blacks?

One instance does come to mind. White males have long experienced and imposed nearly institutionalized access to non-white women. Black autobiographers living in the nineteenth-century American South testify that "often through 'gifts,' but usually through force, white overseers and planters obtained the sexual favors of black women. Generally speaking, the women were literally forced to offer themselves 'willingly' and receive a trinket for their compliance rather than a flogging for their refusal and resistance."[17]

There are no objective twentieth-century data on the subject, but descriptive accounts and participant observations are not difficult to find. Access to domestic house servants illustrates a continuity with the slave experience. Another institution providing ample opportunity for white-black rape is the police. Here is a black Chicago streetwalker of the 1930s telling her pimp about providing services demanded by two white policemen to avoid being booked:

"Blondie" pushed my head down to his lap. Then I got on the back seat with him. That freak bastard, Max, turned around and kept his flashlight on us the whole time. I made "Blondie" holler. I finished with "Blondie." Max got back there with me. For a half hour he called me filthy names. He punched me. I'm sure sore all over. "Blondie" begged him to stop. My ass feels like he split something back there. I had a rough time.[18]

Here is a chronicler of the 1970s visiting a friend in Harlem and watching two white policemen entering the apartment of a recently jailed man who had left behind a young daughter:

Neighbors were standing at windows and stoops all around looking toward that building. Wasn't anyone going to do something? "Look," [the friend] said. "Those cats leave their cars and hitch up that big gun bulge on their hips. They run down into that apartment, they stay about one-half hour. They come out and hitch that bulge again before they get in their cars. They know as long as they hitch that bulge they got us."[19]

With whites in control of the institutions, there are good reasons why a black woman would not report. Thus, in one study an informant disclosed that "no black woman would report being raped by a white man to the police in Oakland. They might report it to the Panthers, but never the police."[20] It is a near certainty, then, that the negligible reported white-black rape rate would rise if all rapes were reported.

The probability of bias in the other reported race patterns is not as great as in white-black rape. Thus, it might be asserted that white-on-black assaults and robberies are also significantly underreported because of conditioned Uncle Tomism and related factors. Yet, because we can be fairly confident about the low white-on-black homicide frequency (most homicide being reported), and because homicide is so similar to assault (as will become clear by the end of the study), we can reasonably assume that a low white-on-black assault frequency in fact is the case. And it is difficult to imagine a large proportion of whites (who have money) robbing blacks (who don't). Contemplating each of the other race combinations for each crime, one can usually find several of the reasons for not reporting to fit very well.

In fact, Ennis has more substantiating evidence. The estimated true victimization rate among blacks remained higher than the white rate for violent crimes, and the extent of and reasons for not reporting were basically the same for both races.[21]

It would appear safe to conclude that the leading reported racial paterns of the national survey police data approximate reality reasonably well, even though biases are inevitably inherent. Except when new methodological difficulties are specified, the most clearcut configurations for the other national survey variables can be regarded with the same qualified confidence.

The *Thunderbolt* cartoon at the beginning of Chapter 2 superimposes one of the "crime clocks" J. Edgar Hoover promoted in the annual FBI *Uniform Crime Reports.* The idea of the clock is to express the volume of crime for the nation as a whole in terms of time frequency. The 30 minutes shown in the cartoon frame the rape rate in the early 1960s (the time period is much shorter today). The clock, however, is based on *all* rapes, not a specific racial pattern, as implied. Thus, the cartoon as a whole is a hateful involution of the objective statistical reality that we have tried to address here. Yet it is a useful illustration that surfaces the lurid black and white undercurrent to much of the debate on "law and order" in the United States and encourages a careful but direct treatment of race in the sections to follow.

A Note on Offender-Victim Trends. Because of the sensitivity of such data and because they play a central role in the interpretations of *Violence, Race and Culture*, it would be interesting to know whether the offender-by-victim racial composition of violent crime has changed over recent years—that is, for any given place, have there been significant trends over time in race of offender by race of victim? Unfortunately, the FBI refuses to publish national data linking offender and victim by race. In fact, the reporting forms that local departments are required to submit to the FBI are constructed so that these data are not even collected. One official reason given for this procedure is that linking offenders to victims in racial data would be too politically explosive for inclusion in the *Uniform Crime Reports.*

However, scraps of trend information have been pieced together in Tables 2-2 and 2-3. The data are based on national survey breakouts for individual cities, some of the published single-city studies, and unpublished recent figures supplied to the author by certain police departments. The information is from different years so that various trend periods are observable.

To the extent that there was any consistency in the reported trends, it was found in violence by blacks on whites. For most crimes and in most cities, there was an increase in the relative percentage of reported black-white violent crime. When there was an increase, it ranged from slight to dramatic. For the most part, the exceptions to this trend were instances where there was little change in the relative black-white percentage (rather than a substantial decrease in the proportion). As illustrated by rape and robbery in San Francisco, this commonly happened when and where the black-white rate was initially high at the beginning of the trend period and remained that way. Figures 2-1 and 2-2 chart the black-white trends across all cities and crimes.

Table 2-2
Trends in Race of Offender by Race of Victim, Major Violent Crimes in Cities with Available Data (Percent)

Crime: Criminal Homicide

Race of Offender by Race of Victim	Philadelphia 1948–1952 — Cases Cleared Only	Philadelphia 1973[2] — Cases Cleared and Uncleared	Washington, D.C. 1967[3] — Interactions Cleared and Uncleared	Washington, D.C. 1972[4] — Interactions Cleared and Uncleared	Washington, D.C. 1973[5] — Interactions Cleared and Uncleared	Detroit 1967[6] — Cases Cleared and Uncleared	Detroit 1972[7] — Cases Cleared and Uncleared	1965[8] — Cases Cleared and Uncleared	Chicago 1970[9] — Cases Cleared and Uncleared	Chicago 1972[10] — Cases Cleared and Uncleared	New Orleans 1967[11] — Interactions Cleared Only	New Orleans 1973[12] — Interactions Cleared and Uncleared	San Francisco 1967[13] — Cases Cleared and Uncleared	San Francisco 1973[14] — Cases Cleared and Uncleared
Black Offender, Black Victim	72.0	82.1	86.3	90.3	85.2	70.0	77.1	77.6	83.3	85.4	69.8	73.1	41.2	43.5
White Offender, White Victim	22.0	8.2	7.8	4.0	3.2	22.5	13.8	15.8	8.5	7.6	30.2	12.3	44.1	22.6
Black Offender, White Victim	4.0	9.0	2.0	3.4	6.4	5.0	6.9	5.3	7.3	5.9	–	14.6	14.7	21.0
White Offender, Black Victim	2.0	.8	3.9	2.3	5.2	2.5	2.2	1.3	.9	1.1	–	–	–	12.9
Total %	100.0	100.0	100.0	100.0	100.0	100.0	100.0	100.0	100.0	100.0	100.0	100.0	100.0	100.0
(N)	(550)	(368)	(51)	(175)	(155)	(40)	(491)	(379)	(633)	(529)	(43)	(171)	(34)	(62)

Crime: Aggravated Assault

Race of Offender by Race of Victim	Philadelphia 1967[15] — Cases Cleared Only	Philadelphia 1973[16] — Cases Cleared and Uncleared	Washington, D.C. April 6, to May 10, 1966[17] — Cases Cleared and Uncleared	Washington, D.C. 1967[18] — Cases Cleared and Uncleared	Washington, D.C. 1967[19] — Interactions Cleared and Uncleared	Washington, D.C. 1972[20] — Interactions Cleared and Uncleared	Washington, D.C. 1973[21] — Interactions Cleared and Uncleared	Chicago Sept. 16, 1965 to March 2, 1966[22] — Cases Cleared and Uncleared	Chicago 1967[23] — Cases Cleared Only	St. Louis 1961[24] — Cases Cleared and Uncleared	St. Louis 1967[25] — Cases Cleared and Uncleared	San Francisco 1967[26] — Cases Cleared and Uncleared	San Francisco 1973[27] — Cases Cleared and Uncleared
Black Offender, Black Victim	70.2	70.9	84.3	82.6	80.9	80.1	82.1	76.2	67.3	79.0	78.9	40.1	38.4
White Offender, White Victim	14.3	15.6	6.6	2.9	4.1	4.5	4.0	17.8	21.3	16.8	14.4	29.4	35.8
Black Offender, White Victim	11.9	11.8	5.9	12.2	12.9	14.2	12.4	4.8	10.6	3.4	6.1	23.5	21.9
White Offender, Black Victim	3.6	1.7	3.2	2.3	4.1	1.2	1.6	1.2	.8	.8	.6	7.0	3.9
Total %	100.0	100.0	100.0	100.0	100.0	100.0	100.0	100.0	100.0	100.0	100.0	100.0	100.0
(N)	(84)	(4,782)	(121)	(173)	(213)	(5,780)	(5,420)	(2,952)	(122)	(238)	(180)	(187)	(2,071)

Table 2-2 (cont.)

Crime: Forcible Rape

Race of Offender by Race of Victim	Philadelphia 1958 1960[28]	Philadelphia 1973[29]	Washington, D.C. 1964[30]	Washington, D.C. 1967[31]	Washington, D.C. 1967[32]	Washington, D.C. 1972[33]	Washington, D.C. 1973[34]	Chicago Sept. 16 1965 to March 2, 1966[35]	Chicago 1967[36]	New Orleans 1967[37]	New Orleans 1973[38]	Seattle 1967[39]	Seattle 1973[40]	San Francisco 1967[41]	San Francisco 1973[42]
Base	Cases Cleared and Uncleared	Cases Cleared and Uncleared	Cases Cleared and Uncleared	Cases Cleared and Uncleared	Interactions Cleared and Uncleared	Interactions Cleared and Uncleared	Interactions Cleared and Uncleared	Cases Cleared and Uncleared	Cases Cleared Only	Interactions Cleared Only	Interactions Cleared and Uncleared	Cases Cleared and Uncleared	Cases Cleared and Uncleared	Cases Cleared and Uncleared	Cases Cleared and Uncleared
Black Offender, Black Victim	76.9	68.2	78.8	76.0	73.7	79.1	75.5	82.0	78.2	50.0	63.0	21.4	14.1	9.5	21.0
White Offender, White Victim	16.3	15.7	8.6	2.0	1.3	1.6	3.0	12.0	11.4	40.6	7.4	35.7	34.1	50.0	37.9
Black Offender, White Victim	4.2	15.8	12.6	20.0	23.7	19.0	21.0	5.0	8.3	9.4	29.1	42.9	51.1	40.0	38.4
White Offender, Black Victim	2.6	.3	–	2.0	1.3	.3	.5	1.0	2.1	–	.5	–	.7	–	2.7
Total %	100.0	100.0	100.0	100.0	100.0	100.0	100.0	100.0	100.0	100.0	100.0	100.0	100.0	100.0	100.0
(N)	(646)	(670)	(151)	(50)	(76)	(739)	(641)	(459)	(96)	(32)	(189)	(14)	(305)	(42)	(578)

Crime: Robbery (Armed and Unarmed)

Race of Offender by Race of Victim	Philadelphia 1960[43]	Philadelphia 1966[44]	Philadelphia 1973[45]	Washington, D.C. 1967[46]	Washington, D.C. 1972[47]	Washington, D.C. 1973[48]	Chicago Sept. 16, 1965 to March 2, 1966[49]	Chicago 1967[50]	San Francisco 1967[51]	San Francisco 1973[52]
Base	Cases Cleared and Uncleared	Cases Cleared and Uncleared	Cases Cleared and Uncleared	Interactions Cleared and Uncleared	Interactions Cleared and Uncleared	Interactions Cleared and Uncleared	Cases Cleared and Uncleared	Cases Cleared Only	Cases Cleared and Uncleared	Cases Cleared and Uncleared
Black Offender, Black Victim	64.6	59.9	48.8	58.9	63.6	62.0	58.0	49.2	5.7	10.0
White Offender, White Victim	12.8	13.0	8.1	1.7	1.3	1.2	13.0	15.4	22.9	19.9
Black Offender, White Victim	21.8	26.3	42.5	39.4	34.8	36.4	27.5	35.4	71.4	69.1
White Offender, Black Victim	.8	.8	.6	–	.3	.4	1.5	–	–	1.0
Total %	100.0	100.0	100.0	100.0	100.0	100.0	100.0	100.0	100.0	100.0
(N)	(201)	(250)	(8,156)	(292)	(8,600)	(7,783)	(4,049)	(65)	(175)	(3,793)

Table 2-2 (cont.)

Notes: The frequency distributions are based only on total numbers of cases or interactions where race was known for both offender and victim and where the races were black, white, or both. Unknowns were excluded, as were other non-whites beside blacks. (In the only exception, the 1961 St. Louis assault data actually used the category "non-white," rather than "black," as shown. To insure comparability, the 1967 national survey assault data from St. Louis also coded for all non-whites, rather than just blacks.) This was done to concentrate on the most frequent race patterns and because unknowns and/or other non-whites were consciously excluded or simply not mentioned in a number of studies.

Data producing trend figures for any particular city-crime type have the same analytic base—the case or the interaction, as defined in Chapter 1. For case based data from the 1967 national survey, the following procedure was used. When a case included two or more offenders or victims, the most frequently occurring race configuration among the interactions in the case was coded. (There were few instances where this problem arose, however.) Ties (e.g., a case involving one victim and two offenders of different races) were thrown out, but ties were rare. The other studies usually did not discuss what was done in such situations.

In most instances, the different data sources are based on clearances and nonclearances combined (see Chapter 1 for definitions). However, in a few instances, only cleared data were available for a city-crime type at a given point in time, and these are compared to cleared plus uncleared data for the same city-crime type at other points in time. (The [minimal] biases so introduced are noted in the text.)

References: [1] Wolfgang (1958, p. 379); [2] Herron (1974); [3] National Survey; [4] Wilson (1974); [5] Wilson (1974); [6] National Survey; [7] Wilt and Bannon (1974); [8] Voss and Hepburn (1968, pp. 502-3); [9] Rochford (1974); [10] Rochford (1974); [11] National Survey; [12] Caruso (1974); [13] National Survey; [14] Feder (1974); [15] National Survey; [16] Herron (1974); [17] D.C. Crime Commission (1966, p. 78); [18] National Survey; [19] National Survey; [20] Wilson (1974); [21] Wilson (1974); [22] Reiss (1967, p. 34); [23] National Survey; [24] Pittman and Handy (1964, p. 468); [25] National Survey; [26] National Survey; [27] Feder (1974); [28] Amir (1971, p. 283); [29] Herron (1974); [30] D.C. Crime Commission (1966, p. 78); [31] National Survey; [32] National Survey; [33] Wilson (1974); [34] Wilson (1974); [35] Reiss (1967, p. 34); [36] National Survey; [37] National Survey; [38] Caruso (1974); [39] National Survey; [40] Seattle Law and Justice Planning Office (1975); [41] National Survey; [42] Feder (1974); [43] Normandeau (1968, p. 166); [44] Normandeau (1968, p. 167); [45] Herron (1974); [46] National Survey; [47] Wilson (1974); [48] Wilson (1974); [49] Reiss (1967:34); [50] National Survey; [51] National Survey; [52] Feder (1974).

Table 2-3

Race of Offender by Race of Victim, Criminal Homicide: New York City Comparison between 1967 and 1971 (Percent)

Year / Race of Offender by Race of Victim[a]	1967[b] Cleared Only	1971[c] Cleared Only
Black Offender, Black Victim	47.9	48.0
Hispanic Offender, Hispanic Victim	18.8	21.0
White Offender, White Victim	20.3	13.0
Black or Hispanic Offender, White Victim	8.3	9.0
Hispanic or White Offender, Black Victim	4.2	4.0
White or Black Offender, Hispanic Victim	−	4.0
Total %	99.5	99.0
(N)	(48)	(100)

[a]The offender-victim racial combinations in this table follow the presentation in Burnham (1973), the source of the 1971 data. Burnham used a case base, worked with clearances only, and omitted reports in which the race information was not available.

[b]The 1967 data are the homicide results for New York City broken out from the national survey. Although the national aggregates in Table 2-1 exclude "others" besides blacks and whites, the New York homicides were recorded for Hispanics to allow for race categories identical to those used by Burnham. Similarly, to work towards comparability, a case base was used, only clearances were counted, and reports in which the race information was unavailable were omitted. When a case included two or more offenders or victims, the most commonly occurring configuration among the interactions in the case was coded. (There were few cases where this problem arose, however.) Ties (e.g., a case involving one victim and two offenders of different races) were thrown out, but ties were rare.

[c]Burnham (1973, p. 1).

As for the other reported racial patterns, the percentage of black-black violence for any one crime tended to either change in different directions in different cities or to remain the same over time. The same was generally true for the white-white percentage.[22] The reported white-black proportion tended to remain insignificant (except in San Francisco homicide).

The conclusions on the reported black-white increase should be treated with extreme caution. Some of the increases were insignificant in any statistical sense. The sample sizes were low in certain instances, and the data were from only a limited number of cities. Often an uptrend was based on only two discrete data points. Some of the changes may have been due to variations in victim reporting to police as well as police recording and disclosure to the public.[23] However, until the more refined data that are urgently needed become available, the considerable uniformity of the reported black-white uptrend across a number of cities and over the 4 violent crimes provides some reason for attaching significance to the pattern, at least in certain places.

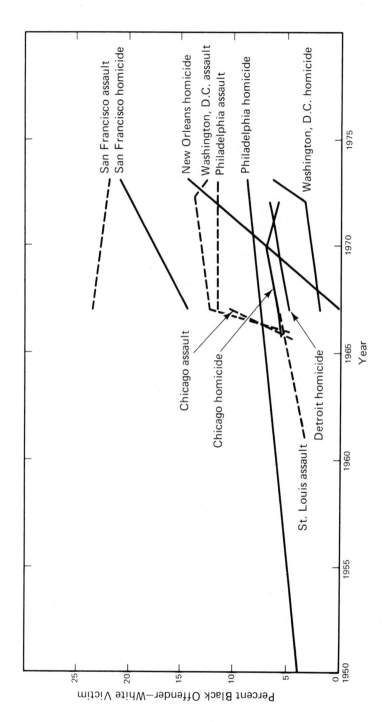

Figure 2-1. Trends in Reported Criminal Homicide and Assault by Blacks on Whites in Cities with Available Data. Source: Table 2-2.

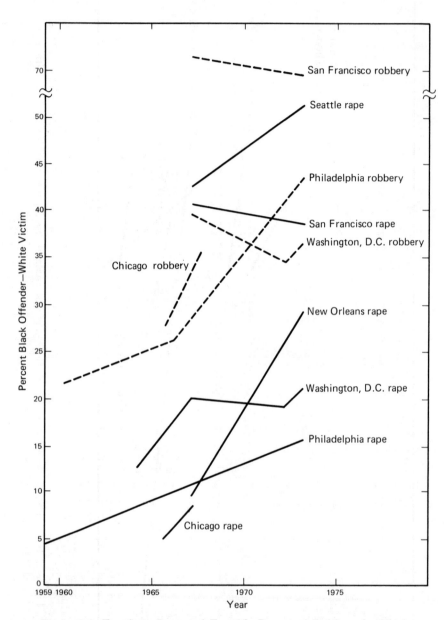

Figure 2-2. Trends in Reported Forcible Rape and Robbery by Blacks on Whites in Cities with Available Data. Source: Table 2-2.

Although they do not directly link the race of offender and victim, other supportive data come from FBI records of killings of police. The number of police officers killed rose nationally from 55 in 1963 to 112 in 1972. Of the officers killed from 1963 to 1967, 87 percent were white; 38 percent of the killers were black. From 1968 to 1972, the proportion of police officers killed who were white was about the same—86 percent; but the proportion of black killers rose to 55 percent.[24] In addition, the FBI national data in Chapter 3 express a clear increase in the proportion of homicides by strangers over the last decade. These data are again indirect. But they are based on the entire reported universe of homicides, not a sample, and interracial killings are more associated with absence of a prior relationship than intraracial killings.[25]

The discussion has been limited to the relative proportions of black-white, black-black, white-white, and white-black criminal violence out of a total or sample volume reported. But to speak of a relative proportion is not to speak of a crime rate per 100,000 population. What, then, is the implication for crime rates of the possible increase in the relative proportion of reported black-on-white encounters? Chapter 1 showed that reported offense rates per 100,000 population have increased dramatically over recent years among all 4 major violent crimes. In addition, special computations done by the FBI and the National Violence Commission showed sharp increases in the reported arrest rates of blacks per 100,000 urban blacks for all 4 crimes, as well as increases in the reported arrest rates of whites per 100,000 urban whites.[26] When combined with our percentage figures linking race of offender and victim, these rate data suggest very tentatively that reported arrest rates per 100,000 race-specific population have probably increased over recent years for all major violent crimes and in all racial patterns (black-black, white-white, black-white, and white-black) but that the black-white rate has probably increased relatively more than the others in some places. This does not, of course, justify the singular emphasis on black-white rape in *The Thunderbolt* cartoon.

Foreign Comparisons

There are relatively few foreign studies that link race of offender to race of victim. These works are mostly on homicide.

As in the United States, the evidence available shows homicide to be committed much more within a sociocultural group than between persons of different groups. Thus, 87 percent of the homicides committed in Israel between 1950 and 1964 involved persons of the same ethnic group—Western Jews (20 percent), Oriental Jews (27 percent), or Arabs (40 percent).[27] Similarly, in the studies of rural Indians, 92 percent of the Maria tribe killings and 84 percent of those in Central India were between persons of the same caste, an especially dramatic phenomenon in the latter study because it included 25 castes, often living adjacent to one another.[28] Of these homicides, 94 percent were among persons of the same religion, mainly Hindu.[29] In the Southern Province of Ceylon, virtually all of the killings were among persons of the same race (mostly Sinhalese).[30]

Of the "robberies under aggravating circumstances" reported in South Africa from 1970 to 1971, 41 percent involved non-whites, but 55 percent were by non-whites on whites. This pattern was not too dissimilar from U.S. robbery. However, 94 percent of "other robberies" reported and 97 percent of the "assaults with intent to do grievous bodily harm" reported were among non-whites in South Africa. No attempt was made in this study to explain the differences.[31]

Sex of Offender by Sex of Victim

The United States

Sixty-two percent of the homicide clearances in the national survey were between males; most of the rest were split between male-female and female-male encounters (Table 2-4). The cleared assault pattern bore a close resemblance except that the second-place frequency was more singularly male-female. Non-clearances that produced higher figures for the paramount male-male pattern in both crimes were also run.[32] The all-male percentages were even more

Table 2-4
Sex of Offender by Sex of Victim, Major Violent Crimes, 17 American Cities, 1967, Clearances (Percent)

Sex of Offender-Victim	Crime				
	Criminal Homicide	Aggravated Assault	Forcible Rape	Armed Robbery	Unarmed Robbery
Male-Male	62.3	56.6	–	84.5	68.9
Female-Female	3.8	7.1	–	0.9	2.9
Male-Female	17.5	27.0	100.0	10.2	26.2
Female-Male	16.4	9.3	–	4.4	2.0
Total %	100.0	100.0	100.0	100.0	100.0
(N)	(668)	(1493)	(617)	(412)	(482)

Base: Interactions
Note: Only those clearances where sex of both offender and victim was known are included. In robbery, clearances where the victim was an "institution" are not included.

preponderant in armed and unarmed clearances and non-clearances. The regional breakdowns were similar for the most part.[33] Other American studies concur.[34]

Foreign Comparisons

There is abundant international material on sex of offender and victim in homicide. Studies in Montreal, Denmark, Finland, Poland, Russia, Yugoslavia, Bulgaria, and Italy have provided findings that, broadly speaking, are consistent with the four-to-one male-female ratio among offenders and the four-to-one ratio among victims that was found in the national survey.[35] Yet, at various points in time, the proportion of female victims has been greater in England and Wales, Scotland, Sweden, Germany, Switzerland, France, Florence, and Moscow.[36]

Male offenders also predominated in Israel, but significant ethnic differences emerged among victims. About half of the Jews killed between 1950 and 1964 were females, but only roughly one-third of the Arabs were women. Landau and Drapkin believe that part of the reason for the relatively lower proportion of female victims among the Arabs may be attributable to the direct property value attached to women in Arab culture, through the tradition of brideprice paid by the groom to the parents or other relatives of the bride.[37]

Overwhelmingly, offenders were male in Africa, even more so than in the Western countries and Israel. The proportion of female victims ran from 17 to about 25 percent in 5 of the tribes studied by Bohannon's group and in Mushanga's study of Western Uganda.[38]

Mushanga relates all-male killings to the high frequency of face-to-face interactions among them. A man is not expected to be in the company of females. It is assumed that he will seek to display "masculinity, superiority, and dominance over other men." Low female homicide participation is consistent with intense conditioning to passivity. Thus, in the Ankole and Kigezi districts, the bridegroom, on his wedding day, is instructed to hit his bride on the head and say to her, "Speak once while I speak twice." Wives who insist on speaking as often as their husbands are very soon in trouble.[39] However, one of the districts Mushanga studied—Toro—departed from this general pattern for Western Uganda. Here the proportion of females killed was considerably higher. Mushanga allows that the institution of marriage has a uniquely high value in this area. There is deep emotional involvement and more prolonged male-female contact, particularly through sharing agricultural work.[40] When conflicts do arise, marriages are difficult to legally resolve, and so the only alternative in some instances may be perceived as physical termination.

In his analysis of 40 non-literate societies, Palmer found males to predominate in homicide as both offenders and victims.[41]

Four males were killed in Delhi, India for every female in 1963, but almost all the offenders were males.[42] In the studies of East-Central and Central Indian tribes, two-thirds of the homicides were all male. Most of the rest involved men killing women. Rural India, as rural Africa, therefore appears to host noticeably fewer intersex killings with female offenders than does the United States. Each of the rural Indian studies relates this to the woman's institutional role. Elwin observes the strong aboriginal belief that it is supernaturally dangerous for a woman to take life. This is why there are no female priests; the priest must offer sacrifice. Women are not supposed to kill even goats or chickens in the course of preparing daily meals.[43] Driver describes how women are expected to manage the household, care for the children, respect the authority of their husbands, and leave the management of business and the settlement of disputes to male relatives.[44]

The Southern Province of Ceylon paralleled India, with 5 times as many male as female victims and with almost all offenders being male. Jayewardene and Ranasinghe lay emphasis on the male role of arbitrator. All conflicts are resolved by him. "Even in the matriarchal fishing villages, violence begins only after the return of the male home from the more fruitful fishing grounds he migrates to during the monsoonal period. The female gets her battles fought then."[45]

Examination of incarcerated Chinese offenders in pre-Communist Peking produced about the same proportion of males as in India and Ceylon.[46] More recent information (1965), however, suggests that the ratio of male to female victims in Hong Kong, Singapore, and Taiwan is generally compatible to American cities, lower than in the Philippines and Thailand, and higher than in Australia and Japan.[47]

Generally, then, the great majority of homicide offenders are males in countries throughout the world, and the percentage of females among victims is usually higher than among offenders. Although local institutions and customs vary, the preponderance of men in homicide is related not only to such socially and culturally defined roles as aggressor, provider, and leader, but to the greater social pressures created by these positions and to the greater frequency of their external contacts.

Vekko's classical hypothesis that the proportion of female offenders and victims will be relatively higher in countries with a relatively higher incidence of homicide, and vice versa,[48] does not appear valid from the evidence set forth.

However, Sutherland's suggestion that the rate of female offenders will show some tendency to approach the male rate in countries where females experience relatively greater freedom and equality[49] does seem to have considerable truth for the places reviewed. Similar results did not emerge for female victims. For example, women are probably more equal vis-à-vis men among Western Jews in Israel and in the United States than in England. Yet the proportion of female victims for Western Jews in Israel is about the same as the proportion of female victims in England and much higher than in the United States. One might expect women to register more on *both* sides of the ledger of death as they increase their interfacings and responsibilities in professional, business, and other activity.

The few foreign studies of the other major violent crimes show no dramatic departures from the American sex of offender by victim pattern.[50]

Age of Offender by Age of Victim

The United States

The leading homicide and assault clearance pattern in the national survey placed both offenders and victims in the 26 and over category (Table 2-5). However, more detailed breakdowns of this broad classification tend to support the findings of other American studies that the most disproportionate offender range covers young adults in their teens and twenties, with modal victims in the same group for assault but slightly older for homicide.[51] Rape offenders in the national survey were most frequently juveniles or young adults as old as or, more commonly, older than their victims. The ascendant armed robbery sequence was for young adults to hold up older persons. In unarmed robbery, offenders were most often juveniles, and the victims were either juveniles or adults over 26. Earlier work in the United States was generally consistent.[52]

Table 2-5

Age of Offender by Age of Victim, Major Violent Crimes, 17 American Cities, 1967, Clearances (Percent)

Age of Offender-Victim	Crime				
	Criminal Homicide	Aggravated Assault	Forcible Rape	Armed Robbery	Unarmed Robbery
17 & under - 17 & under	3.3	13.5	15.7	6.8	31.2
17 & under - 18 to 25	1.6	1.4	2.7	8.5	4.9
17 & under - 26 & over	4.2	2.8	2.5	8.1	21.0
18 to 25 - 17 & under	3.6	3.4	17.1	2.1	1.7
18 to 25 - 18 to 25	10.3	10.1	18.8	13.1	6.4
18 to 25 - 26 & over	19.8	11.1	12.1	36.8	23.2
26 & over - 17 & under	3.5	3.1	14.6	0.8	–
26 & over - 18 to 25	6.7	11.7	7.4	5.4	2.0
26 & over - 26 & over	47.0	42.9	9.1	18.4	9.6
Total %	100.0	100.0	100.0	100.0	100.0
(N)	(542)	(780)	(445)	(255)	(237)

Base: Interactions

Note: Only those clearances where age of both offender and victim was known are included. In robbery, clearances where the victim was an "institution" are not included.

There were some exceptions, but age relationships were compatible over the different regions in the national survey.[53]

Foreign Comparisons

Homicide age patterns in Montreal, England and Wales, Scotland, Poland, Florence, Israel, Africa, India, and Ceylon were reasonably consistent with the United States.[54] This was also broadly true for assaults in Montreal and London[55] and for rapes in Montreal, England and Wales, and Denmark.[56] Age distributions for robbery in London followed the pattern of United States armed robberies. Victims were somewhat younger in Montreal than in American cities and offenders a bit older.[57]

Notes and References

1. Wolfgang and Cohen (1970, p. 5).
2. Sills (1968, Volume 13).
3. However, self-identification was completely implemented in the 1970 census (U.S. Department of Commerce 1972).
4. Although the relatively few interactions involving persons of other races were eliminated here, they are included in the general tables in other chapters, where frequency distributions for all races are aggregated together. In the national survey, the category of "other" races was composed of the *UCR* category of American Indian, Indian, Chinese, Japanese, and "other." Police classify offenders and victims with Spanish surnames as either black or white (although it may be that some Spanish surname participants are classified as "other"). Unfortunately, the national survey did not code separately for Spanish surnames. However, an exception was made in New York City, to produce the survey data in Figure 2-3. For robbery, interactions where the victim was an "institution" were, of course, eliminated from tables in this chapter.
5. For the tables on non-clearances, see Curtis (1972).
6. See Curtis (1972) for the supporting tables.
7. Thus, the most reliable 1967 estimates (U.S. Department of Labor 1970) of the percentage of blacks in the central metropolitan areas (not SMSAs) of the survey cities are as follows:

North Central Cities		*Northeastern Cities*	
Chicago	30%	Boston	15%
Cleveland	34%	New York	19%
Detroit	39%	Philadelphia	33%
Minneapolis	4%	Washington, D.C.	69%
St. Louis	37%		

Western Cities		Southern Cities	
Denver	9%	Atlanta	44%
Los Angeles	18%	Dallas	22%
San Francisco	14%	Miami	N.A.
Seattle	7%	New Orleans	41%

Offender-victim race specific rates per 100,000 population are not available by region. Estimates might have been attempted here using the survey racial percentages, *UCR* crime volumes and Bureau of the Census population volumes, but we prefer to wait until more broad-based race specific offender-victim data come into being.

8. For homicide, Wolfgang (1958, p. 210) found 72 percent of his Philadelphia cases to be all-black and 22 percent all-white. In Houston, Pokorny (1965, p. 484) disclosed that 94 percent of his killings were intraracial. In Washington, the D.C. Crime Commission (1966, p. 42) found only 12 of 172 murders to be interracial. Voss and Hepburn (1968, p. 501) showed only 7 percent of their Chicago killings to be interracial, mostly black-on-white. Seventy-seven percent of the homicides analyzed by Wilt and Bannon (1974) were black-black while 14 percent were white-white. In New Orleans, 73 percent of the killings were all black and 12 percent were all-white (Caruso 1974). The figures in San Francisco were 43 percent, black-black; 23 percent, white-white; 21 percent, black-on-white; and 13 percent, white-on-black (Feder 1974). In the country as a whole, the 1967 FBI *Uniform Crime Reports* (1967, pp. 7, 126) found 58 percent of all offenders and 54 percent of all victims to be black. The lower proportions compared to the national survey reflected the inclusion of non-urban areas. For assault, Pittman and Handy (1964, pp. 467-8) found that 80 percent of their cases were black-black and 17 percent were white-white. In Washington, the D.C. Crime Commission (1966, p. 76) showed only 9 percent of all assaults to be interracial. In Chicago, Reiss (1967, p. 34) concluded that 90 percent of his assaults were intraracial, with most of the rest being black-on-white. In Houston, Pokorny (1965, p. 495) found that 66 percent of the offenders were black, as were 68 percent of the victims. The figures in San Francisco were 38 percent all black, 36 percent all-white, 22 percent black-on-white, and 4 percent white-on-black.

9. Amir (1965, p. 82) reported that 77 percent of the rapes studied in Philadelphia were all-black; 16 percent, all-white; and only 4 percent, black-white. Reiss (1967, p. 34) showed 90 percent of his Chicago rapes to be intraracial, only 3 to 5 percent being black-white. In Washington, the D.C. Crime Commission (1966, p. 54) found that 88 percent of the rapes studied were intraracial, but almost all the rest followed a black-white pattern. Hayman's (1971) later observations in the same city produced a black-white figure of 21 percent. MacDonald (1971, p. 51) found that 18 percent of his Denver rapes were black-white. Forty-nine percent of the Kansas City rapes reported by

Harpold (1973) were black-black; 20 percent, white-white; and 21 percent, black-white. In New Orleans, 63 percent of the rapes were all-black, and 29 percent were black-white (Caruso 1974). Only 14 percent of the rapes in Seattle were all-black; 34 percent were white-white and 51 percent black-white (Seattle Law and Justice Planning Office 1975). Twenty-one percent of the rapes in San Francisco were all-black; 38 percent, all-white; and slightly more than 38 percent, black-white (Feder 1974). In Oakland, 40 percent were all-black and 33 percent black-white (Agopian et al. 1972). Nelson and Amir (1973) found that fully 64 percent of the hitchhike rapes and 57 percent of the non-hitchhike rapes reported in Berkeley between 1968 and 1970 were by blacks on whites.

10. In Washington, the D.C. Crime Commission (1966, pp. 56, 65) disclosed that 56 percent of the victims in all types of robbery were white and 86 percent of the offenders non-white. Reiss (1967, p. 34) concluded that about two-thirds of his Chicago robberies were intraracial and 25 to 30 percent were black-on-white. Normandeau (1968, p. 207) found that 63 percent of his Philadelphia armed robberies were black-black and 23 percent were black-white; among unarmed robberies, 63 percent were all-black and 24 percent, black-on-white.

Thirty-one percent of Silverman's (1971, p. 99) Philadelphia juvenile robberies were black-black and 60 percent were black-on-white. In San Francisco, 10 percent of the robberies were all-black; 20 percent, all-white; and 69 percent, black-on-white.

11. FBI (1967).

12. Ennis (1967, p. 8).

13. LEAA (1974). Other estimates of the gap in rape are even higher than in Ennis or by the LEAA. See, for example, Lear (1972).

14. Black (1971); Skolnick (1966); Tiffany, McIntyre and Rotenberg (1967).

15. Ennis (1967, p. 44).

16. LEAA (1974).

17. Blassingame (1972, pp. 82-83).

18. Iceberg Slim (1969, p. 177). White prostitutes are not immune from such situations; yet a white woman going into prostitution may have a better chance than a black woman of becoming a call girl or otherwise working in a way to avoid the greater abuse encountered on the street.

19. Guy (1972, pp. 74, 80). In this case, the victim was Puerto Rican, but the account applies equally to blacks.

20. Agopian et al. (1972, p. 15).

21. Ennis (196, pp. 30, 47).

22. The only exception to these conclusions on black-black and white-white proportions was in criminal homicide, where the all-black proportion either increased or stayed the same and the all-white proportion uniformly declined.

23. Two other potential problems should be noted. First, when the black-white proportion was lower than the black-black or white-white proportions at the beginning of a city-crime trend period (as was often the case), the same

increase in the number of incidents over time produced a higher percent increase for the black-white proportions than the others. Secondly, several of the trends in Table 2-2 compare cleared data at one point in time to cleared plus uncleared data at another point in time. As discussed in the text, cleared data are likely to produce relatively lower black-white percents than uncleared data (because black-white encounters are relatively more likely to involve strangers, who are more difficult to trace and arrest than non-strangers). Therefore, cleared data are also likely to produce relatively lower black-white percents than cleared plus uncleared data combined. What are the implications? In Table 2-2, initial cleared data are compared to later cleared plus uncleared data in three city-crime types showing an increase over time in the black-white percent (Philadelphia homicide, New Orleans homicide, and New Orleans rape); here it is possible that much or all of the increase would be eliminated if clearances were compared to clearances, non-clearances to non-clearances, or cleared plus uncleared to cleared plus uncleared. Initial cleared data are compared to later cleared plus uncleared data in one city-crime type showing no significant change over time in the black-white percent (Philadelphia assault); here it is possible that a trend decrease in the percent would emerge if clearances were compared to clearances, and so forth. Finally, initial uncleared plus cleared data are compared to later cleared data in three city-crime types showing an increase over time in the black-white percent (Chicago assault, Chicago rape, and Chicago robbery); here it is possible that the black-white increase would be even greater if clearances were compared to clearances, and so forth.

24. FBI (1972, pp, 41, 43, 50).

25. For example, 48 percent of the black-black killings in the national survey aggregate involved non-primary group relationships (mostly strangers or acquaintances), 35 percent of the white-white killings, 65 percent of the white-black killings, and 75 percent of the black-white killings. See Curtis (1972) for the tables.

26. See Mulvihill and Tumin with Curtis (1969, c. 3). The relative levels of the white rates were much lower than the levels of the black rates, however. For example, the computed arrest rate per 100,000 urban blacks in 1964 was 47.2 against 4.9 per 100,000 urban whites. The 1967 rates were 59.9 and 5.4, respectively.

27. Landau and Drapkin (1968, Table 21).

28. Elwin (1943, p. 40) and Driver (1961, p. 98).

29. Driver (1961, p. 98).

30. Jayewardene and Ranasinghe (1963, p. 98).

31. Freed (1973).

32. For the tables on non-clearances, see Curtis (1972).

33. For the regional tables, see Curtis (1972).

34. In homicide, Wolfgang (1958, p. 32) concluded that 82 percent of his Philadelphia offenders and 76 percent of the victims were male. The frequencies

were 81 and 76 percents for Pokorny (1965, pp. 484-5) in Houston, 82 and 69 percents for the D.C. Crime Commission (1966, pp. 36, 42) in Washington, and 83 and 74 percents for Voss and Hepburn (1968, p. 501) in Chicago. For the country as a whole, the 1967 FBI *Uniform Crime Reports* (1967, p. 7) produced an offender ratio of 5:1 male to female and a victim ratio of 3:1 male to female. In aggravated assault, the dominant pattern was male-male for Pittman and Handy (1964, p. 467) in St. Louis and Reiss (1967, p. 34) in Chicago. The D.C. Crime Commission (1966, p. 76) reported that 79 percent of the offenders and 71 percent of the victims in Washington were male. In robbery, 73 percent of Normandeau's (1968, pp. 167-73) Philadelphia cases were male-male. Seventy-seven percent of Reiss's (1967, p. 34) armed robberies and 69 percent of his unarmed robberies were male-male. The D.C. Crime Commission (1966, pp. 56, 64) disclosed that 95 percent of Washington robbery offenders were male; the male-female victim ratio was 3:2.

35. In Montreal, Tardiff (1966, pp. 65-66) found 71 percent of victims and 84 percent of offenders to be male in 1964. In Denmark, Svalastoga (1956) found about 70 percent of offenders to be male over 1934-1939 and 1945-1951. In Finland, Verkko (1951, p. 42) found between 1934 and 1944 that 23 women were killed for every 100 men. In Poland, Holyst (1967, pp. 72-74) found 69 percent of the victims over 1955-1961 to be men, as were 90 percent of the offenders. Conner (1973) reported that over 90 percent of the offenders were male in various Russian studies in the 1960s. For the USSR as a whole, the official Soviet textbook reported that about three-quarters of all homicide victims were male. Verkko (1951, p. 51) reported that less than 10 percent of the homicide victims he studied in Serbia, Bulgaria, and Italy were women.

36. In England and Wales, Gibson and Klein (1969, p. 16) found 47 percent of the 1967 victims were males (convicted offenders were overwhelmingly males). In Scotland, Gibson and Klein (1969, p. 87) showed that 51 percent of victims between 1966 and 1968 were males (convicted offenders were again almost all males). Verkko (1951, p. 47) reported that in Sweden between 1921 and 1940, there were 63 female victims per every 100 male victims. Von Hentig (1940, p. 305) disclosed that 44 percent of German victims slain between 1928 and 1930 were males. Ting and Tan (1969, p. 245) showed that in 1965 the ratio of male to female victims was 1:1 in Switzerland and 1.2:1 in France. Simondi (1970) found 82 percent of the homicide offenders he studied in Florence to be male, but the percent of male victims dropped to 62. For the late 1960s, 51 percent of the homicide victims in Moscow were female (Conner 1973, p. 112).

37. Landau and Drapkin (1968, pp. 39, 41, 42).

38. Bohannon (1960, pp. 218-20) and Mushanga (1970, p. 24).

39. Mushanga (1970, pp. 20-24).

40. Mushanga (1970, p. 24).

41. Palmer (1973).

42. Rao (1968, pp. 17, 19).

43. Elwin (1943, p. 162).

44. Driver (1961, p. 56).

45. Jayewardene and Ranasinghe (1963, pp. 99-100).

46. Yen (1929).

47. Ting and Tan (1969, p. 245) give these 1965 ratios of male to female victims based on reported homicide rates:

Hong Kong	3.2:1
Singapore	
Chinese	6:1
Indian	2.7:1
Malay	3.6:1
Taiwan	3.5:1
Philippines	14.7:1
Thailand	7.8:1
Australia	1:1
Japan	1.9:1

48. Verkko (1951, p. 51) presented the hypothesis as two "static laws," one for victims and one for offenders. He also proposed "dynamic laws" for victims and offenders: when homicide is on the increase in a country, the increase mainly involves male victims and offenders, and when it is on the decrease, the decrease as well mainly involves male victims and offenders. Although the "dynamic laws" could not be tested here from the international data available, Wolfgang (1958, pp. 61-64) found inconsistent fluctuations over a five-year period in Philadelphia.

49. Sutherland (1947).

50. In Montreal assaults, Tardiff (1966, pp. 65-71) found somewhat higher proportions of males as both offender and victim than in the U.S. More than 90 percent of the assaulters in London were males. (McClintock 1963a, pp. 42-45.) The proportion of male victims was about the same for assaults in public houses, streets, and other places away from home; yet it was only slightly higher than the female percentage in family disputes, producing an aggregate victim distribution closer to U.S. cities than Montreal. Robberies in Montreal (Tardiff 1966, pp. 65-68) and London (McClintock and Gibson 1961, pp. 18-22) generated sex distributions resembling unarmed encounters in the U.S.

51. For homicide, the modal range among Wolfgang's (1958, p. 66) Philadelphia offenders was 20-24, and victims were most concentrated from 25 to 34. Pokorny's (1965, p. 493) modal offender range was 25-29 for Houston offenders and 30-34 for victims. In Washington, the D.C. Crime Commission (1966, pp. 37, 43) found that 37 percent of all offenders and 25 percent of all victims were 18 to 29. The modal offender range for Voss and Hepburn (1968, p. 502) was

20-24, and 25-29 was the modal victim span. Burnham (1973) found the largest single group of victims in New York to be aged 30 to 39 (26 percent) and the leading offender group to be 20 to 29 (34 percent). For the country as a whole in 1967, the FBI *Uniform Crime Reports* (1967, p. 123) found arrested offenders most concentrated from 18 to 25 and victims from 20 to 29. For assault, Pittman and Handy's (1964, p. 467) St. Louis offenders as well as victims were most frequently aged 20 to 34. In Washington, the D.C. Crime Commission (1966, pp. 71, 77) found 32 percent of all offenders to be 18 to 29; the victim proportion was the same.

52. For rape, the median age Amir (1965, p. 104) found for Philadelphia offenders was 23.0, compared to 19.6 for victims. However, Chappell and Singer (1973, p. 34) found that almost 50 percent of the rapists studied in New York were aged 25 or over (compared to only 30 percent in Philadelphia). In Washington, the D.C. Crime Commission (1966, pp. 49, 52) reported that 36 percent of all offenders were aged 16 to 20 and 29 percent aged 21 to 29, but that 54 percent of the victims were 15 and under. Fifty percent of the rapists MacDonald (1971, p. 54) studied in Denver were between 15 and 25, whereas victims were younger on the average. For robbery, Normandeau's (1968, pp. 167-73) offenders were generally much younger than victims. Twenty percent of the Washington robbery offenders reported by the D.C. Crime Commission (1966, pp. 59, 65) were 15 and under, with 62 percent 16 to 29; but 38 percent of the victims were 30 to 49 and 32 percent were 50 years or older.

53. See Curtis (1972) for the regional tables.

54. In Montreal, Tardiff (1966, pp. 67, 68, 71) found the most frequent victim range to be 25-44 and the most frequent offender range 20-34 in 1964. In England and Wales, Gibson and Klein (1969, pp. 16, 26, 28) showed the most frequent victim range to be 16-49 in 1967; the majority of offenders were under 30. In Scotland, the 1966-1968 results of Gibson and Klein (1969, p. 76) had victims peak between 16 and 49, while two-thirds of the offenders were between 18 and 30. Holyst (1967, pp. 29, 30, 76) found the peak offender range in Poland to be 26-30, followed closely by the 22-25, 18-21 and 31-35 groups. The highest victim range was 31 to 40, followed by 41 to 50. The most common age bracket among the offenders Simondi (1970) studied in Florence was 21 to 30. The highest victim frequency was for ages 45-60. In Israel, Landau and Drapkin (1968, p. 42) found 49 percent of the victims between 1950 and 1964 to be 15 to 39; 47 percent of the offenders were 20 to 29. Among the African Gisu (1948-1954 data) and Soga (1952-1954 data) tribes studied by the Bohannon group (1960, pp. 83, 108), killers were most common between ages 25-30 and 21-35, respectively. Mushanga (1970, p. 26) reported that offenders in Western Uganda were most often 25 to 29, then 20 to 24. Victims were highest in the 25 to 29 range also, followed by the 35 to 39 bracket. The peak victim range was 16-30 and the peak offender group 22-30, according to Rao (1968, pp. 17, 20) in Delhi for 1963. In the Southern Province of Ceylon, Jayewardene and

Ranasinghe (1963, p. 101) found the mean age for suspected offenders to be 28.8 in 1960; the victim mean was 29.8.

55. In Montreal, Tardiff (1966, pp. 65-71) found the most common age range for assault offenders as well as victims to be 15-44. In London, McClintock (1963a, pp. 42-45) found the majority of offenders to be over 21, with victim somewhat older.

56. In Canadian rapes, Tardiff (1966, pp. 67, 68, 71) found that the peak victim range was 15-44 and the peak offender range 20-44 in 1963. In 1950 "sexual offenses" occurring primarily in urban parts of England and Wales, Radzinowicz (1957, p. 85) found that the majority of female victims were 16 and under and the proportion over 21 was small. Rapes only made up a small part of the sex offenses, however, and it is likely that the resulting age distribution was downward biased compared to the distributions of rape alone in England and Wales as well as in other countries. In Denmark, Svalastoga (1962, p. 49) reported that about half of all rape victims between 1946 and 1958 were between 15 and 19, and 71 percent of the offenders were between 15 and 29. In an earlier investigation, between 1929 and 1939, LeMaire (1946) found the most common offender range to be 15-19.

57. McClintock and Gibson (1966, pp. 46-48) found the majority of London robbery victims to be between 21 and 50 and most offenders to be between 17 and 30. In Montreal, Tardiff (1968, pp. 65-68) reported the peak victim range to be 10-24 and the peak offender range 15-34.

3

Interpersonal Relationships

Fear of strangers is impoverishing the lives of many Americans. People stay behind the locked doors of their homes rather than walk in the street at night. Poor people take taxis because they are afraid to walk or use public transportation. Sociable people are afraid to talk to those they do not know. Society is suffering from what the economist would label opportunity costs. When people would stay home, they are not enjoying the pleasurable and cultural opportunities in their communities; they are not visiting their friends as frequently as they might. The general level of sociability is diminished.

—Jennie McIntyre,
The Annals, November 1967

Summary of the National Survey

Just how great is the stranger's role in criminal violence? Table 3-1[1] arranges degree of prior knowledge according to "husband-wife relationships," "other family relationships," "other primary group relationships" (close friend,[2] heterosexual lover, homosexual lover[3]) and "non-primary group relationships" (prostitute, acquaintance,[4] neighbor, business relation, sex rival or enemy,[5] stranger,[6] police officer, or felon[7]).

A considerable number of clearances were, in fact, comprised of strangers in 1967. The frequency of strangers was relatively low in homicide (16 percent) and assault (21 percent). However, the possibility exists that a disproportionate number of the instances where relationship was not known entailed strangers. It is usually more difficult for police to accumulate information when the offender has no previous relationship with the victim. The proportion of strangers took primacy in forcible rape (53 percent) and dominated in armed (79 percent) and unarmed robbery (86 percent). The percentage of non-primary group relationships steadily rose from homicide to robbery, whereas the frequency of family and other primary group relationships uniformly declined.

We can hypothesize that crimes by strangers gravitate to the impersonal street, whereas violence within primary group relationships tends to indoor privacy. The survey data on locations (Appendix A) are largely supportive. Although there was a relatively even split between indoor and outdoor places in armed robbery, that points to the many commercial targets, unarmed robbers kept to the street for the most part. The odds for outside locations declined in assault and even more for homicide. As in homicide, rape occurred most frequently indoors. However, Amir and MacDonald found that the place of first

Table 3-1
The Interpersonal Relationship between Offender and Victim, by Type of Crime, 17 American Cities, 1967, Clearances (Percent)

Relationship	Major Violent Crime Type				
	Criminal Homicide	Aggravated Assault	Forcible Rape	Armed Robbery	Unarmed Robbery
Husband (V) Wife (O) (legal)	6.3	1.9	0	0	0
Wife (V) Husband (O) (legal)	6.0	5.3	0	.6	0
Husband (V) Wife (O) (common)	1.5	.5	0	0	0
Wife (V) Husband (O) (common)	2.0	1.7	0	0	0
SUBTOTAL: Husband-Wife	15.8	9.4	0	0.6	0
Parent (V) Child (O)	2.0	0.9	0.2	0	0
Child (V) Parent (O)	3.9	1.2	2.0	0	0.1
Brother-Sister (V or O)	1.4	1.4	0.3	0	0
Other Family	1.6	1.0	4.4	0	0.4
SUBTOTAL: Other Family	8.9	4.5	6.9	0	0.5
Close Friend	5.6	3.6	1.6	0.1	0
Heterosexual Lover	3.2	2.9	1.7	0.3	0.1
Homosexual Lover	0.2	0.2	0	0	0

SUBTOTAL: Other Primary	9.0	6.7	3.3	0.4	0.1
Prostitute (V or O)	0.9	0.2	0	0.6	0.1
Acquaintance	15.4	16.0	28.5	8.8	8.0
Neighbor	3.1	3.8	3.3	0.5	2.6
Business Relation	1.9	1.3	0.1	0.9	0
Sex Rival or Enemy	6.8	3.0	0.7	1.4	0.2
Stranger	15.6	20.6	52.8	78.6	85.7
Felon or Police Officer (V or O)	1.7	10.1	0.3	0	0.2
SUBTOTAL: Non-Primary	45.4	55.0	85.7	90.8	96.8
SUBTOTAL: Unknown	20.9	24.3	4.1	8.2	2.6
GRAND TOTAL	100.0	100.0	100.0	100.0	100.0
	(668)	(1493)	(617)	(509)	(502)

Base: Interactions

meeting was more often outside, and Chappell and Singer also observed a higher percentage of outdoor places for initial contact than for the rape itself.[8]

In sum, the popularly conceptualized fear that violent attack will come from a stranger on the street is justified by the national survey for robbery and relevant for rape, but less valid for assault and homicide.

Criminal Homicide

The United States

Yet, even in homicide, the role of strangers appears to be growing in this country. National homicide relationship trends, at least for the last decade, can be derived from the FBI *Uniform Crime Reports*. Covering all offenses known, Table 3-2 was pieced together from the FBI tabulation of "Murder by Circumstances."[9] The data show that homicides for all types of relationships have increased in volume over the 10-year period from 1963 to 1972, but the relative proportion of killings by strangers has risen at the expense of the other categories.[10] Complementary findings come from a survey in Washington, D.C. and show that the proportion of strangers in homicide rose from 25 percent in 1966 to 73 percent in 1969.[11]

The FBI does not relate offender and victim by race in the killings by strangers chronicled in Table 3-2. However, as discussed in Chapter 2, the data on the proportion of non-primary group killings in intraracial against interracial contexts from the national survey and other studies and the data on the rise in police killings (mostly by strangers and increasingly black-on-white) support the speculation that the increase in the percentage of stranger killings in Table 3-2 may be disproportionately black-white. A stream of journalistic investigations—impressionistic, of course, and not based on scientific samples—provides ample illustration of such encounters. Consider, for example, the following case studies, all on black offenders previously unknown to their white victims, in a 1971 *National Observer* survey:

... Bob Aleshire, a brilliant 29-year old antipoverty consultant, had just left his office to begin a vacation with his wife and four small children. It was rush hour in downtown Washington, D.C., as he nosed his car into traffic and headed toward his suburban Montgomery County, Maryland home. Two blocks from the office an approaching car crossed the center stripe and sideswiped his car and two others. Startled, Mr. Aleshire got out to survey the damage. So did the driver of the car that hit him—but that driver had a gun. Without a word he stepped up to Bob Aleshire and fired. The victim slumped to the ground, one bullet lodged in his head, another in his stomach. He died minutes later. His assailant waited until police arrived and turned himself in.

... *Mrs. Charlotte Cooper, 47, of Miami and her husband William, a disabled carpenter, were driving home from a visit to a daughter one evening last winter. As they passed through the Liberty City ghetto area, someone lobbed a*

Table 3-2
Criminal Homicide Relationships Nationally, Offenses Known, All Years Available (1963-1972) (Percent)

Relationship	1963[b]	1964[b]	1965[b]	1966	1967	1968	1969	1970	1971	1972
Family	31.0	31.0	31.0	28.8	28.2	25.7	25.2	23.3	24.7	24.3
Friends, Neighbors, and Acquaintances (*UCR* categories of "Romantic triangle and lovers' quarrels" and "Other arguments")	51.0	49.0	48.0	49.4	50.3	49.4	48.3	47.9	47.8	48.3
Non-Primary Relationships—Mostly Strangers (*UCR* categories of "known felony type", and "suspected felony type"[a])	17.0	20.0	21.0	21.8	21.5	24.9	26.5	28.8	27.5	27.4
TOTAL	100.0 (8,500)	100.0 (9,250)	100.0 (9,850)	100.0 (10,920)	100.0 (12,090)	100.0 (13,650)	100.0 (14,590)	100.0 (15,810)	100.0 (17,630)	100.0 (18,520)

[a]Felony homicide is defined in the *UCR* as "killings resulting from robberies, sex motives, gangland slayings and other felonious activities."
[b]Only rounded figures available.
Source: FBI *Uniform Crime Reports*

firebomb into their car. She died of burns. The killer was apprehended and committed to a state mental hospital.

... Robert Lafleur, 21, a Boston College senior, was sharing a six-pack of beer with some friends at a high school parking lot in the interracial Dorchester area of Boston late last month. Two strangers got out of a car nearby, and one began firing. The friends scattered, but the assailant pursued Mr. Lafleur into a car and shot him in the abdomen. He died four hours later. The killer has not been found.

... At 11:15 p.m., August 15, Stephen Borg, a vacationing Elmira, N.Y., junior high school teacher, who was white, and his wife, who is black, pulled their car to the curb at 37th Street and Broadway. They opened a newspaper to check whether there was dancing at a hotel 20 blocks away. A black couple approached them with a gun and ordered them into the back seat. Instead Mr. Borg stepped on the gas. The gunman fired two shots, fatally wounded Mr. Borg in the face and back. The killer has not been apprehended. [1][2]

The dynamics of race and relationship need to be carefully traced in years to come, but the considerable amount of homicide that remains among intimates should not be forgotten. One-third of the interactions in the 17-city survey were primary group in 1967. Most involved family relationships. The percent reported that year by the FBI for all areas of the country, urban and rural, was about the same (Table 3-2). Significant primary group percentages also have been found in the single-city studies—for example, Philadelphia, Houston, Washington and Chicago. [1][3]

Although spouses, lovers, and close friends are a main source of pleasure in one's life, they are equally a main source of frustration and hurt. Few others can anger one so much, and there is more social transaction time for ego picking, as well as spine stroking, in comparison to less close relationships. Not uncommonly, intimates are often locked in a pattern that satisfies both positive and negative emotional needs:

In an intimate relationship . . . one or both persons can come to feel that the other is unfair or wrong but a redress of the imbalance is difficult to achieve, because both are convinced that they have already overextended their resources, and already done enough for the other. Being emotionally close, each is vulnerable, and knows how to hurt the other, while neither can easily retreat to the comfortable, civil formulas and masks that are permissible and common with mere acquaintances or strangers.

Letting go is painful, because both individuals once fed each other's emotional needs, and the need remains, while no other person is exactly a substitute. Breaking off is hurtful also because one or both may feel that the other is getting away scot free without a just revenge being inflicted, without a fair and final balance of the emotional books. . . .

One consequence is that many people remain in a relationship which they have come to detest and which they know may even be physically dangerous. . . . In addition, the pressure of friends and the sheer practical difficulty of starting and maintaining a new household can seem insurmountable.

Many men and a goodly number of women have finally come to the conclusion that homicide is a cleaner, neater solution than the dragged out, acerbic destruction of ego and dignity that is inherent in breaking off.[14]

Shakespeare, long before Freud, recognized that an individual can both love and kill the object of his or her desire if the normal expression of feelings is denied, or perceived as such. Without love and consequent jealousy, Othello might not have killed Desdemona.

The theme of violence among intimates also was a useful differentiating pattern when the regional groupings of the 1967 survey cities were examined. A greater proportion of killings occurred in the family for the western aggregate (38 percent) than in the Northeast (26 percent), South (23 percent) and the north central cities (19 percent).[15] Homicide relationships compose one of the few survey categories where the FBI publishes regional information for all reporting areas. In 1967, the *Uniform Crime Reports* also showed the West to lead in family killings. We can only speculate on the reasons behind the difference. Geis, for one, has suggested that perhaps there is something selective about the migration to California,[16] so that, when a murder is committed, there may be a greater likelihood than in other regions that it reflects "a heightened isolation and ensuing willingness to take out hostility in overt ways—aggression and divorce."[17] However, when the family percentages are multiplied by regional rates of homicide, the resulting estimates of rates of family homicide by region are highest in the South, with the West in second place.[18] (By contrast, the West had the highest rate in assault as can be seen below).

Foreign Comparisons

Table 3-3 summarizes the international data.[19] The very high proportion of stranger killings in Montreal should be noted, but the Canadian data resemble the urban United States more if it is assumed that the unknowns in the national survey disproportionately involved strangers. There were relatively more family killings in England and Wales than the United States, but less in Scotland.

Of the homicides examined in Denmark, 57 percent were within the family, which is higher than in any other study. This was not so much due to the murder of spouses as to killings within other family relationships. In particular, many of the female offenders killed their newborn babies. Svalastoga's observation periods were directly before and after World War II, so the actions might have been related to the social chaos and resulting personal hardship. Updated findings are needed to bear any such speculation out. The frequency of non-primary group killing in Denmark was also lower than in other countries of the West.

Family killings figured prominently in the reports based on all of Poland (41 percent), from Moscow (42 percent) and from two (mixed urban-rural) prov-

Table 3-3
Interpersonal Relationships by Crime and Country (Percent)

	Criminal Homicide				
Crime, Country, Geographic Scope, Year / Relationship	United States Urban (17 City Survey, Clearances) 1967	Canada[1] Urban (Montreal) 1964	England[2] and Wales Entire Country 1967	Scotland[3] Entire Country 1957-1968	Denmark[4] Entire Country 1934-1939 1946-1951
Family-Kinsman-Relative	24.7	27.1	36.1	17.1	57.0
Husband-Wife	15.8	8.3	16.7	7.3	12.2
Other Family-Kinsman-Relative	8.9	18.8	19.4	9.8	44.8
Other Primary Group	9.0	10.4	9.7	8.5	10.4
Non-Primary Group	45.4	62.5	54.2	74.4	32.6
Acquaintance	15.4	12.5	34.7	39.0	–
Stranger	15.6	47.9	19.4	34.8	12.3
Unknown	20.9	0	0	0	0
TOTAL	100.0	100.0	100.0	100.0	100.0
	(668)	(48)	(72)	(164)	(172)

Table 3-3 (cont.)

	Criminal Homicide				
Crime, Country, Geographic Scope, Year / Relationship	Poland[5] Entire Country 1955-61	USSR[6] Urban (Moscow) Late 1960s	USSR[6] Urban-Rural (Briansk, Kalinin and Vladimir Provinces) 1963	USSR[6] Urban-Rural (Rostov Province) 1961-1962	Italy[7] Urban (Florence) 1951-1963
Family-Kinsman-Relative	40.7	42.0	40.8	36.2	25.5
Husband-Wife	20.0	–	–	–	–
Other Family-Kinsman-Relative	20.7	–	–	–	–
Other Primary Group	3.6	– } 58.0	– } 59.2	– } 63.8	19.1
Non-Primary Group	40.2	–	–	–	47.9
Acquaintance	–	–	–	–	19.1
Stranger	–	–	–	–	16.0
Unknown	15.5	0	0	0	7.5
TOTAL	100.0	100.0	100.0	100.0	100.0
	(420)	(100)	(Unknown)	(Unknown)	(94)

Table 3-3 (cont.)

Crime, Country, Geographic Scope, Year / Relationship	Criminal Homicide			
	Israel[8]			
	Entire Country (Jewish Population 2/3 Urban, Non-Jewish Population Rural) 1950-1964			
	Western Jews	Oriental Jews	Non-Jews	Total
Family-Kinsman-Relative	40.0	44.0	41.0	42.0
Husband-Wife	22.0	25.0	5.0	16.0
Other Family-Kinsman-Relative	18.0	19.0	36.0	26.0
Other Primary Group	9.0	5.0	4.0	6.0
Non-Primary Group	51.0	51.0	55.0	52.0
Acquaintance	–	–	–	–
Stranger	20.0	22.0	16.0	19.0
Unknown	0	0	0	0
TOTAL	100.0	100.0	100.0	100.0
	(65)	(91)	(115)	(271)

Table 3-3 (cont.)

Crime, Country, Geographic Scope, Year / Relationship	Criminal Homicide				
	Africa[9,10]				
	Rural				Rural and Urban
	1945-1954	1948-1954	1952-1954	1931-1949	1955-1968
	Alur	Gisu	Soga	Tiv	Western Uganda
Family-Kinsman-Relative	22.5	38.0	56.0	44.2	41.0
Husband-Wife	8.9	11.0	37.0	8.8	10.0
Other Family-Kinsman-Relative	13.6	27.0	19.0	35.4	31.0
Other Primary Group	0	17.0	8.0	2.2	3.0
Non-Primary Group	77.7	20.0	16.0	30.9	30.0
Acquaintance	–	–	–	–	–
Stranger	8.9	0	10.0	0	0.4
Unknown	0	24.0	20.0	23.3	25.6
TOTAL	100.0	100.0	100.0	100.0	100.0
	(47)	(99)	(49)	(90)	(501)

Table 3-3 (cont.)

Crime, Country, Geographic Scope, Year / Relationship	Criminal Homicide			
	India[11]	India[12]	India[13]	Ceylon[14]
	Urban (Delhi)	Rural (Maria tribe)	Rural (Central India)	Southern Province (Both Urban and Rural)
	1963	1921-1941	1946-1956	1960
Family-Kinsman-Relative	27.0	62.0	48.6	25.0
Husband-Wife	8.0	21.0	18.0	4.6
Other Family-Kinsman-Relative	19.0	41.0	30.6	20.4
Other Primary Group	17.0	7.0	11.1	21.6
Non-Primary Group	56.0	28.0	40.3	46.8
Acquaintance	23.0	–	–	–
Stranger	20.0	–	9.0	5.7
Unknown	0	3.0	0	6.9
TOTAL	100.0	100.0	100.0	100.0
	(52)	(100)	(144)	(88)

Table 3-3 (cont.)

Crime, Country, Geographic Scope, Year / Relationship	Aggravated Assault			
	United States	Canada[15]	England[16]	
	Urban (17 City Survey Clearances)	Urban (Montreal)	Urban (London)	
	1967	1964	1950	1957
Family-Kinsman-Relative	13.9	18.5	19.3	14.6
Husband-Wife	9.4	10.1	11.6	9.4
Other Family-Kinsman-Relative	4.5	8.4	7.7	5.2
Other Primary Group	6.7	5.9	13.8	12.9
Non-Primary Group	55.0	75.6	66.9	72.5
Acquaintance	16.0	17.6	–	–
Stranger	20.6	42.8	11.5	12.6
Unknown	24.3	0	0	0
TOTAL	100.0	100.0	100.0	100.0
	(1493)	(119)	(1111)	(1893)

Table 3-3 (cont.)

Crime, Country, Geographic Scope, Year / Relationship	Forcible Rape			
	United States	Canada[17]	England and Wales[18]	Denmark[19]
	Urban (17 City Survey, Clearances)	Urban (Montreal)	Urban (Emphasis on London and Urban Areas)	Entire Country (Mostly Rural Areas and Provincial Cities)
	1967	1964	1950	1946-1958
Family-Kinsman-Relative	6.9	9.0	14.4	8.0
Husband-Wife	0	1.0	–	–
Other Family-Kinsman-Relative	6.9	8.0	–	–
Other Primary Group	3.3	1.0	34.5	14.0
Non-Primary Group	85.7	90.3	51.1	75.0
Acquaintance	28.5	24.8	31.1	–
Stranger	52.8	58.4	16.3	54.0
Unknown	4.1	0	0	4.0
TOTAL	100.0	100.0	100.0	100.0
	(617)	(113)	(588)	(141)

Table 3-3 (cont.)

Crime, Country, Geographic Scope, Year / Relationship	Robbery				
	United States		Canada[20]	England[21]	
	Urban (17 City Survey, Clearances)		Urban (Montreal)	Urban (London)	
	1967		1964	1950	1957
	Armed Robbery	Unarmed Robbery			
Family-Kinsman-Relative	0.6	0.5	0		
Husband-Wife	0.6	0	0		
Other Family-Kinsman-Relative	0	0.5	0	5.2	2.8
Other Primary Group	0.4	0.1	0		
Non-Primary Group	90.8	96.8	100.0	94.8	97.2
Acquaintance	8.8	8.0	3.0	–	–
Stranger	78.6	85.7	97.0	82.3	81.9
Unknown	8.2	2.6	0	0	0
TOTAL	100.0	100.0	100.0	100.0	100.0
	(509)	(502)	(202)	(287)	(462)

Table 3-3 (cont.)

Note: A dash ("–") means data for the particular category are not available. The years cited show the time spans over which data were collected.

References: [1] Tardiff (1966, p. 117); [2] Gibson and Klein (1969, Tables 14, 15, 16); [3] Gibson and Klein (1967, pp. 74-75); [4] Svalastoga (1956, Table 1); [5] Holyst (1967, p. 90); [6] Connor (1973, p. 113). It was impossible to separate the "Other Primary" category and the "Non-Primary" category from the data published by Connor.); [7] Simondi (1970, p. 39); [8] Landau and Drapkin (1968, p. 47. The original relationship table in this study had a classification called "Friend-Acquaintance." The percentages were small—around 3.5 percent. In the above table, half of this frequency was lumped into the "Primary Group" total and half into the "Non-Primary Group" total.); [9] Bohannon (1960, p. 222); [10] Mushanga (1970, p. 49); [11] Rao (1968, p. 23); [12] Elwin (1943, p. 104 and tabulation from Appendix); [13] Driver (1961, pp. 58-59); [14] Jayewardene and Ranasinghe (1963, p. 93); [15] Tardiff (1966, p. 117); [16] McClintock (1963a, Tables 11 and 15, Appendix III. The percentages here are for all the "Crimes of Violence" in the study, though within this group the great majority are "malicious wounding," the British equivalent of "aggravated assault." Because of insufficiently precise breakdowns in the study, some of the assaults classified in the table under "Other Primary Group" may in fact fall under "Non-Primary Group."); [17] Tardiff (1966, p. 117); [18] Radzinowicz (1957, p. 90. This distribution covers "sex offenses" committed on females. "Indecent assault" dominates and "rape" has a relatively small role. See note 53, c. 1. Because of insufficiently precise breakdowns in this study, some of the offenses classified under "Other Primary Group" should probably be in "Non-Primary Group."); [19] Svalastoga (1962, p. 53); [20] Tardiff (1966, p. 117); [21] McClintock and Gibson (1961, Table 6).

inces of the Soviet Union (41 percent and 36 percent). Little analysis of these contemporary findings is available. However, if Thomas and Znaniecki's monumental study of the turn of the century Polish peasant still holds truth, one would expect the family and primary group percentages to be even higher if rural areas alone were isolated. Analyzing why murders of strangers are rare among peasants, they emphasize that the social contacts between the individual and the world outside his community are relatively few and superficial. The peasant needs "really strong motives for any abnormal acts because of the stable and regulated character of his habitual life and because of the strength of his desire for security."[20]

The highest European frequency for other primary relationships, outside of the family, was in Florence, where 19 percent of the killings were between fiances and lovers.

Homicide among family and relatives was considerable in Israel. The most interesting ethnic variation was a significantly lower proportion of spouse slayings among non-Jews than Jews. The possibility was raised in Chapter 2 that the direct property value attached to women may discourage Arab men from killing their wives in conflict situations. More pervasively, the male plays the dominant role in Arab society, as omnipotent master of his family. The Arab wife usually is given a much more passive and inferior role compared to the Western Jewish wife. "Therefore, the probability of sharp marital disputes and conflicts between husband and wife is much lower among Arab Moslem couples."[21] It is difficult to question the Western Jewish wife's role vis-à-vis her Arab counterpart, but one should be aware that a number of social, economic, and legal means are available today through which a Moslem woman and her family may effectively counterbalance the husband's seemingly unlimited legal powers (for example, deferral of part of brideprice until subsequent divorce or any time the woman chooses to demand it).[22]

In Africa, killings among family and kinsmen and non-primary group percentages for the Alur were broadly consistent with the United States and Canada. But Gisu, Soga, Tiv and Western Ugandan killings within the family clan were much more frequent and the non-primary percentages noticeably lower.[23]

The relationship profile for Delhi was closer to the urban United States and Montreal than to the rural, primitive societies observed in the other two Indian studies. In certain ways akin to Mushanga's account of the marital institution in the Toro district of Western Uganda, Elwin suggests that the closeness of marriage and the joint family system are primarily responsible for the 62 percent figure under family and kinsmen relationships among the Indian Maria tribe killings. Marriage is apparently much more of a partnership than in many other Indian tribes. Husband and wife share the entire spectrum of experience, from work and social life to mourning, and the principle source of marital conflict seems to arise when the union is disturbed by another person. Long established traditions promote such contexts—for example, the privileged relationship a younger brother has with his older brother's wife, the custom that allows a married woman to visit her mother's house, and the option of the husband to take more than one wife.[24]

Although the respective sociocultural contexts might make the opposite pattern more intuitively reasonable, the Southern Province of Ceylon resembles urban rather than rural India: one-fourth of the killings were set in family relationships mostly *not* involving spouses, one-fourth in other primary relationships, and the rest in non-primary contexts. In Ceylon, husband and wife (the latter playing a very passive role) conform to traditional pressures for harmony and consanguinity, which produces a minimal "disjuncture between the expected and actual interactions" in marriage. Yet custom and society do not expect this among kinsmen and relatives outside of the immediate family, so that "considerable disjuncture between the expected and the actual" exists here.[25] How this notion of a variable disparity between expected and actual behavior might apply to other relationships is unfortunately not discussed by Jayewardene and Ranasinghe. For example, no light is shed on the very low proportion of strangers in homicide (6 percent).

In retrospect, one is not very successful in identifying an order underlying these diverse themes. Distinctions between West and non-West or between more and less advanced industrial societies are not particularly useful. The American, Canadian, and Indian urban settings give some reason to expect city homicides with greater anonymity, consistent with Thomas and Znaniecki's observations. Yet the data from Moscow are an exception to any city-specific phenomenon imposed upon a more universal locus of violence among intimates.

The real lesson simply may be that the unique social institutions, roles, and expectations that develop in a country over time become important in understanding the relationship patterns between offender and victim. Thus, note how in Ceylon conflict is ostensibly discouraged through social expectations of harmony and female subservience, how among Arabs in Israel the passiveness of women and their treatment as property similarly discourages spouse killings, but how the comparatively less obtrusive passivity expected of and generally received from British women does not seem to do so, how the emphasis on real partnerships in rural India works to increase husband-wife killings, and how the relatively lessened emphasis on such life-long partnerships in America exists along with a not insignificant proportion of mate slayings. Observe that the larger family group is closely bound in some societies, especially rural ones, so that happiness as well as homicide often are byproducts of the sustained contacts that result, whereas the family institution has little positive or negative influence in other places. Realize that other primary and non-primary contacts, between friends, acquaintances and the like, are normal in some cultures but less so in others, where the likelihood of interpersonal friction may accordingly be diminished.

Homicide, then, is driven by deep social and cultural currents. It extends beyond the interpersonal "dyad" on which Von Hentig centered his analysis.[26]

Aggravated Assault

The United States

Table 3-1 shows that 14 percent of all assaults in the 1967 survey were between family members (mostly husband and wife), 7 percent entailed other primary group associations, and 55 percent occurred in non-primary group settings (with the remaining relationships mostly unknown). Primary group involvement was higher in the one earlier study—Washington, D.C.—with a comparable tabulation.[27] The intimates pattern appears understandable through the same reasoning used for homicide. In the U.S. regional breakdowns, the West again had a greater proportion of family conflicts than the other regions (25 percent, versus 16 percent in the South, 13 percent in the North Central aggregate, and 10 percent in the Northeast).[28] When these percents were multiplied by the regional assault rates published in the *UCR* for 1967, the estimated family assault rate for the West was also higher than for the South.[29]

Foreign Comparisons

The proportion of family assaults in Montreal and London was roughly comparable to the urban United States (Table 3-3). However, the percentage of strangers was much greater in Montreal than London, where McClintock dismissed the importance of deliberately planned assaults by street gangs of "Teddy-boys."[30]

Forcible Rape

The United States

From a legal perspective, the kind of personal relationship between victim and offender is probably more important in forcible rape than in any of the other major violent acts. The law and informal ethical codes recognize degrees of moral weakness and culpability that partly depend on the relationship. A young woman is considered a blameless victim in incest rape, for example, but she is thought (often erroneously) to be less innocent if drinking is mutual or a close relationship existed prior to the offense.[31]

Only 10 percent of all forcible rape relationships were primary group in Table 3-1. However, the figure is probably too low because victims may be less likely to report, and even if they do, police may be less likely to record acts between intimates. Strangers and acquaintances, respectively, prevailed in the non-primary group. The studies in Philadelphia and Washington, D.C., based on data prior to the 1967 national survey, had somewhat lower stranger frequencies. Investigations with data later than 1967 produced about the same proportion of strangers in Kansas City, but higher percentages in Denver and Seattle.[32]

The FBI does not publish national trend data on relationships in rape, as is the case for homicide. But Table 3-4 constructs a trend in New York City from 1967 through 1972. The proportion of reported rapes by strangers has clearly increased.[33] Because we know that the proportion of strangers in interracial rape is greater than in intraracial rape,[34] these data are indirect support for the tentative conclusion in Chapter 2 that there may have been a recent rise in the relative proportion of reported black-white rapes (resulting, when rates are computed, in a possible increase in the reported black-white rape rate greater than the presumed increases for other reported offender-victim race combinations in some places).

The national survey results differed little between blacks and whites, except that black victims, more than white victims, had primary group associations other than the family. The frequency of incest rape offenders was higher among whites than blacks.[35]

Foreign Comparisons

The rape configuration was almost identical in Montreal, Denmark, and the United States, with non-primary relationships, especially strangers, the leading

Table 3-4

Interpersonal Relationships, Forcible Rape: New York City Comparison between 1967 and 1970-1972 (Percent)

Relationship[a] Year	1967 Cleared and Uncleared	February 1, 1970 through December 31, 1972[b] Cleared and Uncleared
Relative	8.8	3.2
Close Friend/Boy Friend/Family Friend	0.9	2.8
Neighbor	4.4	–
Acquaintance	21.0	15.9
Stranger	64.9	78.1
Total %	100.0	100.0
(N)	(114)	(314)

[a]The relationship aggregates in this table follow the format of Chappell and Singer (1973), who combined clearances and non-clearances, used a case base, and omitted cases where relationship data were unavailable. This was also done for the 1967 data, broken out from the national survey. When a case included two or more offenders or victims, the most commonly occurring relationship configuration among the interactions in the case was coded. (There were few such cases where this problem arose, however.) Ties (e.g., a case involving one victim and two offenders, each with a different relationship with the victim) were thrown out, but ties were rare. Chappell and Singer did not discuss what they did in such situations.

[b]Chappell and Singer (1973, p. 65).

category (Table 3-3). There was a much higher frequency of primary group contacts and a much lower percentage of strangers in urban England and Wales, however. This may largely be because the British results were aggregated for all "sexual offenses against women" and therefore composed mostly of attacks less serious than rape. Yet, if the lessened fear of street attack that Londoners seem to have in comparison to urban Americans[36] is any source of validation, the lower rate of rape in the English metropolis[37] may in fact also be accompanied by a lower proportion of stranger rapes.

Robbery

The United States

The only other relationship category of note beyond the reign of strangers in survey robberies was a prior acquaintanceship (8 percent in armed and 9 percent in unarmed encounters). There was little variation by race, except that blacks almost exclusively bore the few primary group relationships.[38] Normandeau's Philadelphia results and Feeney and Weir's Oakland findings concurred.[39]

Strangers played a greater role in northeastern unarmed robberies than in the other regions (92 percent, against 79 percent in the North Central group, 75 percent in the West and 70 percent in the South).[40]

Foreign Comparisons

Strangers also were the general rule in Montreal and London robbery (Table 3-3).

Notes and References

1. Table 3-1 used the "interaction," not the "case" as the unit of analysis (see Chapter 1). It might be contended that an attack by more than one offender has a greater likelihood of occurring when the offenders are strangers to the victim or have some other non-primary group relationship. Therefore, it can be hypothesized that these interaction based figures are biased and yield significantly higher non-primary relationship percentages and significantly lower primary relationship percentages than data based on cases. This hypothesis was tested in Curtis (1972) by comparing the interaction-based distribution with the case-based distribution. The interaction percentages were almost uniformly lower for primary relationships and higher for non-primary relationships. But the disparities were small and showed very similar interaction and case frequencies.

2. A "close friend" was defined as a person with whom frequent direct and intimate (but not sexual) contact had been maintained.

3. A "lover" was defined as any sexual partner other than a spouse or a prostitute.

4. An "acquaintance" relationship was defined as one involving recognition, but no fellowship or friendship.

5. An "enemy" was defined as a traditional foe avoided in normal social relations.

6. A "stranger" was defined as a person with whom no previous contact had been made.

7. This relationship mainly refers to situations where felons escaping arrest attack police officers, though it is possible for an officer to attack a felon and be prosecuted for brutality.

8. Amir (1965, pp. 283-5); MacDonald (1971, p. 33); Chappell and Singer (1973, p. 61).

9. The Chief of the FBI's Uniform Crime Reporting Section has verified that

the relationship categories that we restructured from the FBI "Murder by Circumstance" categories are accurate and valid. (Personal communication from Inspector Jerome J. Daunt, November 17, 1971). The FBI does not publish comparable data for the other crimes being considered here.

10. Note that the FBI data in Table 3-2 refer to all offenses known, not just clearances (although during this period 8 or 9 out of every 10 homicides known were cleared). If only clearances had been used, one partial explanation of the stranger uptrend might have been a disproportionate increase in police efficiency in clearing homicide cases involving strangers, compared to other relationship categories. It can be argued that the uptrend is explicable as an increase in the misclassification of offenders as strangers in uncleared killings over recent years (and/or a reduction in misclassification to the other categories). But such claims are hard to substantiate, and given the relatively low volume of non-clearances, it is unlikely that such a tendency would explain away the trend. Finally, it can be argued that police have become relatively more efficient in detecting killings by strangers, so that offenses known in this category have risen disproportionate to the other relationship categories. But it is generally agreed that most killings do become known, particularly in comparison to the other violent crimes. And overall police efficiency in homicide, at least when measured by clearance rates, has actually gone down slightly over the trend period (from a 91 percent level in 1963 to 82 percent in 1972, according to the *UCR*). Thus, this position, too, is not easy to support.

11. *Washington Evening Star*, 1 April 1970. Many of these killings began as street robberies.

12. Arnold (1971). See also Cook (1971) and Greider (1971).

13. Wolfgang (1958, p. 207) registered 25 percent of the Philadelphia killings he studied as family affairs. Thirty-nine percent were other primary group relationships and 36 percent non-primary (including 12 percent for strangers). In Houston, Pokorny (1965, p. 483) found that 23 percent of the homicides were within the family, 35 percent between other primary group relations, and only 1 percent by strangers. Thirty-seven percent of the D.C. Crime Commission's (1966, p. 42) homicides were in the family and 21 percent by strangers. The rest involved at least a casual prior relationship. Voss and Hepburn's (1968, p. 506) Chicago homicides had 47 percent in the primary and 53 percent in the non-primary group (including 20 percent strangers). Zimring's (1968, Table 1) Chicago homicides included 20 percent spouse-lover-other family, 22 percent strangers, and most of the rest in varying friendships-acquaintanceships.

14. Goode (1969, p. 958).

15. See Curtis (1972) for the supporting tables. It should also be pointed out that although the percent change varied, all regions experienced a decline in husband-wife killings and a rise in stranger homicides from 1966 to 1972, the years with the published data. See the FBI *Uniform Crime Reports*, 1966-1972.

16. The California cities dominated the western regional aggregate in the survey.

17. Personal communication from Gilbert Geis, 11 April 1970.

18. This was so using both the national survey and FBI estimates of percent family killings in 1967. The 1967 homicide rate was 4.9 in the West and 9.4 in the South. With the survey family proportion of 38 percent in the West and 23 percent in the South, the estimated family killing rates were 1.9 per 100,000 in the West and 2.2 in the South. The FBI family proportion in 1967 was 33 percent in the West and 27 percent in the South, which produces estimated rates of 1.6 in the West and 2.5 in the South.

19. The discussion in this section is based on the cities in Table 3-3, except when noted otherwise.

20. Thomas and Znaniecki (1927, p. 1756).

21. Landau and Drapkin (1968, p. 221).

22. Rosen (1970, pp. 34-35).

23. Bohannon (1960, p. 221).

24. Elwin (1943, pp. 104-5).

25. Jayewardene and Ranasinghe (1963, p. 94).

26. Bohannon (1960, pp. 27-28) was probably the first to emphasize this point.

27. The D.C. Crime Commission (1966, p. 76) reported primary group relationships in 58 percent of the assaults where relationships were known (11 percent between mates, 10 percent other family, and 37 percent other primary group) and non-primary group contexts in 42 percent.

28. See Curtis (1972) for the supporting tables.

29. Regional assault rates in 1967 were reported by the FBI to be 138.3 in the West and 163.5 in the South. When multiplied by the family proportions (25 and 16 percent, respectively), the resulting rates were 34.6 in the West and 26.1 in the South.

30. McClintock (1963b, p. 30).

31. Amir (1965, p. 482).

32. In Philadelphia, Amir (1965, p. 490) registered 13 percent for primary group relationships (2 percent family and 11 percent other primary), 86 percent non-primary (including 42 percent strangers), and 1 percent unknown. The D.C. Crime Commission (1966, p. 53) came up with a 14 percent primary group frequency in Washington (2 percent family, 12 percent other primary), with 82 percent non-primary (including 36 percent strangers), and 4 percent unknown. In Kansas City, 54 percent of the rapes involved complete strangers in 1973 and 45 percent, some previous contact (Harpold 1973). In Denver, 12 percent of MacDonald's (1971, p. 78) rapists were friends, 17 percent casual acquaintances, and 60 percent strangers (most of the rest falling into primary relationships). Giacinti's (1973) even more recent Denver data had 15 percent well known or related, 14 percent casual acquaintances, and 67 percent strangers. In Seattle, 63 percent of the rapes studied in 1973 were by strangers, 27 percent by acquaintances and 7 percent by friends, ex-boy friends or ex-husbands. (Seattle Law and Justice Planning Office 1975.)

33. With a reported 1967 New York City rape rate of 23.3 per 100,000 (from Mulvihill and Tumin with Curtis 1969) and a reported 1972 rate of 41.4 (calculated from the 1972 rape volume in Chappell and Singer 1972 and the 1970 Census Bureau population volume), the relative proportion of increase in strangers in Table 3-4 is, of course, associated with an increase in the rape rate by strangers. To illustrate for two of the other leading categories in Table 3-4, the decrease in the proportion of rapes by relatives is associated with a rate decrease, but the decrease in the proportion of rapes by acquaintances still corresponds to an increase in the rate for that category.

34. For example, in the 17-city aggregate of the national survey, 85 percent of the black-black rapes involved non-primary group relationships (mostly strangers or acquaintances), whereas the figure was 97 percent in black-white rapes. See Curtis (1972).

35. See Curtis (1972) for the supporting tables. The regional breakdowns also produced a greater proportion of incest rape in the South than for the other groupings (Curtis 1972). However, we cannot be confident about the representativeness of this pattern because the sample size for rape was low in the Southern cities. If the same results were demonstrated for rape *rates* and with a geographic area centered more on the Old South (rather than our crude aggregate, which includes Miami and Dallas with Atlanta and New Orleans), some interesting questions could be raised. For example, to the extent that the nineteenth-century plantation culture's emphasis on sheltering white women (Smith 1963) and maintaining family and social cohesion (Hackney 1969) still holds today, could it be applied to explaining a higher real incidence of incest rapes and a higher rate of reporting them in the South compared to other regions?

36. See, for example, West (1968).

37. For comparative data on rape rates in the United States and England and Wales, see Mulvihill and Tumin with Curtis (1969).

38. See Curtis (1972) for the supporting tables.

39. There was no previous relationship in 85 percent of Normandeau's (1968, p. 119) robberies. Almost all the robberies in Oakland were by strangers. (Feeney and Weir 1973.)

40. See Curtis (1972) for the supporting tables.

4 Motive

Summary of the National Survey

The term "motive" is too imprecise to imply conscious design, planning, or the underlying sociopsychological processes that result in a crime. Motive should not be confused with intent, which is essentially a legal concept referring to the offender's ability to comprehend the nature of his act and his resolve to commit it. Whereas intent has to do with degree of determination to reach a specific goal, motive deals with the reasons for wanting to do so. Motives are informal terms in police investigations. Some probe a state of mind (for example, "jealousy") and others a social situation (for example, an "altercation"). To a certain degree, however, motives can describe the precipitants of a crime (see Chapter 5) and give clues to its explanation as a behavioral phenomenon. In the national survey, the coders who read the police reports were instructed to list what appeared to be the *original* motive leading to the crime reported (for example, an event ending in homicide or assault could have begun as a robbery or a sexual attack).

Table 4-1 shows the motive categories used. With minor changes, they are based on Wolfgang's classifications in *Patterns in Criminal Homicide*. The original plan was to add categories uniquely responsive to assault, rape, and robbery. However, the coders soon found the homicide categories also covered the full range of possibilities in assault. As for rape and robbery, the homicide labels made little sense, and it was hardly enlightening to list the Table 4-1 category of "sexual" as the motive for rape and "robbery" as the motive for robbery. In fact, the police reports on rape and robbery did not give information usable in any typology of a concept comparable to motive in homicide and

65

Table 4-1

The Motive of the Offender in Criminal Homicide and Aggravated Assault, 17 American Cities, 1967, Clearances (Percent)

Motive	Major Violent Crime Type	Criminal Homicide	Aggravated Assault
Family quarrel		7.7	5.8
Altercation		35.7	29.6
Self-defense		5.5	1.7
Jealousy		4.4	3.0
Revenge		2.5	2.9
Robbery		8.8	2.3
Sexual		2.1	1.0
Riot		0	0
Psychopathic		0.9	1.0
Halting felon		0.3	0.2
Escaping arrest		0.5	7.9
Other		10.6	4.5
Unknown		21.0	40.1
Total		100.0	100.0
(N)		(668)	(1493)

assault, so analysis has been limited to these latter crimes. Minor altercations stood out clearly as the most frequent triggering events for each in Table 4-1.

Criminal Homicide

The United States

The overall importance of altercations plus the findings that altercations were more frequent for men than women and in all-black than all-white killings were consistent with previous studies.[1] The seeming triviality of motivation in many altercations that become lethal among black men is illustrated by the following observations:

"Murders result from little ol' arguments over nothing at all," noted a veteran Dallas homicide detective. "Tempers flare, a fight starts, and somebody gets stabbed or shot. I've worked on cases where the principals had been arguing over a 10¢ record on a juke box, or over a one dollar gambling debt from a dice game."

Detectives say a dialog that ends in homicide may begin:
"You got a cigaret?"
"Naw, I ain't got any."

Or, the fateful conversation may begin like this:
"Hey, you're lookin' at me."
"No, I ain't."
"Yes you are. Why you lookin' at me?"

A man was shot in the back in front of a tavern because, police said, he had refused to lend his assailant a dollar.

"Deceased and suspect had been arguing over a $5 bet and became involved in a scuffle," says the beef sheet concerning another shooting.[2]

Among other homicide motives with some importance in Table 4-1 are robbery and family quarrels. White male victims were killed in proportionately more situations beginning as robbery than white females or blacks. The percentage of victims in homicides that began as robberies tended to increase with age.[3] Older white males are prime robbery targets because they are thought to carry a relatively great amount of money. Social expectations and physical strength encourage men to resist robbers more than females, and offenders no doubt believe that force is more needed with male victims, regardless of whether they fight back. Perhaps younger men resist more than older men, but the latter probably cannot defend themselves as effectively.

Female victims were much more likely than males to be in killings brought on by family quarrels. The same was true for offenders.[4] Women are relatively more limited to family contexts than men in their daily lives, so the likelihood of physical attack arising out of these situations is accordingly greater.

Considering the attention often given to crazed killers in the media, the insignificant proportion of homicide motives judged to be "psychopathic" by the coders is conspicuous. Of course, the police recording and the coders reading the national survey homicides were not professional diagnosticians, so it can be reasonably argued that there are more "psychopathic" killers than implied in Table 4-1. Nonetheless, there is widespread scholarly agreement that legally insane persons form a very small proportion of homicide offenders.[5]

We were unable to make an accurate count of premeditated homicides from the information available, but, here again, legal and behavioral experts concur that careful planning over a considerable period of time has minimal import for the bulk of American homicides. It has been estimated, for example, that less than 5 percent of all killings in the United States are premeditated.[6] Today, perhaps some of the few homicides that can be so classified form the core of the exceptions to the relative infrequency of juvenile gang involvement in these crimes; they may be "jappings," small scale, planned attacks by several gang members on a member of another gang (see *Violence, Race and Culture*[7]).

Foreign Comparisons

As in the United States, foreign records usually give only superficial motives and little insight into the underlying reasons for an offender's behavior. Many motives are merely the judgement of some third observer, and there are often overlapping themes. The labels used in different foreign studies are often not totally comparable, and the same ostensible classifications can have somewhat variable meanings in different societies.[8] With these pitfalls in mind, Table 4-2[9] was built up in an ad hoc way from several studies of criminal homicide that promised some semblance of comparability. The motive categories evolved by modification as each successive study was integrated into the table.

The first broad classification, "Immediate Physical and Verbal Conflict," seeks to capture flare-ups of the moment, conflicts over seemingly trivial subjects and with little past history. "Altercations" are typical. Excluded are most sexually motivated situations that cannot be considered necessarily trivial. The vagaries of the information mean that some sexually based homicides or those directly grounded on a theme built up over time have been inadvertently incorporated. It is difficult to assess the validity of this measurement or the purity of the category.

The same time and seriousness criteria apply to the second classification in the table, but here "Self-Defensive Responses" are isolated.

The third category, "Revengeful Response," refers to events in which the offender strikes back at the victim for some perceived injustice, sexual or non-sexual. Good examples are killing an unfaithful spouse and upholding the family name in the course of a blood feud. There might have been a dramatic verbal and physical outburst immediately prior to the killing, but the absence of such conflict and, more importantly, the build-up of hostilities over time are especially characteristic here.[10]

The fourth classification in Table 4-2 is meant to specify robbers and sex assaulters who eventually kill their victims (although in some primitive countries instances where robbery victims killed the thieves could not be separated out). Record ambiguities probably also resulted in the inclusion of some events where the offender did not set out to rob but rather directly to kill in order to gain money and goods.

The remaining categories cover a miscellaneous group: motives with certain significance in some countries, motives with considerable import in one or two countries that could not easily be lumped into the earlier categories, and cases where motive could not be determined.

Immediate conflicts and homicides originally motivated by robbery were key patterns in Canada and England and Wales. Unlike the United States, however, revengeful responses also were frequent in Britain.

Data from all of Germany in 1931 showed robbery to be the leading homicide motive. Country-wide French reports from the same year listed 70 percent of the killings due to quarrels, mostly over money.[11] More compatible with U.S. urban homicides, Simondi's analysis of Florentine murder from 1951 to 1963 produced immediate conflicts as the leading motive.

Table 4-2 shows very high percentages of immediate conflict killings for the Soviet research summarized by Conner. However, most of these homicides were originally listed as having "hooligan" motives in the original studies. The only explanation of "hooligan" killings was that they occur in the course of "public order violations." Assuming that if more were known, some of these homicides would be better classified under other motive categories in Table 4-2, we can infer with reasonable confidence from the information given by Conner that the proportion of Soviet immediate conflicts is roughly on the same plane as the United States. Parallel to our remarks on the triviality of many American altercations, Conner, quoting a Russian criminology text, observes:

The management of impulse, the insulation from stress producing problems on a daily basis, are commodities in relatively short supply among those Soviet citizens, mainly the urban semiskilled and unskilled working class, whose lives are "beset by . . . high rates of desertion, separation, promiscuity, drinking, brutality, and incompatibility." These, it may be argued, make up the main part of the recruiting pool of homicide offenders.[12]

Table 4-2 also indicates that motives of revenge and jealousy may play a relatively greater role in the USSR than in the United States.

It was impossible to fit Holyst's results from modern-day Poland into Table 4-2. His leading motives were "economic," "threat of feeling of personal value," and "erotic," respectively.[13] However, in their monumental study, Thomas and Znaniecki conclude that in effect revengeful responses and long gestation periods were most typical of killings among rural peasants in turn of the century Poland. "Greed, fear, sexual desire, jealousy, revenge, mostly exaggerated by long brooding, constitute the usual facts of murder [in peasant life], and it is clear that situations giving rise to such emotions are apt to develop solely within the individual's own group."[14]

Tracing the changes that occurred when these peasants resettled in American cities, Thomas and Znaniecki show how the close social ties engendered by rural Polish life were loosened in North American urban culture. Part and parcel, revenge-related motives lost their leading importance in assaultive violence:

There is no need of recurring to violent means in order to get rid of one's undesirable family members, for one can merely desert them. A house or a sum of money which the individual may inherit after the death of his parents does not mean here even approximately as much as in the smallest farm in the old country either in its bearing on the individual's social position or even from the purely economic standpoint. . . .Sexual desire can be satisfied outside of the one legal way of marriage. Jealousy still exists but is in most cases weakened by the consciousness that it is possible to have many other men or women beside the

Table 4-2

Motive in Criminal Homicide by Country (Percent)

Motive \ Country	United States Urban (17 City Survey, Clearances) 1967	Canada[1] Urban (Montreal) 1964	England and Wales[2] Entire Country 1967	Italy[3] Urban (Florence) 1951-1963	USSR[4] Urban (Moscow) Late 1960s	USSR[4] Entire Country Early 1960s
Immediate Physical and/or Verbal Conflict:	43.4	29.2	31.1	41.5	39.0	50.1
Quarrels, Fights, Rage, Brawls, Altercations						
(Family, Lover's Quarrel)	7.7	20.1	–	21.3	–	–
(Altercation)	35.7	–	–	20.2	–	–
Self-Defensive Response to Provocation and/or Physical Assault	5.5	0	0	0	0	0
Revengeful Response:	6.9	4.2	31.1	8.5	26.0	30.4
Sexual Jealousy–Revenge–Infidelity–Rivalry; Feud–Vendetta–Non-Sexual Revenge–Ongoing Dispute						
(Sexual Jealousy, etc.)	4.4	4.2	–	8.5	–	–
(Feud, etc.)	2.5	–	–	0	–	–
Original Motive Robbery–Theft–Gain–Sexual Attack, or Other Crime	10.9	22.9	15.6	10.6	19.0	8.8
(Robbery, Theft, Gain)	8.8	22.9	15.6	10.6	–	–
(Sexual Attack)	2.1	0	0	0	–	–
Mental Illness–Psychopathic–Depression	0.9	10.4	0	0	0	0
Halting Felon or Escaping Arrest	0.8	0	2.2	8.5	0	0
Other and Unknown	31.6	33.3	20.0	30.8	16.0	10.7
(Public Embarrassment)	–	–	–	–	–	–
(Dispute over Property–Land)						
(Abuse–Neglect of Primary Kin)						
(Alcohol)	–	–	–	–	–	–
Total	100.0 (668)	100.0 (48)	100.0 (90)	100.0 (94)	100.0 (100)	100.0 (Unknown)

Table 4-2 (cont.)

Motive	Israel[5] Entire Country (Jewish Pop. 2/3 Urban, Arab Pop. Rural)				African Tribes[6] Rural	
	Western Jews	Oriental Jews	Arabs	Total	1948-1954 Gisu	1952-1954 Soga
Immediate Physical and/or Verbal Conflict:	28.0	34.0	30.0	30.0	27.0	67.0
Quarrels, Fights, Rage, Brawls, Altercations (Family, Lover's Quarrel)	9.0	13.0	3.0	7.0	10.0	48.0
(Altercation)	19.0	21.0	26.0	23.0	–	–
Self-Defensive Response to Provocation and/or Physical Assault	0	1.0	3.0	1.0	10.0	0
Revengeful Response:	19.0	21.0	41.0	30.0	4.0	0
Sexual Jealousy–Revenge–Infidelity–Rivalry ; Feud–Vendetta–Non-Sexual Revenge–Ongoing Dispute (Sexual Jealousy, etc.)	19.0	14.0	9.0	13.0	–	0
(Feud, etc.)	0	9.0	32.0	16.0	–	0
Original Motive Robbery–Theft–Gain–Sexual Attack, or Other Crime	7.0	5.0	6.0	6.0	0	3.0
(Robbery, Theft, Gain)	–	–	–	–	0	–
(Sexual Attack)	–	–	–	–	0	–
Mental Illness–Psychopathic–Depression	25.0	18.0	4.0	14.0	0	0
Halting Felon or Escaping Arrest	0	0	0	0	17.0	15.0
Other and Unknown	21.0	21.0	16.0	19.0	41.0	15.0
(Public Embarrassment)	–	–	–	–	–	–
(Dispute over Property–Land)	–	–	–	–	15.0	0
(Abuse-Neglect of Primary Kin)	–	–	–	–	–	–
(Alcohol)	–	–	–	–	–	–
Total	100.0	100.0	100.0	100.0	100.0	100.0
	(69)	(87)	(116)	(272)	(99)	(100)

Table 4-2 (cont.)

Motive \ Country	Western Uganda[7] Rural 1955-1968	India[8] Urban (Delhi) 1963	India[9] Rural (Maria Tribe) 1921-1941	India[10] Rural (Central India) 1946-1956	Ceylon[11] Southern Province (Both Urban and Rural Areas) 1960
Immediate Physical and/or Verbal Conflict:	36.0	0	16.0	4.1	21.6
Quarrels, Fights, Rage, Brawls, Altercations (Family, Lover's Quarrel)	13.0	–	16.0	–	–
(Altercation)	–	–	0	–	–
Self-Defensive Response to Provocation and/or Physical Assault	10.0	8.0	0	5.6	0
Revengeful Response:	10.0	58.0	23.0	21.5	31.9
Sexual Jealousy–Revenge–Infidelity–Rivalry; Feud–Vendetta–Non-Sexual Revenge–Ongoing Dispute (Sexual Jealousy, etc.)	9.0	22.0	17.0	21.5	6.8
(Feud, etc.)	1.0	36.0	6.0	0	25.0
Original Motive Robbery–Theft–Gain–Sexual Attack, or Other Crime	10.0	10.0	8.0	11.9	2.3
(Robbery, Theft, Gain)	10.0	10.0	8.0	–	2.3
(Sexual Attack)	0	0	0	–	0
Mental Illness–Psychopathic–Depression	9.0	6.0	5.0	0	2.3
Halting Felon or Escaping Arrest	1.0	0	0	0	0
Other and Unknown	24.0	18.0	48.0	56.9	42.0
(Public Embarrassment)	–	0	0	23.6	–
(Dispute over Property–Land)	5.0	18.0	15.0	17.3	34.2
(Abuse-Neglect of Primary Kin)	3.0	–	0	6.9	–
(Alcohol)	–	–	19.0	–	–
Total	100.0	100.0	100.0	100.0	100.0
	(501)	(50)	(100)	(144)	(88)

Table 4-2 (cont.)

Notes: A dash ("–") means data broken down for the particular category are not available.

The subtotals in parentheses under some major headings need not add up to the major heading percentage (although in some cases they do because all of a country's percentage under a major heading happens to fit into the subheadings given). The subheadings refer to important motives that can often be broken out from the aggregate or, in the case of "Other and Unknown," to otherwise unclassifiable motives important to one specific country.

References: [1] Tardiff (1966, Table 12); [2] Gibson and Klein (1969, Tables 17, 18, 19); [3] Simondi (1970, p. 50); [4] Conner (1973, p. 116); [5] Landau and Drapkin (1968, p. 53); [6] Bohannon (1960, p. 233); [7] Mushanga (1970, p. 63); [8] Rao (1968, Table 12); [9] Elwin (1943, Table 14); [10] Driver (1961, pp. 58-59); [11] Jayewardene and Ranasinghe (1963, computations made from c. 15).

unfaithful one. The fear of social opinion can hardly compel the average individual to murder as an alternative to some shameful disclosure, for social opinion has much less influence and can be easily avoided by moving away. The desire for revenge cannot be as deep as in the old country for here an individual has less chance to inflict a really serious wrong upon another and since the claims of solidarity have lost most of their old meaning, a break of solidarity is less resented as such.[15]

Thomas and Znaniecki's thesis, therefore, is that the motives in homicide shifted from long-term intragroup conflict to killings in more anonymous, or at least non-primary group, situations. Typically involved were people with whom the Polish immigrant interacted—mistrustfully and defensively—in the new urban environment. The relatively low U.S. percentage under revenge in Table 4-2 and the relatively high proportion of immediate conflict altercations give credence to this hypothesis, although European Americans do not, of course, have the highest homicide rates in the United States today.

As could be expected, motives for homicides committed in Israel followed different ethnic pathways. The percentage of feud and vendetta killings among Arabs was considerably higher than among Jews. There is a long tradition of rural blood feuds and mass conflicts among the Arabs. One of the social duties of an individual is to help fellow clansmen in disputes with persons from other clans. As a result, trivial altercations between two members of different clans sometimes escalate into prolonged, bitter group conflicts and a vicious circle of homicides and blood feuds.[16] Personal altercations were also more frequent among Arabs than Jews. But the Jewish proportions were considerably greater in altercations over money (which generally occurred in urban areas, where the Jewish population is concentrated), marriage conflicts (which may again reflect the less subservient posture of Jewish women vis-à-vis Arab women) and "mental illness."

Immediate conflict killings took on about the same, substantial import in Mushanga's study of Western Uganda and within the African Gisu tribe covered by Bohannon's group as in Canada, England and Wales and Israel. Beer party brawls were brought out in the African studies, and alcohol seemed to play an important catalytic influence,[17] as in this country.

About half of the killings among the African Soga tribe were family quarrels. Much of the explanation appears to lie in conflicts produced by strong lineage bonds. A wife in Busoga has close ties with and is constantly visiting her natal home, even though tradition simultaneously gives the husband great authority over her. Showing insecurity over the competition from the wife's lineage group, the husband can become a household tyrant. The wife, in turn, can feel oppressed and has more reason to return home to her father. Extramarital affairs are also an assertion of freedom against a domineering husband. The sex act often becomes a central and symbolic confrontation within the conflict of authority. If and when a husband perceives his dominance to be slipping away, he may imagine himself as losing his virility as a result of sorcery directed against him by his wife. "In a number of the cases in our sample, sexual intercourse appeared to have immediately preceded homicide or suicide."[18] Whether or not sex is directly involved, the continually spiraling tension that can be produced results in many arguments with a potential for assaultive violence.

Table 4-2 is arranged so that family quarrels are part of the immediate conflict totals, but it is certain that, in the case of the Soga, cumulative animosities and infidelity often come into play. Consequently, the Soga percentage under immediate conflicts is too high. If more complete information were at hand, we would expect a substantial percentage of the family conflicts to better fit under the revengeful response heading.

The killing of thieves or unknown intruders in the night also emerged with importance in the societies examined by Bohannon and his associates. Here was perhaps the central reason behind the relatively high percentages (17 and 15, respectively) under "Halting Felon or Resisting Arrest" for the Gisu and Soga tribes and the 10 percent figure under Gisu "Self-Defensive Responses." Some of these cases provided good illustrations of a colonial administration defining, reporting, and prosecuting as a crime an act which is normatively acceptable to native tradition. And so, a British judge sentenced a Gisu tribesman who one night had speared to death a suspected cattle thief:

The accused has probably reached manhood in a society which regarded the killing of thieves as a praiseworthy act. I much doubt if he understands what all this fuss is about. However, he is not entitled to acquital as the extent of the wounding far exceeded that necessary to apprehend a thief.[19]

Of the Gisu killings, 15 percent were property disputes. That figure was slightly higher in Delhi, but most cases were motivated by various feelings of revenge (22 percent involving sexual jealousy and 30 percent feuds).[20]

Revenge motives, mostly sexual in origin, were also prominent in Maria tribe murders. The Maria are "passionately concerned about female chastity, and a wife's infidelity is constantly a source of murder."[21] The men are "jealous and possessive by temperment, passionate as lovers, suspicious and exacting husbands. Divorce is rare; adultery is dangerous, a crime the end of which cannot be foreseen."[22] When males set out on sexual revenge, they express their intentions through symbolic ritual. "They pull out their pubic hairs; they remove a few handfuls of grass from an enemy's roof; they whistle loudly the dreaded *sui* whistle."[23]

The other leading motives among the Maria were property disputes, immediate conflicts within the family, and "alcohol." Killings over property usually arose over the partition of the family goods. They were not committed for gain in the ordinary sense, but arose as disputes about rights and privileges. "In several cases, indeed, murder has been a form of self-defense against someone who tries to take away land or other property that the murderer believes to be his by right."[24]

Elwin observes that unlike the Maria, the neighboring Muria tribe is characterized by an absence of jealousy, a lack of attachment to property and personal possessions, strong civic and social instincts, and gentleness and kindness. He believes that these differences can largely be traced to the presence among the Muria and absence among the Maria of the Ghotul, or village dormitory, in which boys and girls grow up under a high degree of discipline and are trained in the tribal virtues. A system that is almost "prenuptial sexual communism" teaches Muria children the impropriety of jealousy. The habit of sharing in the dormitory is said to weaken individual attachment to property.[25]

The large number of apparently motiveless family quarrels for the Maria tribe in Table 4-2 were interpreted by Elwin as reflecting "exhaustion and fatigue," not other precipitating factors, like drinking, that may have been present. When "alcohol" was listed as the primary motive, the transaction usually appeared to be an immediate conflict.

Sexual jealousy and property disputes were integral to conflicts among rural peoples in Central India as well. Situations where "the victim refused to apologize for or to desist from actions which were publicly embarrassing" added to the totals. "Of major importance in this regard were habitual disobedience or other inappropriate conduct by the wife and derogatory references to the offender, his kin or caste, by neighbors."[26] These encounters, and most of the other murders, were based more on violations of conduct norms and a build-up of hostility over time, "in spite of personal appeals, mediation by community leaders, legal threats, and other social devices, rather than on a sudden impulse, mental aberration or the influence of intoxicants."[27]

Unlike rural India, husband-wife quarrels and sexual motives were not very relevant to the Southern Province of Ceylon, which is consistent with the low proportion of spouse killings there. But land disputes in Ceylon, as in India, were very prominent. Land and property disputes were in fact the formative configuration (34 percent), and many of the feuds (25 percent) and even immediate conflicts (22 percent) were related to land one way or another.

There is a long history to these land disputes. The social system of ancient Ceylon demanded as a right unlimited access to the land. As the property holdings of a family were outrun by its needs, new lands were opened and remained available through the period of the Sinhalese Kings. But eventually the supply-demand balance became critical, and the government began to jealously safeguard its preserves. In recent times, the phenomenal decrease in the death rate has combined with a corresponding increase in the birth rate to create increased pressure. "An obvious result of this situation is the aggravation of the struggle for existence and the ready availability of a basis for dispute." The hunger for land and its socioeconomic effects, especially in the non-urban areas of the Southern Province of Ceylon, where homicide rates are highest, continue to promote discord today.[28]

In perspective, a number of patterns have no universal applicability and appear to be the result of classification problems fused with social and cultural institutions and structures that are genuinely unique. The absence of immediate conflicts in Delhi, the non-applicability of family quarrels and jealousy to Ceylon and the high frequency of "mental illness" among Jewish homicides in Israel are examples. Although there were exceptions, immediate conflicts appeared somewhat more consistently relevant to the West and populations more advanced technologically. Forms of revenge arising out of long, drawn-out hostilities were somewhat more consistently relevant to the non-West and populations less technologically advanced. If correct, this coarse dichotomy, balancing more superficial motives set in an impersonal, hostile, complex, modern urban environment against motives of retribution built up over long periods of time in a more traditional culture, suggests that Thomas and Znaniecki's analysis far transcends the case of the Polish peasant. The one trend that stood out clearly from the data was the importance of property-land disputes in the non-West and the less advanced countries. The motive was irrelevant in other nations for the most part, although it can be maintained that American blacks who respond with violence to structural constraints are expressing similar desires for a stake in their society (see *Violence, Race and Culture*).

Aggravated Assault

The United States

The percentage of unknowns in national survey assaults was very high in Table 4-2. Yet, as in homicide, altercations were the leading motive context for the country as a whole and in each region. Similar evidence from other American studies was at hand, and altercations were even more frequent in all-black than all-white assaults.[29] These findings appear interpretable in the same ways as homicide. Support is given this position by Zimring's conclusion that, "There is a good deal of overlap between the structure, intention and motivational background of most serious but non-fatal attacks and most homicides in Chicago."[30]

Foreign Comparisons

The only comparable reports on assault that proved consistent with the urban United States were from Montreal; altercations, fights, brawls, and family or lover's quarrels led as motives.[31]

A Note on Foreign Perspectives in Forcible Rape and Robbery

The inability of the national survey police reports to yield insights upon which to build a comparable analysis for rape and robbery was matched by a dearth of such material in other American and foreign studies. However, two bits of information—on rape among the African Gusii tribe and on robbery in London—are appropriate here.

Gusii custom encourages male force in sexual intercourse; yet young men also experience intense sexual frustration. There are several reasons. One is the provocative behavior of Gusii women, combined with their sexual inhibitions (see Chapter 5). Another is the high bride-wealth rate, which often postpones marriages. A third is that men can only marry women from another clan. Clans were originally located far apart, and strong tribal sanctions existed against intergroup rape. As a result, a more or less formal pilgrimmage was made to select a bride. When Gusiiland came under British administration, however, tradition was disrupted; penalties for interclan rape were reduced and a pacification program encouraged settlements close together, which created possibilities for interclan heterosexual contact. In effect, there was an increase in sexual "temptation opportunities" and a decrease in personal risks.[32]

Obviously, more than surface motives are encompassed here, and one must again acknowledge the statutory labeling and social engineering of colonial bureaucrats imposing their brand of civilization on "primitive" cultures. But if sexual frustration can be regarded as a rationale for coerced intercourse, then a case might be made that the men of Gusiiland live under more pressure than black Americans.

In a very different setting, McClintock's emphasis on premeditation in English robbery contrasts to the lack of premeditation and triviality of immediate conflicts in homicide and assault. "Impulsiveness and romanticism are not the main characteristics of robbers." Typical robberies in London were predicated by a careful assessment of the situation. Robbers "may not possess tables showing their actual chances of success and impunity, but they are well aware of the large scale failure to enforce the law."[33]

Notes and References

1. In Philadelphia cleared homicides, Wolfgang (1958, p. 191) found the most frequent motive was "altercation of relatively trivial origin," followed by "family quarrel," "jealousy," "altercation over money," and "robbery." "Altercation of relatively trivial origin" had a slightly higher percent for white male than black male victims as well as offenders, but the black male figures were higher when the category "altercation over money" was added in. (The survey "altercation" category did not make this finer distinction.) In Washington, D.C. (D.C. Crime Commission 1966, p. 79), 72 percent of the homicides had altercations as the ostensible motives. In his study of 500 homicides, Harlan (1950, p. 750) also found that killings among white males were less the result of momentary arguments than those among black males. In Chicago homicides, Voss and Hepburn (1968, p. 505) found trivial altercations to be the motive for 20 percent of white victims but 42 percent of non-white victims. For the survey breakdowns by sex and race, see Curtis (1972). Altercations were also the leading motives across all regional aggregates.

2. *Dallas Morning News* (27 October 1968, p. 18A).

3. For the supporting tables, see Curtis (1972).

4. For the supporting tables, see Curtis (1972).

5. See, for example, Wolfgang and Ferracuti (1967, p. 141).

6. Wolfgang and Ferracuti (1967, p. 141). However, it should be added that, although "premeditation may have started out as the clearly distinct concept of lying in wait, as the concept grew the distinction between premeditated and unpremeditated intentional killings became progressively metaphysical. Distinguishing between killings with malice and killings without malice, if that distinction rests on anything other than the simple intention to kill, is also a task best left to word-magicians or judges and juries trying to conform results in homicide cases to personal instincts about rough justice." (Zimring 1972, p. 121).

7. See also the discussion of multiple offenders in Appendix A.

8. See Bohannon (1960, pp. 229-30) for a more complete discussion of these classification problems.

9. The analysis in this section is based on the data in Table 4-2 unless the text cites a different source.

10. In the (few) cases where it was definitely known that hostilities had built up over time but there also was a fight over a trivial subject directly before the crime, category three was used. Similarly, with regard to property disputes (subcategorized in the "Other and Unknown" classification), a long-term dispute over land, for example, was placed under the "Revengeful Response" heading, but a more on the spot, one time conflict was recorded under "Dispute over Property-Land."

11. Von Hentig (1948, p. 398).

12. Conner (1973, p. 116).

13. Holyst (1967, pp. 46-47).

14. Thomas and Znaniecki (1927, p. 1757).

15. Thomas and Znaniecki (1927, pp. 1757-8).

16. Landau and Drapkin (1968, p. 55).

17. Bohannon (1960, p. 205) and Mushanga (1970, pp. 68-82).

18. Bohannon (1960, pp. 80-82).

19. Bohannon (1960, p. 103).

20. Because no "Immediate Conflict" cases were registered, however, it is likely that part of the high "Revenge" figure is misclassified.

21. Elwin (1943, p. xxxv).

22. Elwin (1943, p. 6).

23. Elwin (1943, p. xxxv).

24. Elwin (1943, p. 99).

25. Elwin (1943, p. ix).

26. Driver (1961, p. 58).

27. Driver (1961, pp. 57-58).

28. Jayewardene and Ranasinghe (1963, pp. 32, 34, 139).

29. See Curtis (1972) for tables on regional and racial breakdowns. Among the comparable American studies, the D.C. Crime Commission (1966, p. 79) found that 63 percent of Washington assaults involved altercations.

30. Zimring (1972, p. 110).

31. Tardiff (1966, Table 12).

32. LeVine (1959, pp. 965-990).

33. McClintock and Gibson (1961, p. xiii).

5 Victim Precipitation

Prof. Heinrich Applebaum is a criminologist who feels that unless the police start cracking down on the victims of criminal acts, the crime rate in this country will continue to rise.

"The people who are responsible for crime in this country are the victims. If they didn't allow themselves to be robbed, the problem of crime in this country would be solved." Applebaum said.

"That makes sense, Professor. Why do you think the courts are soft on victims of crimes?"

"We're living in a permissive society and anything goes," Applebaum replied. "Victims of crimes don't seem to be concerned about the consequences of their acts. They walk down a street after dark, or they display jewelry in their store window, or they have their cash registers right out where everyone can see them. They seem to think that they can do this in the United States and get away with it."

—Art Buchwald,
Washington Post, February 4, 1969

Summary of the National Survey

To the recipient of a violent crime, Art Buchwald's anecdote is grim humor. But, like all good parody, his involutions often catch more than an insubstantial glimpse of reality, for it is not difficult to imagine a contribution by the victim to each of the major violent crimes. During an altercation, one party hands the other a gun and, knowing full well the other's hostile mood, accuses him of not having the "guts to shoot." A young woman agrees to intercourse and engages in heavy petting but resists her date at the last moment. A man flashes a great deal of money at a bar and then staggers home alone on a dark street late at night.

The extent to which culpability is legally recognized when situations such as these lead to acts reported to the police varies considerably according to the type of crime. American homicide laws recognize provocation by allowing for mitigation of the offense from murder to excusable homicide. Comparable outcomes are allowed in felonious assaults not resulting in death, but there is no acknowledgment of culpability in robbery. Statutory recognition of the victim's role in rape has mainly been entered through corroboration rules. At one extreme, New York State law long provided that every material element of a rape—penetration, force, and the identity of the rapist—had to be corroborated by evidence besides the victim's testimony. Largely as a response to pressures from feminists and other groups, the corroboration requirement was removed from the books in March 1974 for all sex offenses where lack of consent results from "forcible compulsion" or "physical helplessness."[1] There are now only a few remaining jurisdictions with corroboration rules.

From a behavioral science point of view, the concept of victim precipitation was probably first suggested by Von Hentig in the 1940s. He observed that "the victim shapes and moulds the criminal" and that "the victim may assume the role of the determinant."[2] The actual term "victim precipitation" was later coined by Wolfgang.[3] Over recent years, there has been increased interest in the role of the victim in the etiology of crime, culminating in the First International Symposium on Victimology held in Jerusalem in 1973. Seeking to examine the empirical validity of victim precipitation, the national survey tailored a definition of the term to each of the violent crimes and used as guides the definitions in earlier studies wherever possible. The coders reading the police reports then judged for presence or absence of provocation.[4] On the basis of the definitions used, precipitation appeared not uncommon for homicide and assault, less frequent but still empirically noteworthy for robbery and perhaps least relevant for rape. Table 5-1 has the data on clearances.

Criminal Homicide

The United States

From a psychoanalytic perspective, there is much to theorize about the death wish and a victim's precipitative inclinations, but mapping the unconscious was hardly amenable to operationalization in the survey. The definition had to be

Table 5-1
Victim Precipitation by Type of Crime, 17 American Cities, 1967, Clearances (Percent)

Presence of victim-Precipitation	Criminal Homicide	Aggravated Assault	Forcible Rape	Armed Robbery	Unarmed Robbery
Victim Precipitation	22.0	14.4	4.4	10.7	6.1
No Victim Precipitation	33.8	34.6	82.9	81.4	83.8
Unknown	44.2	51.0	12.6	7.9	10.1
Total	100.0 (668)	100.0 (1493)	100.0 (617)	100.0 (509)	100.0 (502)

Base: Interactions

more overt, and so, following Wolfgang, provocation was considered to occur whenever the victim was first to use physical force against the subsequent slayer.

As originally conceived by Wolfgang, this straightforward definition, relatively easy to operationalize, seeks a level of behavioral technicality and political neutrality. It does not automatically assume that certain situational contexts (such as gang fights for homicide-assault or hitchhiking for rape) are precipitative per se. There is further inquiry into what precisely happens when the participants meet. Each offender-victim interaction is examined to see whether the victim engages in a specific kind of behavior at a specific time. In addition, the decision on whether or not an event is precipitated is made by a coder reading a police report and implementing a predetermined definition. It is not based on the offender's judgement of self-perceived precipitation, nor the victim's judgement. Degrees of precipitation are not operationalized.

Here are some illustrations of precipitation as defined in this way by Wolfgang and replicated in the national survey:

... A husband accused his wife of giving money to another man, and while she was making breakfast, he attacked her with a milk bottle, then a brick, and finally a piece of concrete block. Having had a butcher knife in hand, she stabbed him during the fight.

... *During a lover's quarrel, a man hit his mistress and threw a can of kerosene at her. She retaliated by throwing the liquid on him, and then tossed a lighted match in his direction. He died from the burns.*

... A drunken husband, beating his wife in their kitchen, gave her a butcher knife and dared her to use it on him. She claimed that if he should strike her once more, she would use the knife, whereupon he slapped her in the face and she fatally stabbed him.

... *During an argument in which a man called a woman many vile names, she tried to telephone the police. But he grabbed the phone from her hands, knocked her down, kicked her, and hit her with a tire gauge. She ran to the kitchen, grabbed a butcher knife, and stabbed him in the stomach.*[5]

Unfortunately, there was not enough information for coders to make a judgement on many reports in the national survey, but 22 percent of all the clearances and 14 percent of the non-clearances were determined to be precipitated.[6] Wolfgang found 26 percent of the Philadelphia slayings he studied to be provoked[7] and, using the same definition, Voss and Hepburn put the figure at 38 percent in Chicago.[8] Complementary results were provided when the national survey data were grouped by region; higher frequencies of precipitation fell in the North Central cities than in the Northeast.[9] It would be interesting to explore the extent to which these differences reflect truly divergent behaviors rather than idiosyncrasies in police reporting.

Among the race specific patterns, precipitation was lowest (6 percent) when the offender was black and the victim white, a finding consistent with an initial motive of robbery and the absence of previous relationships—typical indicators of interracial killings. Of the all-black killings, 28 percent were judged precipitated, as against 20 percent of the all-white killings, but there were high percentages of unknowns.[10]

Males of both races were considerably more likely than females to precipitate cleared homicides in the survey. Age, relationship, and location were not important considerations.[11] Wolfgang's results were about the same,[12] but variations in Chicago included frequencies of precipitation for non-white victims that were higher than in the national survey.[13]

Foreign Comparisons

Several bits of information begin to validate the cross-cultural significance of precipitation in homicide.

Examining homicides in Scotland and sensitive to both intent and motive, Avison distinguishes three categories that in reality blend into one another along a continuum: crimes with no victim involvement or minimal involvement, crimes with some degree of "participation" and crimes where there is clear victim responsibility.[14]

The first group is largely characterized by deliberate offender premeditation—as in "problem solving homicides." The second group is perhaps best illustrated by quarrels that escalate from verbal to physical violence and end in a fatal assault. Alcohol consumption is a common correlate. There is usually an absence of intent, and the offender is commonly remorseful afterwards. The third category covers incidents where the subsequent victim seeks to detain a criminal or intervenes in a fight, the victim colludes in a criminal act and disregards the possibility of being killed (e.g., a woman in an illegal abortion), the victim seeks revenge after a quarrel or over a long series of episodes, or the victim is a member of a gang attacked by another group. Intent usually is present.

Notice that the first category, of little victim involvement, and the third, of considerable involvement, both usually witness intent by the offender, whereas the role of both offender and victim are typically more ambiguous in the second grouping. In addition, there is a tendency for Avison's instances of clear precipitation to move away from Wolfgang's offender-victim specifics and toward a definition in terms of certain situational contexts per se.

Avison found that two-thirds of the homicides studied fell into categories two or three. He does not further distinguish this proportion—presumably because the emphasis on a continuum of participation often made it difficult to neatly classify an event as either group two or three. His conclusion is that "the phenomenon of participation is far more widespread than has been indicated [in prior research]."[15]

In another study, Holyst refers to a "predestined guilty victim group" within a total of 470 Polish homicides, although the exact proportion is not given. These victims engaged in illegal or quasi-illegal activities (for example, prostitution), experienced personal problems (alcoholism), acted anti-socially (through, for example, "brutal behavior"), worked in target-prone legal jobs (taxi drivers, police officers, cashiers) and were "incidentally" or "permanently" careless, according to whether or not exposure to danger occurred regularly.[16]

The question of provocation is explored within this unspecified "predestined guilty" subsample. No formal definition of "victim precipitation" is given, but a much broader conception than used here becomes apparent. In illustrating his range of precipitation, Holyst specifies active and passive forms, conscious and unconscious provocation, and from the point of view of "moral and social criteria," "pejorative, positive and indifferent provocation." So conceived, "provocation" was applicable to 49 percent of the Polish cases with "predestined guilty" victims.[17]

Using a definition more in keeping with Wolfgang's and ours, Pecar found that the victim verbally or physically provoked homicide in 51 percent of the 271 cases studied in Slovenia between 1954 and 1967.[18]

Palmer uses a broader definition, but one that still focuses on specific offender-victim transactions. He found that the victim made "the first aggressive move physically or orally or by gesture" in over half of the homicides in 15 of the 29 non-literate societies examined.[19]

A final source of information is derivable from the case-by-case summaries included in the survey of African homicides by Bohannon and in Elwin's classic account of killings among the Maria tribe in India. We have judged these cases for presence of victim precipitation as defined in the national survey. The results are in Table 5-2. The only primitive societies that seemed to approach the American figures for precipitation were the Gisu and Luyia tribes in Africa (where 20 and 16 percent of the cases, respectively, were judged to be precipitated). No differences in traditions or institutions encouraging physical provocation could be discerned from the available information to make these cultures unique when set against the other primitive societies. More detailed work is necessary—it would be a valuable undertaking—before any conclusions can be reached on the quality and extent of assaultive provocation in American ghettos, say, compared to experiences in Africa.

Aggravated Assault

The United States

Victim precipitated aggravated assault was defined in the national survey as occurring when the victim was first to use either physical force or insinuating

Table 5-2
Victim Precipitation in Criminal Homicide Estimated for United States and Primitive Tribes (Percent)

Country Geographic Scope Year / Presence of Victim Precipitation	United States Urban (17 City Survey, Clearances) 1967	Africa[a] Rural						India[b] Rural (Maria Tribe) 1921-1941
		Gisu 1948-1954	Luo Years Not Available	Luyia 1949-1954	Nyoro 1935-1955	Soga 1952-1954	Tiv 1931-1949	
Victim Precipitation	22.0	20.2	4.5	15.8	0	7.0	9.9	11.0
No Victim Precipitation	33.8	53.5	59.1	64.9	97.1	72.0	78.9	76.0
Unknown	44.2	26.3	36.4	19.3	2.9	21.0	11.2	13.0
TOTAL	100.0 (668)	100.0 (99)	100.0 (44)	100.0 (114)	100.0 (34)	100.0 (100)	100.0 (122)	100.0 (100)

[a]Compilation from case summaries in Bohannon's (1960) Appendix.
[b]Compilation from case summaries in Elwin's (1943) Appendix.

language and gestures against the subsequent attacker. Large numbers of unknowns remained a problem, but 14 percent of the clearances and 21 percent of the non-clearances[20] were judged to be precipitated.

There have been no other estimates of provocation in assault to triangulate with these results, but the congruence with homicide is attested by clinical observations on the similar personality types of many assault and homicide victims, particularly when the offender is a friend or intimate. For example, Schultz has observed that many victims in both homicide and assault have aggressive-tyrannical personality types. They often complement submissive-passive offender types, who seek to avoid conflict whenever possible and will play the masochistic role if it gains them affection. But the eventual victim sadistically exploits these traits in the eventual offender by threatening to withhold love and affection. Finally, the victim oversteps the offender's "previously overcontrolled hostility threshold."[21]

As in homicide, precipitation in national survey assault clearances was not drawn to any particular victim age range, blacks invited attacks more than whites and men more than women.[22]

Foreign Comparisons

No international material has been found for provocation in assault.

Forcible Rape

The United States

Precipitation is a particularly volatile question for rape. Illustrating attitudes that are commonly revealed, one man recently ventured on a Los Angeles television program that "in the majority of women who are raped, I think that probably 75 percent of them are actually enjoying it or are asking for it."[23]

Victim-precipitated rape was defined in the national survey as a situation ending in forced intercourse where a female first agreed to sexual relations, or clearly invited them verbally and through gestures, but then retracted before the act. Amir used this conception in his Philadelphia study. It can be argued that there is clear bias toward the offender, that too much is necessarily labeled precipitative. Does not a woman have the right to be receptive, but up to a point? Nonetheless, the definition is still closer to seeking offender-victim specifics than to blanketing certain situational contexts as precipitative per se.

Whereas Amir judged 19 percent of the rapes studied in Philadelphia to be precipitated,[24] only 4 percent of the survey clearances at the national level and 6 percent of the non-clearances were so designated by the coders.[25] The survey sample of clearances from Philadelphia (N = 44) was lower still: 2 percent of the interactions were judged to be precipitated, 96 percent not, and 2 percent could not be determined.

It is plausible to argue that Amir's results are more reliable than the survey frequencies. He was able to review backup material in the Philadelphia police records, whereas all the information was often not sent for cases with extensive write-ups in the national survey. Amir's definition is sufficiently vague to raise questions of accurate replication. A number of different coders worked on the rapes in the survey, and Amir, working alone, might have built up a deeper understanding and more sensitive decision-making ability. Clinical material on sexual precipitation—for example, the work of Weiss, Halleck and Schultz[26]— can be found.

Amir also asked whether rape victims had a "bad reputation"—whether they were known as promiscuous, admitted having sexual relations before with the offender, admitted having sexual relations before with anyone (for young women under age 18), or admitted being raped before but didn't prosecute. On this basis, 19 percent of the black women and 23 percent of the white victims had "bad reputations."[27] Although the D.C. Crime Commission did not measure for provocation, it did inquire into "poor reputations." Determination of "poor reputation" was based on whether the victim engaged in a criminal occupation; had a prior record for sex offenses, habitual drunkenness, disorderly conduct and drug offenses; or had a history of prior specious complaints of sexual assault. Also used were substantiated statements by the offender(s) that the victim was known to be a "loose or easy object of sexual assault."[28] By these criteria, 24 percent of the black victims and 25 percent of the whites had "poor reputation."[29] If one interprets bad or poor reputation as associated with the likelihood of precipitation, then added support is given Amir's position.[30]

A decline in Philadelphia and perhaps national victim precipitated rapes from Amir's 1958 to 1960 period to 1967 might be theorized to explain some of the discrepancy with the survey findings, but the institutional filters that help confound the results should always be remembered. As discussed in Chapter 2, the gap between true and reported levels of rape is as great as or greater than the gap for the other serious violent crimes (or any of the FBI Index crimes), so our confidence—as well as Amir's—about any reported rape configuration is commensurably weakened. Police are usually more skeptical about the victim in rape than in homicide, assault, or robbery, because, among other reasons, rape is such a personal crime, often lacking witnesses and therefore squarely pitting the victim's word against the defendant's.

One possible consequence—there is little proof—might be that the low level of precipitation registered in some cities in the national survey reflected police rejection of questionable complaints because they assumed the cases would not survive the criminal justice process. Yet, one can argue in the other direction that police bias against the victims in some cities resulted in their filing more reports interpretable as precipitative by our coders than were warranted. Some police departments are skilled and tactful in their interrogation of the victim and construction of offense reports, yet accounts of insensitive treatment are common, and many feminists are outraged at what they see as the unfairness of the criminal justice system. They argue that there can be no clearer example of women's place in society. When a person is robbed or murdered, the offender is put on trial. "But when a woman is raped, it is the woman and not the rapist who is put on trial."[31] Although opinion abounds, there is in fact little objective evidence that victims in rape lie more than, say, victims in robbery. The procedural need is for a better balance, eliminating the second class citizenship pressed on many rape victims while still protecting offenders from grave injustice. The New York Police Department's largely female staffed and directed Sex Crimes Analysis Unit is an example of welcome reform in this direction.[32]

The national survey departure from Amir need not be written off, then, as long as it is recognized that issues of factual accuracy are interwoven with biases from institutions filtering the data. In addition, compared to homicide and assault, the frequency of unknowns in estimating national survey rape precipitation was relatively low; the coders seemed to be expressing some degree of confidence. They were all males, which discounts the possibility of female coders intentionally not recording precipitation. Because precipitation was low both in non-clearances (where only accounts by victims are recorded) and clearances (where offender accounts may be attached), it cannot be claimed that the findings reflect a victim reporting bias. Perhaps Amir projected biases; with a number of recorders, the survey gained a better chance of having subjective currents neutralized or diluted. Feminists can easily shoot down the material on bad and poor reputations on the basis of sexism[33] and point out that white males have done most of the clinical studies—which, in addition, have meager generalizability because of few subjects.

The jury is far from in, and may never be, on whether the occurrence of provocation in rape follows the minority but still highly significant pattern apparent in homicide and assault, gravitates towards insignificance or holds a middle course. Yet, at present, there is sufficient reason to de-emphasize the typical rape victim's contribution. This tentative conclusion will be useful in the conceptual discussion of rape in *Violence, Race and Culture.*

The 15 to 17 age range had a higher proportion of precipitating victims than other ages in the national survey, but no clearcut interracial or intraracial patterns could be specified with confidence. Amir's results on age were generally consistent, but 29 percent of his white victims precipitated rape, against 17 percent for black females. His all-white versus all-black precipitation figures were 41 and 14 percents, respectively.[34]

The survey frequency of precipitation was higher between close friends, paramours, and the like than when the rapist was a relative or when the relationship was non-primary. Amir concurred. It is, of course, consistent with accepted sexual behavior among blacks and whites as well for a female to assume a more receptive posture to the advances of a boy friend than an uncle or stranger. Provocation was slightly more common nationally in home locations than when the rape happened elsewhere. Amir, however, found Philadelphia precipitation higher in outside places excluding cars than in residences or in cars. When the victim was injured in the survey, she was about as likely to have provoked attack as when she was not, but Amir found more precipitation in cases where the offender used physical force than when he did not.[35]

In a later study, Amir, with Nelson, found that 20 percent of the rapes sampled in Berkeley from 1968 to 1970 involved hitchhiking. The Philadelphia definition of precipitation is not applied in this research. Rather, the authors conclude that hitchhike rape "is interesting because it is a 'victim precipitated' offense, in which the victim's behavior contributes to her victimization."[36] As with evidence that some law enforcement officials consider prior association by white women with black men as tantamount to a request for rape,[37] here is a good illustration of precipitation defined in terms of a situational context per se.

Foreign Comparisons

Empirical findings are not readily available, but several different conceptual approaches to provocation come to light.

Consider again LeVine's work on the Gusii tribe of Kenya. The reported rape rate in Gusiland is very high (for example, 47 per 100,000 in 1955, compared to 15 per 100,000 in the United States for the same year). Much, perhaps most, of the reason may prove to be embedded in reporting discrepancies. But courting traditions, acceptable feminine role-playing, familial obligations, and religious interdicts coalesce to produce incidents that might reasonably be called victim precipitated rape:

Gusii girls who have no desire for sexual relationships deliberately encourage young men in the preliminaries of courtship because they enjoy the gifts and attention they receive. Some of them act provocative, thinking they will be able to obtain the desired articles and then escape the sexual advances of the young man. . . . An aggressive conclusion is particularly likely if the girl is actually married. In the early stages of marriage brides spend a good deal of time in their home communities visiting their parents. Such a girl may . . . pretend to be unmarried in order to be bribed and flattered. No matter how emotionally and financially involved in her a young man becomes, the bride is too afraid of supernatural sanctions to yield to him sexually. After she fails to appear at several appointments . . . he may rape her in desperation the next time they meet, and she will report the deed.[38]

Had LeVine been interested in operationalizing a definition of precipitation, it seemingly would have concentrated on offender-victim specifics. What he does contribute is some sense of the developmental history of the relationship that touches more on offender motive than intent. If such information had been available on the national survey police reports, instead of data covering a very discrete segment of time, more accurate judgements on precipitation might have emerged. Thus, behavior during a single recorded incident that could be interpreted as a woman's right takes on different implications if repeated again and again.

By contrast, the following illustrations have affinities to Nelson and Amir's assumption that certain contexts are precipitative per se.

In Nigeria, Nkpa describes an incident among the Igbo people in which a girl came to market wearing a mini skirt. When she bent down, her thighs and underwear were exposed. Seeing this, a young man "lost control of himself" and raped her. Nkpa says the girl "prepared the ground" for the assault because of her dress, which contrasts to the traditional Igbo garment, flowing down almost to the ankle.[39]

Among orthodox Moslems in many less Westernized Mideast and Central Asian Countries, like Afghanistan and Pakistan, a woman must wear the traditional veil, or burqa, when she leaves home. This is part of "purdah," the nunlike existence in which women are shut off from contact with all but their closest relatives. Orthodox Moslem men see purdah as protecting women and preserving their sanctity. When several young Pakistanis were recently asked by a reporter what would happen if the veil were taken away, one member replied that "men would become crazy. They couldn't control themselves. There would be nothing but crime and anarchy—the same as in [the United States]."[40]

In Bangladesh, Roy interviewed a sample of women raped by Pakistani soldiers during the 1971 war for liberation. He reports that the victims did not know their offenders, had no prior contacts with them, and were fearful of any kind of direct or indirect involvement with the Pak army. Roy concludes that victims therefore were "not responsible for their victimization either consciously or by default. No rape event can thus be said to have been precipitated by victims.."[41]

The status quo is threatened by change in the first two examples. In the eyes of men, who establish the standards of behavior, the change is associated with a Westernizing influence in the dress of women. Rather than recognizing the possibility of or adjusting to the change, the response is to label it remissive. There is also a renunciation of social responsibility for what is predicted to happen if the behavior continues—based on an assumption that men have an innate sexual appetite that is difficult to control. The potential importance of a particular cultural setting in the definition of precipitation is clearly brought out, just as Chapter 3 recognized broader normative influences in the analysis of interpersonal relationships and violence.

Whereas the first two examples show how victim precipitation can be used to defend the existing social order, the last illustration, where an entire context is defined as *non*-precipitative per se, demonstrates how the provocation concept can be reversed and used as a tool with which to attack the offender. The central assertion in Roy's paper, which his discussion of precipitation helps make, is that rape by soldiers was ordered by the top Pakistani commanders as part of an overall military strategy to terrorize a rebellious people.

Robbery

The United States

Victim precipitation in armed and unarmed robbery was defined in terms of "temptation-opportunities" where the victim clearly had not acted with reasonable self-protective behavior in handling money, jewelry, or other valuables. The orientation was to personal victims, but applicability to institutions was not ruled out. This conception was taken from Normandeau. As with Amir's original definition of precipitation in rape, the emphasis here is more on accepting Wolfgang's use of case-by-case offender-victim specifics rather than on assuming that all events of a certain context are precipitated per se. But, also as for rape, the definition for robbery has more conceptual and operational ambiguities than for homicide. There is not that cutting point neatness of the subsequent victim striking the first blow.

Careless, precipitating behavior was determined to be present in 11 percent of the national survey armed clearances, 5 percent of the non-clearances, 6 percent of the unarmed clearances, and 10 percent of the unarmed non-clearances.[42] Unknowns were low. Normandeau found a roughly compatible 11 percent of his Philadelphia robberies to fit the description.[43]

In his recent Boston study, Conklin confirms that robbers look for such invitations. Less skilled, non-career robbers, who casually stole on the street as the opportunity arose, were concerned with obvious signs of vulnerability in personal victims, such as being old and out alone at night. Their level of awareness in effect converged quite closely to the transactions recorded as precipitative in the survey. But Conklin also found that career professionals, who were usually older and had a relatively greater interest in robbing institutions, conceived of vulnerability in broader terms, as circumstances that might yield potential payoffs after careful planning. Thus, a vulnerable bank might have a rear exit, a poor alarm system and a highway nearby.[44]

DeBaun, writing while serving a sentence for armed robbery, has described how such professionals find their "marks." Some targets are sought out by the professional himself—e.g., armored cars making deliveries or women appearing in public "festooned like Christmas trees." Other "marks" are tipped off by ostensibly honest people, and more than a few are prearranged: the truck driver wishing to share the value of the cigarettes or whiskey he is carrying; the jeweler wanting to beat his insurance company; the bank manager seeking to cover his embezzlements.[45]

The high degree of emotion and irrationality in homicide and assault would seem to make warnings against precipitating attack rather futile. In spite of the seemingly lower prevalence of provocation in robbery, a public response, in terms of greater personal care and public and private target hardening, is more feasible. Thus, Camp concludes that banks could do much to make thefts more difficult[46] and Normandeau lectures on the responsibilities of individuals.[47] Buchwald comes into his own, almost.

Male victims precipitated armed robbery more than female victims, and the percentage was higher for blacks than whites in the national survey. Temptation opportunities appeared to surface more in all-black than all-white or black-on-white situations. Victims 18 to 20 and 26 to 30 were more likely to invite armed robbery than other ages, and offenders were almost invariably strangers. Interestingly, victim precipitation took place almost entirely in all-white clearances for unarmed robbery.[48]

There was a higher percentage of armed robbery temptation opportunities in the Northeast (19 percent) than in the north central (5 percent) and western (6 percent) cities and a greater proportion of victim precipitated unarmed robberies in the West (10 percent) and Northeast (8 percent) than in the north central region (1 percent). The sample size was too small to say anything about the South. The relatively high overall northeastern figure invites further work to test the hypothesis that the location, physical structure, and practices of businesses handling money as well as the habits of private individuals with money make them more robbery prone in Bos-Wash than in other parts of the country.[49]

Foreign Comparisons

In the absence of international findings of an empirical nature for robbery, two examples serve to demonstrate how the concept of precipitation has been employed qualitatively in the analysis of foreign data and how the search for robbery victims carries across national and cultural boundaries.

McClintock and Gibson conclude that many London robberies could have been avoided if victims had taken very elementary precautions. In spite of police warnings to merchants and others against making the same journey with money at the same time each week, a sizable number of robberies were carefully planned precisely because offenders were able to observe the regular movements of subsequent victims. Other victims walked across parks, commons, or poorly lit side streets late at night instead of taking longer routes along main thoroughfares.[50]

In Nigeria, Nkpa describes how "easy marks" for robbery are sought out among the Igbo. The emphasis on material success is so great in Igbo society, says Nkpa, that many people will go to any length to achieve it. One manifestation is acceptance—indeed, often approval—of theft, as long as it is conducted in towns other than where one was born.[51] Here, then, the impact of interceding cultural interdicts seems to result in a very broad perception of precipitation in robbery by potential offenders outside village boundaries that sharply diminishes with declining distance to the village—until there is minimal or no response to even the easiest of marks.

Discussion

Based on the data and definitions in the national survey, the ranking of homicide-assault, robbery, and rape in terms of greater to lesser precipitation by the victim is attenuated by the definitional, conceptual and operational questions that have been raised.

One step in conceptually refining precipitation as a notion applicable to all crimes with victims would be to standardize a scale of victim availability as a replacement for Wolfgang's either-or version replicated here. Even though both incidents can be considered precipitative, there is surely a difference in degree between a person walking alone through Central Park late at night and someone who hands his assailant a gun and dares him to shoot. Von Hentig's original thoughts on provocation in fact acknowledged a victim range from "complete indifference to conscious impulsion."[52]

A modest innovation would follow Avison into three categories of precipitation, from deliberate provocation to some degree of involvement to little or no involvement. (Figure 5-1.) But most past work—Avison excluded—may be deficient in not systematically recognizing that victim precipitation simultaneously must be defined by offender intent. Figure 5-1 does this. There are five categories: 1—"pure victim precipitation" (clear victim provocation and little or no offender intent); 2—events short of this extreme, where victim involvement is still more pronounced than offender intent; 3—events where the involvement-intent levels are roughly equivalent; 4—events, short of the extreme, where offender intent is more pronounced than victim involvement; and 5—"total offender responsibility" (deliberate offender premeditation and little or no victim involvement). Whereas those following the Wolfgang approach might concentrate on all events in the column headed "clear provocation" (and also possibly events in the column headed "some involvement"), this scheme asserts that only in category 1 can one think confidently in terms of distinct victim responsibility alone. The relative focus remains on the victim in category 2, though the offender intent-victim responsibility disparity is not as clearcut. In part, category 3 argues that even if there is clear provocation or at least some involvement by the victim, it may be misleading from conceptual and policy viewpoints to collapse into category 1 events where there is a standoff in terms of responsibility.

Offender intent \ Victim involvement	Clear provocation	Some involvement	Little or no involvement
Deliberate premeditation	3A	4A	5 "Total offender responsibility"
Some intent	2A	3B	4B
Little or no intent	• 1 "Pure victim precipitation"	2B	3C

Key: See text.

Figure 5-1. Offender Intent and Victim Involvement.

Conceptually, a distinction might be made between a homicide where the victim hands the offender a gun and dares him to shoot (category 1) and a gang shootout where the victim wings the offender first but then is killed (category 3A). For rape, the distinction might be between an event where the victim, after drinking a great deal, succumbs or agrees to intercourse with her boss but then claims rape when discovered by her husband (category 1) and a party where the victim, when dancing, physically encourages a stranger on the make, who then takes her into a bedroom and forces sex against her will (category 3A). For robbery, compare a scene where a dude happens on a drunken older man and, on the spot, decides to take advantage of him (category 1) and the planned postal office heist of a professional robber that is facilitated by most of the staff being asleep (a category 3A event that has been reported in Italy). Similar distinctions are possible between cells 3B or 3C, on the one hand, and cell 1 on the other. A mirror image analysis in terms of offender responsibility can be done with categories 3, 4, and 5.

The potential implications for victim compensation illustrate the policy relevance that might be developed from this scheme. If policy were to look at the victim alone, then an event falling into cell 4A, with some victim involvement, would not promise much compensation for the victim. But if the relatively higher level of offender intent were jointly taken into account, the victim could expect more favorable consideration.

A modification of Figure 5-1 might also consider how voluntarily the victim entered into the episode concluding in rape. Thus, it can be argued that a woman who voluntarily accepts a hitch has more responsibility for her attack than a woman who is pushed into a car. The crucial query then becomes whether or not degree of voluntariness is necessarily always positively associated with degree of precipitation.

Another critical question is the perspective from which victim precipitation should be defined. The studies replicated in Chapter 5 are based on the researcher's definition, applied to a reading of police reports. But Silverman offers a definition in terms of the offender's perception:

Victim precipitation occurs when the offender's action in committing or beginning to commit a crime is initiated after and directly related to an action (be it physical or verbal, conscious or unconscious) on the part of the victim. The offender perceives the victim's behavior as a facilitating action (including temptation, invitation) to the commission of the crime. The action of the victim might be said to have triggered the offender's behavior.[53]

An advantage to Silverman's definition is that it acknowledges the demonstrably important role of culture but still avoids automatic conclusions that certain contexts are precipitative per se. The normative standards held by the offender presumably help mold his perception of what is precipitating behavior. Thus, for example, leaving a car door unlocked in a small town may not be perceived as a temptation opportunity, but this may indeed be the case in a large city.[54] Or, applying Igbo values, the unlocked car is not a temptation opportunity in one's own small town, but it is in the small town just across the river.

Yet does Silverman place too much importance on the offender? His definition threatens to yield figures for victim precipitation that are so high as to severely reduce any discriminating capacity the concept may have. A short skirt—even (or especially) in Los Angeles—might do for rape. If, after reading the paper, a professional thief decides to rob the latest lottery winner, is this not the genesis of a victim precipitated episode? At the extreme, the offender may interpret the mere existence of an individual as victim precipitation—for example, a child not wanted by an unmarried woman.[55] With as much justification, an argument might be made to define precipitation in terms of the *victim's* perception (except, of course, in homicide). Thus, Conklin interviewed robbery offenders on their perceived vulnerability,[56] and it would be easy to proceed a bit further into a more formal victimization survey on self-interpreted involvement.

Victim-defined precipitation would likely produce figures as low as offender-defined figures may be high. Both versions incorporate cultural influences—yet the relativity of the definition to a participant's normative references and social milieu means that comparisons across different cultures will be difficult if not impossible to make. The definition of precipitation will change. Here is where a constant, researcher-defined concept, as used in Chapter 5, has greatest advantage.

The implication is that there is no "correct" definition of precipitation. Each version has advantages and disadvantages. Accordingly, why not triangulate offender-, victim-, and researcher-based definitions and incorporate into each some kind of more refined scale of degrees of victim involvement like the one suggested? A comparative analysis could then identify the upper- and lower-bound percentage figures of precipitation in a specified sample, depending on the different definitions. Although it may not necessarily be the ideal toward which researcher should aim, a more unified consensus definition of precipitation could emerge from such analysis. One might even conceive of a Delphi exercise among offenders, victims, and researchers.

The discussion has mainly been conceptual. But it will not be easy to measure and compare even sizeable gradations of offender intent and victim involvement. Investigations that apply several definitions will have to face difficult problems of operationalization and replication. At least for researcher-defined precipitation, it may be that only blatant physical actions, like striking the first blow, are employable and that "suggestive gestures," "temptation opportunities," and the like are too subtle to be captured and replicated.

However, in spite of the crude measurement tools presently available to social science, much progress can be made simply if better data are obtained. Future research on victim precipitation should avoid police reports and other institutional filters. Instead, the need is for detailed clinical interviewing and projective testing of incoming victims and offenders on a scale large enough to retain a significant and stratified sample. Whenever possible, the developmental history of any prior relationship between offender and victim should be reconstructed from accounts by the participants as well as significant others. Teams of researchers with different personal attributes should be used for interviewing. Will, for example, conclusions by investigators of the same race and sex of the offender or victim be greatly different from what is now mainly viewed through the eyes of white male scholars? In addition, comparisons of persons who, faced with an offender, have escaped victimization to those who have succumbed may yield valuable insights—for instance, on the merits of aggressiveness by women against rapists. (Touching on this question, Reiss found that the "completion rate" for Chicago rapes in public places was higher for black than white women. Whether white women were in fact more skilled at thwarting attacks could not be determined.[57])

This course of proposed research embraces the writer's preference for a relatively more neutral, Wolfgang-type approach to precipitation based on offender-victim specifics, rather than one blocked out of certain contexts defined as precipitative per se. We believe that the latter path assumes too much, that precipitation should be based on the details of what actually happened and on the participants' perceptions, not on blanket assumptions of increased risk and responsibility for all situations of a given kind. Such assumptions are likely to be unequally applied to different crimes. Thus, is there something about the kind and intensity of sexual as against economic values in the United

States that dissuades those who perceive of short skirts and hitchhiking as sexually precipitative per se from adding that the same might apply in robbery to women whose purses are observable on the street? In addition, the same extreme positions that could result from a definition based on offender perception alone are possible from the blanket definitions. To give the most volatile current political example: for some, the mere existence of Israel may be ground for attack.

Nonetheless, situational context definitions can be expected as long as man remains subjective and political. And such definitions should be encouraged, as interpretations of classes of behavior rather than criteria or standards in any absolute sense. An unlimited variety of new definitions begins to unfold as the sphere of conceptual relevance expands beyond the offender-victim interaction and encompasses the moral demand systems of any society or subgroup within it. By blaming a woman for her own rape, by parallel application to other crimes, the notion of precipitation can be used to resist change and defend the institutionalized order. But victim precipitation has considerable potential for use by the political left as well. The view that the student of victims shares with the labeling theorist invites turning conventional wisdoms inside out and criticizing the established dominant cultural value system. As discussed in *Violence, Race and Culture*, what does precipitation mean if we see American blacks less as violent crime offenders and more as casualties of institutional racism, adapting to economic and racial constraints with contracultural responses that use physical violence to pass the victim identity onto others? To the extent that violent crimes encourage governmental repression, reactive police measures, massive expenditures on hardware, and reaffirmed institutional racism rather than social change, these crimes themselves can be interpreted as precipitative.

Notes and References

1. Forcible compulsion is defined as "physical force that overcomes earnest resistance or a threat, express or implied, that places a person in fear of immediate death or serious physical injury to himself or another person or in fear that he or another person will immediately be kidnapped." Physical helplessness means ". . . that a person is unconscious or for any other reason is physically unable to communicate unwillingness to an act." Corroboration is still required when the victim is less than 17 years or when she is mentally defective or incapacitated. Proof of penetration (usually supplied by a sperm test) is still required. (*Legal Division Bulletin*, 1974.) See also Lear (1972).

2. Von Hentig (1948, p. 384). See also Von Hentig (1940). The historical development of victim precipitation is summarized in Silverman (1973).

3. Wolfgang (1958).

4. Coders were instructed to record "unknown" unless they were reasonably certain from the information provided that an interaction definitely did or did not involve victim precipitation.

5. From Wolfgang (1958, p. 253).

6. For the tables on non-clearances, see Curtis (1972).

7. Wolfgang (1958, p. 252).

8. Voss and Hepburn (1968, p. 506).

9. See Curtis (1972) for the supporting tables.

10. See Curtis (1972) for the supporting tables.

11. See Curtis (1972).

12. Wolfgang (1958, pp. 256-7).

13. Voss and Hepburn (1968, pp. 506-7).

14. Avison (1973).

15. Avison (1973, p. 8).

16. Holyst (1967, p. 79).

17. Holyst (1967, p. 80).

18. Pecar (1971).

19. Palmer (1973).

20. See Curtis (1972) for the supporting tables on non-clearances.

21. Schultz (1969, pp. 139-40).

22. See Curtis (1972) for the supporting tables.

23. Csida and Csida (1974, p. 18).

24. Amir (1967, p. 533).

25. For the supporting tables on non-clearances, see Curtis (1972).

26. Weiss et al. (1955), Halleck (1965), Schultz (1968).

27. Amir (1965, p. 250).

28. D.C. Crime Commission (1966, p. 941).

29. D.C. Crime Commission (1966, p. 50).

30. Peters (1973) also discloses from the first interviews in an ongoing study of rape in Philadelphia that adolescent victims (aged 13 to 17) were judged by the social workers "to lack discretion or have some complicity in over 40 percent of the cases." However, the N was low (47) and the figure was 10 percent for adults (N = 84).

31. Anderson (1971). As indicated here, criticism is not limited to police but to the entire criminal justice system. In fact, Holmstrom and Burgess (1973)—both women—found in their Boston study that, contrary to stereotype, two-thirds of the rape victims interviewed believed the police to have treated them well. The authors conclude that, at least in Boston, more painful to the victim and more in need of reform than treatment by police is the experience in court, particularly crossexamination by the defense lawyers.

32. *Time Magazine* (1973).

33. The National Organization for Women argues that a woman's activities with men other than the accused are irrelevant. Consonant with this position,

Iowa and California have recently passed laws barring defense lawyers from asking questions in court about a woman's past sexual conduct; in Florida, such queries must first be screened in the judge's chambers. (*Time Magazine*, 1974.)

34. Amir (1965, p. 546). See Curtis (1972) for the national survey tables supporting this paragraph.

35. See Curtis (1972) for the tables supporting the survey results and reported in this paragraph. The references to Amir are (1965, pp. 550-1).

36. Nelson and Amir (1973, p. 26).

37. See, for example, Peterson (1973).

38. LeVine (1959, p. 988).

39. Nkpa (1973).

40. Bordewich (1973).

41. Roy (1973, p. 6).

42. For the supporting tables on non-clearances, see Curtis (1973).

43. Normandeau (1968, pp. 291-2).

44. Conklin (1972, pp. 89-90).

45. DeBaun (1950, p. 70).

46. Camp (1967).

47. Normandeau (1968, p. 290).

48. See Curtis (1972) for the supporting tables.

49. See Curtis (1972) for the supporting regional breakdown tables.

50. McClintock and Gibson (1961, p. 23).

51. Nkpa (1973).

52. Von Hentig (1948).

53. Silverman (1973, p. 17).

54. Silverman (1973).

55. Avison (1973).

56. Conklin (1972).

57. Reiss (1967, p. 106).

6 Injury and Weapon Used

What if that pestle had not been in sight, had not been lying on the shelf from which it was snatched by the prisoner, but had been put away in a cupboard? It would not have caught the prisoner's eye, and he would have run away without a weapon, with empty hands, and then he would certainly not have killed any one. How then could I look upon the pestle as a proof of premeditation?

—Fyodor Dostoyevsky
The Brothers Karamazov

Summary of the National Survey

"Injury" was broadly defined in the survey as physical harm of more than a very minor nature (such as scratches or slight abrasions). The victim was assumed injured whenever hospitalized, but hospitalization was not a sine qua non for injury. The data were insufficient to allow for psychological trauma.

The weapons chosen were usually direct, quick, and commonplace. Firearms prevailed in survey homicides, but knives and sharp instruments were turned to with greater frequency in aggravated assault, where the rate of injury was high (Table 6-1). Relatively few armed robbery victims were hurt, but roughly one-quarter of the rapes and unarmed robberies were scenes of injury, usually by bodily means (hands, fists, feet, and the like).

Criminal Homicide

The United States

Forty-seven percent of the survey clearances and 57 percent of the non-clearances were committed with firearms.[1] Knives and other sharp instruments were in second place (29 and 21 percent, respectively). The greater impersonality and efficiency at longer distances of firearms may enhance the relative chances of escape by the offender. This could explain why the proportion of firearms killings was higher in non-clearances than clearances, whereas the opposite was true for homicide with knives.

The complete FBI tabulation of the twelve-odd thousand 1967 homicides, in rural as well as urban areas, produced a somewhat higher proportion of firearms than in the survey, but the same rankings of weapons.[2] From 1962 when these

Table 6-1

Means of Inflicting Injury by Type of Crime, 17 American Cities, 1967, Clearances (Percent)

Injury Status and Means of Inflicting Injury \ Major Violent Crime Type	Criminal Homicide	Aggravated Assault	Forcible Rape	Armed Robbery	Unarmed Robbery
Firearm	46.6	13.0	1.4	2.0	0
Knife or Other Sharp Instrument	29.2	25.9	0.7	1.2	0
Blunt Instrument	3.2	11.7	0.6	3.8	0
Poison	0.2	0.1	0	0	0
Body	10.8	22.4	17.7	3.7	26.7
Other Weapon or Weapon Unknown	9.8	7.0	1.0	3.0	1.0
Subtotal Injured	100.0	80.1	21.4	13.7	27.7
Subtotal Not Injured	0	18.0	76.0	82.5	66.1
Subtotal Injury Status Unknown	0	1.9	2.6	3.8	6.2
Grand Total	100.0 (668)	100.0 (1493)	100.0 (617)	100.0 (509)	100.0 (502)

Base: Interactions

FBI figures were first published to 1972, the relative proportion of shootings out of all homicides has risen 22 percent, at the expense of stabbings and other methods (although the absolute numbers in all categories have risen).[3] The gradual increase correlates with the rise in interracial killings by strangers over the same period (Chapter 3).

Most of the prominent single-city studies have placed firearms on top.[4] The notable exception is Wolfgang's Philadelphia investigation, where knives were more popular (38 percent, versus 33 percent for firearms, from 1948 to 1952).[5] The divergence has withstood the test of time: knives still led over firearms (33 percent to 29 percent) when the 1967 Philadelphia cleared homicide sample (N = 52) was broken out from the national survey data. Part of the explanation may lie in knife-carrying associated with gang activity. The incidence of street gangs is extremely high in Philadelphia. However, it is also possible that regional patterns of weapons preference and availability are operating. When the survey clearances were broken down by regional aggregates, knives were most popular in the Northeast (42 percent, versus 26 percent for firearms), whereas firearms led in the southern, north central and western homicides (67, 58 and 55 percent, respectively).[6]

Foreign Comparisons[7]

The widespread use of firearms in American homicides is accompanied by ineffective firearms licensing and control in the United States and estimated handgun ownership rates far above a number of European countries examined by the Eisenhower Violence Commission.[8] In reviewing the distribution of weapons among foreign homicides, it will be instructive to similarly compare the importance of firearms and the presence or absence of effective regulations. Table 6-2 summarizes some of the abundant international material on weapons employed.[9]

Firearms weigh heavily in Canada. Tardiff found that 56 percent of the homicide attempts and completions he studied in Montreal involved firearms. Throughout all of Canada, about half of the killings were with firearms in 1967.[10] Firearms must be registered, but regulations are modest compared to, say, European countries. Although the Canadian handgun ownership rate is far below the United States (3,000 per 100,000 against 13,500 per 100,000), Canada nonetheless had the second highest ownership rate among the countries in the Violence Commission poll. Ownership of hunting weapons, especially outside the cities, is considerably more widespread than handgun ownership in Canada.[11]

There are so many exceptions to the gun-carrying laws in Panama that many persons own firearms. But shootings are still rare, and most violent crimes are committed with machetes, clubs, and knives. The use of knives is reported to be common throughout South America.[12]

Blunt instruments and bodily means were most frequent in English, Welsh, and Scotch homicides, with firearms having minor importance. This was even more the case for London alone. The burden of proof in the recently amended British Firearms Act rests on the citizen for pistols and rifles, but the initiative to prevent ownership of shotguns is left to the police.[13]

The proportion of firearms in homicide was equally low among the Scandinavian countries, which have very similar regulations. The main interest in firearms is a sporting one. Revolvers and automatic pistols are virtually unobtainable. Killing by gunshot was negligible in West Germany, where a gun permit is granted only if a person is "reliable," legally accountable for his actions, not previously convicted, and in need of the weapon. Possession, importation, exportation, or transportation of guns is strictly forbidden in the Netherlands, where only 15 firearms crimes of all types took place in 1967. Firearms control is fairly strict in France, especially for pistols and revolvers. About equally popular, shooting and stabbing remained the primary methods in homicides, however. Firearms were strongly preferred in Florence, despite Italian gun control laws. The great majority of Greek murders were by firearms. Handguns are strictly controlled by police in Greece, but hunting guns do not require permits.[14]

Table 6-2

Means Used in Criminal Homicide, by Country (Percent)

Country, Geographic Scope, Year — Means	United States — Urban (17 City Survey, Clearances) 1967	Canada[1] — Urban (Montreal) 1964	England and Wales[2] — Entire Country 1967	England[3] — Urban (London) 1946-1962	Scotland[4] — Entire Country 1957-1968	Italy[5] — Urban (Florence) 1951-1963	Poland[6] — Entire Country 1955-1961	USSR[7] — Urban (Moscow)	USSR[7] — Urban-Rural (Briansk, Kalinin and Vladimir Provinces) 1963	USSR[7] — Urban-Rural (Rostov Province) 1961-1962	Israel[8] — Western Jews	Israel[8] — Oriental Jews	Israel[8] — Arabs	Israel[8] — Total
Firearms	46.6	56.2	12.3	5.1	9.2	42.2	12.7	4.0	32.4	20.8	37.0	19.0	20.0	24.0
Knives, Other Sharp Cutting Instruments and Arrows	29.2	18.8	34.4	27.6	37.8	25.6	44.5	64.0	50.0	55.9	24.0	47.0	44.0	40.0
Blunt Instruments	3.2	20.9	13.3	59.0	10.7	11.1	27.6	18.0	16.7	10.0	16.0	12.0	19.0	16.0
Body: Hands, Feet, Etc.	10.8	2.1	35.6		33.5	16.7	10.2	18.0	16.7	12.5	8.0	12.0	5.0	8.0
(Strangulation, Asphixiation)				37.2		16.7	10.2							
(Drowning)						0	0							
Other Methods or Methods Unknown	10.0	2.1	4.4	8.3	8.8	4.4	4.9	0	0	0	16.0	12.0	13.0	13.0
(Arson-Burning)			0				0							
("Infanticide")							0							
(Poison)	0.2					1.1	4.9							
("Riots")						0	0							
Total	100.0 (668)	100.0 (48)	100.0 (90)	100.0 (156)	100.0 (185)	100.0 (90)	100.0 (836)	104.0[7] (100)	115.8[7] (Unknown)	99.2 (Unknown)	100.0 (63)	100.0 (86)	100.0 (110)	100.0 (259)

Israel[8]: Entire Country (Jewish Population 2/3 Urban; Non-Jewish Population Rural), 1950-1964

Means	Ghana[9] Urban (Accra and Kumasi) 1960-1963 (Accra) 1960 (Kimasi)	African Tribes[10] Rural — Alur 1945-1954	Gisu 1948-1954	Luo Years not available	Luyia 1949-1954	Nyoro 1935-1955	Soga 1952-1954	Tiv 1931-1949	Western Uganda[11] Rural 1955-1968	India[12] Urban (Delhi) 1962-1964	India[13] Rural (Maria tribe) 1921-1941	Ceylon[14] Southern Province (Both Urban & Rural areas) 1960	Singapore[15] Urban 1955-1964	Japan[16] Urban (Tokyo) 1967
Firearms	36.9	0	0	0	0	2.9	0	1.1	1.0	4.1	0	14.8	7.8	Neg.
Knives, Other Sharp Cutting Instruments and Arrows	44.6	34.0	38.3	54.5	41.1	61.8	30.0	71.4	43.0	58.5	26.0	53.6	50.2	22.9
Blunt Instruments	12.3	51.0	46.5	34.3	44.8	11.8	32.0	17.2	19.0	4.8	62.0	26.9	25.6	28.2
Body: Hands, Feet, Etc.	1.5	4.2	0	0	0	8.8	3.0	0	10.0	19.7	11.0	3.4	5.7	24.7
(Strangulation, Asphixiation)	1.5	–	0	0	0	8.8	3.0	0	3.0	10.2	8.0	–	5.7	22.4
(Drowning)	–	–	0	0	0	0	0	0	0.2	7.5	2.0	–	0	2.3
Other Methods or Methods Unknown	4.6	10.6	15.2	11.2	14.1	14.7	35.0	10.3	27.0	12.9	1.0	2.3	10.6	24.3
("Arson-Burning")	–	–	–	–	1.8	8.8	–	–	1.0	5.4	0	–	–	–
("Infanticide")	–	–	–	–	–	–	–	–	2.0	0	0	–	–	14.4
(Poison)	–	–	–	–	–	–	–	–	1.0	–	6.1	–	1.2	3.4
("Riots")	–	–	–	–	–	–	–	–	0	–	0	–	8.8	–
Total	100.0 (65)	100.0 (47)	100.0 (99)	100.0 (44)	100.0 (114)	100.0 (34)	100.0 (100)	100.0 (87)	100.0 (501)	100.0 (147)	100.0 (100)	100.0 (88)	100.0 (506)	100.0 (174)

Notes: A dash ("–") means data broken down for the particular category are not available. "Neg." means negligible.

The subtotals under "Body Means" and "Other Means" are illustrative breakdowns of important methods in certain countries and are not necessarily meant to add up to the major category total.

References: [1] Tardiff (1966, p. 38); [2] Gibson and Klein (1969, p. 24); [3] West (1968, p. 250); [4] Gibson and Klein (1969); [5] Simondi (1970, p. 53); [6] Holyst (1967, p. 32); [7] Conner (1973, p. 114. Conner notes, "Totals greater than 100 percent are attributable to rounding errors. The identical figures in the two lower rows of cols. 1 and 2 suggest misprints in the original sources."); [8] Drapkin and Landau (1968, p. 35); [9] W.N. Laing, C.G. Farnilo, G.Y. Ahlijah, *Forensic Science in a Developing Country*, Table 2; [10] Bohannon (1960, p. 227); [11] Mushanga (1970, p. 32); [12] Rao (1968, p. 13); [13] Elwin (1943, p. 43); [14] Jayewardene and Ranasinghe (1963, p. 119); [15] Ting and Tan (1969, p. 246); [16] "The Forensic Sciences in Japan," *Inform*, International Reference Organization in Forensic Medicine, January 1970, Vol 2, No. 1, p. 5.

Knives prevailed by a considerable margin in Poland and the Soviet Union, which have stringent gun control laws.[15] In turn, Moscow had a much lower proportion of firearm homicides (4 percent) than the Soviet province-wide studies compared in Table 6-2. The Moscow figure appears to be anomalous; the official Russian textbook reference to the USSR as a whole attributes about one-fifth of the homicides in the country to firearms. Pointing out that the vast majority of firearms used in Russian homicides are rifles, Conner argues that people in the provinces have more opportunity to hunt and hence greater access to arms by Soviet law, even though they are not necessarily more violence-prone than Muscovites.[16] Although there is no indication that the prevalence of weapons in the Soviet Union is anywhere near as widespread as in the United States, it is interesting to note that in recent years all the Soviet republics have conducted a drive against possession of illegal firearms. The most dramatic effort was made in Georgia, where several "underground gun factories" have been discovered near the port of Sukhumi.[17]

Firearms were most used by Western Jews committing homicide in Israel, and knives were second most popular. Yet the priorities were reversed among Oriental Jews and Arabs, who have a long tradition of carrying knives. The possession of a dagger is both a means of defense and a sign of masculinity in traditional Arab society.[18] Strict firearms control in Israel may serve to reinforce this pattern. The impact of restrictions on possession, however, is neutralized to a degree because many Israeli civilians have been granted gun permits as protection from guerilla attacks and border raids. Then, too, most Israelis are in the military reserve, so that there is widespread knowledge of gun use even though officially citizens cannot return home from the field with weapons.[19]

Ownership and sale of firearms necessitates government registration in Ghana, Kenya, and Uganda. Still, 40 percent of the killings in Accra and Kumasi were with guns, even though knives and other cutting instruments proved slightly more popular in these Ghanan cities. Conversely, firearms were the means in less than 1 percent of the 1967 homicides in Kenya, where gun controls are relatively more severe. Regulations were passed in 1953 when Kenya was a British colony and experienced the first Mau Mau uprisings. No one can own firearms or ammunition without a permit, which is refused to persons with "intemperate habits or unsound mind."[20] Besides the unavailability of firearms in Western Uganda, the precolonial tradition of carrying spears or sticks for self-defense and to symbolize masculinity have lagged into modern times in spite of British proscriptions. Thus, cutting and blunt instruments were most resorted to in Mushanga's study.[21]

The individual tribes examined by Bohannon et al. in Nigeria, Kenya, and Uganda present more primitive lifestyles than found in the African city-wide or country-wide studies. There was a total absence of firearms in 5 of the 7 African tribes listed in Table 6-2, and the remaining 2 had almost negligible percentages.

Killings were nearly always with knives, arrows, other sharp cutting instruments, and blunt instruments. Palmer reached similar conclusions in his study of 40 non-literate societies.[22]

Very few guns appeared in Delhi murders, the killer usually choosing a knife or dagger. There is a rigid firearms licensing system in India, and "traditional usages which permit the carrying of small knives and daggers are an important factor in this type of killing."[23] No firearms were reported among homicides in the rural Maria tribe; blunt instruments were in greater abundance (62 percent), followed by bows and arrows (17 percent). As in primitive Africa, these weapons have a cultural history and are commonly agricultural tools. For example, the godel axe, used in daily work, often doubled as a blunt weapon.[24]

Firearms appeared more in the Southern Province of Ceylon than the Indian tribes, but knives, other sharp instruments, and blunt objects continued to lead. A man wishing to possess a firearm in Ceylon "must obtain a license, which involves an elaborate procedure of checking and rechecking the antecedents and bona fides of the applicant."[25] Yet, as in India, "the occupational pursuits of most individuals make it essential for them to always carry some sharp cutting instrument."[26]

The distribution of weapons used, British influenced gun control laws, and knife-carrying customs in Singapore very much paralleled Ceylon.[27]

Tokyo reported negligible usage of firearms, with blunt objects, bodily methods, and knives being about equally important. Pistols in Japan are stringently forbidden, except to marksmen under close supervision and to police. "Even toy pistols are frowned upon. They may be made only of plastic and they must be colored red or white to keep them from being mistaken for the real thing. Possession of a pistol is considered a serious offense subject to drastic punishment." Rifles and shotguns are allowed for hunting and target shooting, but rigid controls again guide their use.[28]

Overall, the weapons used in criminal homicide largely appear to be a function of their availability and the culture-technology's tradition of implements for work and protection. Thus, handguns are easily obtainable in America; they are the epitome of capitalist efficiency; the sacredness of their possession is proclaimed by the Constitution; and like Ban, Feminique, and Lavoris, they are extremely sanitary. All of this is irrelevant to the Maria tribesman, who is prevented by the government from owning a gun, hunts with bow and arrow, repairs his hut with a crude stone hammer, and without a knife at night, might be caught dead by a cattle thief.

The various countries offer a relationship between the proportion of firearms in killings and the presence of licensing and control that is not completely unambiguous. But the percentage is generally higher where no controls or weak, ineffective ones exist, and it is usually lower or negligible under rigid and strongly enforced interdicts. There are often special explanations behind the exceptions to the rule, as in Israel, where personal defense needs in an atmosphere of continuous seige appear to somewhat counter the effect on Western Jews of strong control laws.

Aggravated Assault

The United States

Victims were estimated to have escaped injury in 18 percent of the national survey cleared assaults in Table 6-1. When there was injury, knives were most favored (26 percent of all clearances), followed by bodily methods and firearms. The percentages and rankings were similar for survey non-clearances[29] and in the complete national account for 1967 by the FBI.[30] Knives led by a greater margin in Pittman and Handy's 1964 St. Louis work.[31]

There are at least two alternative explanations for why firearms are less popular in assault than homicide. The crimes can be viewed as very similar in circumstance, with the differential in their seriousness largely explained by the fact that homicide offenders happen to have more deadly weapons at hand. This can be thought of as the accessibility argument. Or, it might be suggested that the homicide offender is more determined to kill and therefore chooses the weapon most capable of achieving his end, whereas the aggravated assault offender does not have such a goal in mind. This can be thought of as the differential intent argument.

Each interpretation undoubtedly has significance. But we are persuaded, along with Dostoyevsky, that special credence be given to the accessibility argument. The consistent similarity between homicide and assault across all the variables reported in this volume does not support differential intent nor does the low level of premeditation in homicide (Chapter 4). In particular, the fact that altercations are the leading surface rationales in both American homicides and assaults suggests that motives do not determine weapon used. Pittman and Handy's careful comparison of homicide and assault is consistent with this position.[32] Supportive clinical findings can also be found. "Every psychiatrist has treated patients who were thankful that guns were not around at one time or another in their lives. Temper tantrums, fits, seizures, hysterical episodes all make the presence of guns an additional and possibly mortal danger."[33] Berkowitz has some experimental evidence to suggest that for certain persons, even the casual sight of a gun may catalyze violence.[34] Perhaps the most objective validation yet comes from Zimring's data on fatal versus non-fatal assaults in Chicago. He concludes that whether or not someone is killed, most violent attacks with dangerous weapons "are pursued with ambiguous intentions as to whether the victim should die."[35] This is not the kind of information with which one can argue that persons arrested for aggravated assault have a lesser desire to kill than people arrested for criminal homicide.

Trends in assault weapons used by the offender (regardless of whether or not the victim is injured) are derivable from the nationally reported FBI data over the years 1964 to 1972. The proportion of firearms in homicides for 1972 was 67 percent greater than in 1964. But the relative proportion of knives fell 35 percent over the same period.[36] (The volume of knife assaults actually rose, but the relative proportion of knife assaults declined because of a huge increase in the volume of reported firearm assaults.)

We can speculate that whatever the reasons for the sharp reported rise in violent crimes over the 1960s (see Chapter 1), they motivated or were associated with an intensification of American traditions of gun possession, especially in the ghetto, and an expansion of gun availability, marketed with the help of protect-your-person-and-property advertising. More and more did firearms become the weapons at hand—hence their increased use in both assault and homicide. There are no assault trend data on interpersonal relationships and offender by victim race, but the similarity to homicide encourages an hypothesis of increased stranger and black-on-white assaults—correlated with the rise in assault firearms use.

Knives were most used against males of both races, but bodily methods led against females in the national survey. Offenders turned increasingly from bodily means to cutting instruments as they became older, perhaps as a hedge against real or perceived diminution of physical strength. Black assaulters used knives more than other weapons, whereas bodily means were highest for white male offenders and blunt instruments for white females. The likelihood of black as well as white female assaulters injuring their victims was consistently higher than for males. Although there are fewer female assaulters than males, women would appear more dangerous than men when they actually become offenders. Knives were ascendant in intraracial and black-on-white assaults. Firearms led in the few white-on-black encounters. Injury occurred with greater frequency in intraracial attacks than incidents between the races. When the victim was injured, assaulters favored knives over firearms in each survey regional aggregate except the South, where firearms led.[37]

Foreign Comparisons

Comparisons of injury in the few foreign works with usable information were hazardous because, as in the United States, records often lacked precision and problems arose in converting to the definitions used in the survey. Qualified by these realities, the proportion of Montreal assaults ending in injury appeared about the same as in the American cities (where 80 percent of the victims were hurt). Knives were also the leading assault weapon in Montreal.[38] The percentage of injuries seemed to be smaller in London, probably because hands, feet and fists were used in the majority of assaults.[39]

A Note on Firearms, Firearms Control,
and the Homicide Rate

There has been considerable scholarly and popular debate on the relationship
between firearms control and the homicide rate. At this point in Chapter 6, we
are in a position to address the issue.

Some maintain that even if restrictions effectively limited the possession of
firearms, killers would achieve their ends by substituting other weapons so that
few homicides would be avoided. Wolfgang has taken this position,[40] and it is
allied with the differential intent argument above. Conversely, one implication
of the accessibility argument with which we are more comfortable is that while
not reducing the number of people who attack with the intent to injure, firearms
control would require less lethal weapons to be used, which would perhaps result
in an increased assault rate and a correspondingly decreased homicide rate.

Seitz has pointed out that Wolfgang's position leads to the assumption that
no correlation exists between the firearm homicide rate and the total homicide
rate. This, maintains Seitz, is because we would expect a proportional decrease
in the firearms homicide rate in places where firearms access is relatively
restricted, but no change in the total homicide rate. In fact, however, Seitz
found a positive Pearsonian correlation of .98 between the two rates for U.S.
state-level data from 1967. Thus, "it is almost impossible to conclude that the
relation between firearms and criminal homicide is merely coincidental."[41]

To give perspective to Seitz's results, we have constructed as Figure 6-1 a
scattergram in the same form as the one he presented but by using data from
different countries rather than states. Admittedly, the data are crude. The
statistics needed are not easy to come by, and data from many more countries
could produce a very different scattergram. For example, South American
countries, which are not represented in Figure 6-1, could be expected to have
both high total homicide rates and high firearms homicide rates, as is the case
rather uniquely for the United States. Further, in an attempt to gain as many
data points as possible, different units of analysis were allowed—that is, not only
country-level data but also that of specific cities, tribes, and regions within a
country.

With these considerable limitations in mind, we computed the correlation for
the data points. The r of +.55 was deceptively high because of the influence of
the two extreme U.S. points. Clearly, Seitz's strong relationship does not hold
when developed and underdeveloped, Western and non-Western societies are all
included (although the correlation may still be high among regions within any
particular society). When the cluster of data points from Ceylon and Africa were
removed, the r was +.96, but again this was due to the great influence on the
coefficient of the few extreme data points. Thus, when in addition to the
Ceylon-Africa cluster, the data points of urban U.S., total U.S., Montreal, and
total Canada were removed, the r was −.92 for the remaining points covering
Western European countries, Israel, Singapore, Delhi, and Tokyo.

One partial interpretation might be that a more single-minded intent to kill

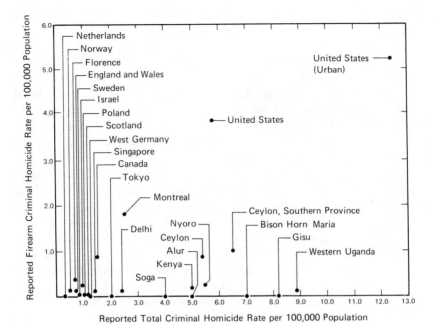

Sources:

Country	Criminal Homicide Rates per 100,000 Population (Years in Parenthesis)	Percent Firearms Involvement in Criminal Homicide (Years in Parenthesis)	Criminal Homicide by Firearm Rates (Column) 1 Times Column 2)
Alur Tribe, Africa	5.0 (1945-1954 mean)[1]	0 (1945-1954)[1]	0
Bison Horn Maria Tribe, India	6.9 (1921-1941 mean)[2]	0 (1921-1941)[2]	0
Canada	1.6 (1967)[3]	49.9 (1967)[3]	.8
Ceylon	5.4 (1955)[4]	15.2 (1955)[4]	.8
Ceylon, Southern Province	6.6 (1960)[5]	14.8 (1960)[5]	1.0
Delhi, India	2.4 (1963)[6]	4.1 (1962-1964)[6]	.1
England and Wales	0.7 (1965)[8]	12.3 (1967)[7]	.1
Florence, Italy	0.7 (1956)[9]	42.2 (1951-1963)[9]	.3
Israel	0.9 (1965)[11]	24.0 (1950-1964)[10]	.2
Gisu Tribe, Africa	8.2 (1945-1954 mean)[1]	0 (1945-1954)[1]	0
Kenya	5.0 (1967)[3]	1.0 (1967)[3]	.1
Montreal, Canada	2.8 (1964)[13]	56.2 (1964)[12]	1.6
Norway	0.5 (1964)[8]	10.0 (1964)[3]	.1
Netherlands	0.4 (1965)[8]	0 (neg) (1967)[3]	0
Nyoro Tribe, Africa	5.5 (1945-1954 mean)[1]	2.9 (1935-1955)[1]	.2
Poland	1.0 (1963)[8]	12.7 (1955-1961)[14]	.1
Scotland	1.1 (1965)[8]	9.2 (1967)[7]	.1
Singapore	1.4 (1965)[11]	7.8 (1955-1964)[11]	.1
Soga Tribe, Africa	4.0 (1952-1954 mean)[1]	0 (1952-1954)[1]	0
Sweden	0.7 (1965)[8]	13.9 (1966)[3]	.1
Tokyo, Japan	2.2 (1965)[11]	0 (neg) (1967)[11]	0
United States	6.1 (1967)[15]	64.0 (1967)[15]	3.9
United States: Urban	11.9 (1967)[15]	46.6 (1967)[16]	5.6
West Germany	1.2 (1964)[8]	0 (neg) (1967)[3]	0
Western Uganda	8.8 (1965-1968 mean)[17]	1.0 (1955-1968)[17]	.1

References: [1] Bohannon (1960); [2] Elwin (1943); [3] *Washington Post* (1969); [4] Jayewardene (1964); [5] Jayewardene and Raneinghe (1963); [6] Rao (1968); [7] Gibson and Klein (1969); [8] Demographic Yearbook, United Nations, New York; [9] Simondi (1970); [10] Landau and Drapkin (1968); [11] Ting and Tan (1969); [12] Tardiff (1966); [13] "Crime Statistics (Police)," Dominion Bureau of Statistics, Health and Welfare Division, Queen's Printer, Ottawa, Canada, 1965; [14] Holyst (1967); [15] F.B.I. (1967); [16] Chapter 6; [17] Mushanga (1970).

Figure 6-1. The Total Reported Criminal Homicide Rate and the Reported Firearm Criminal Homicide Rate.

does indeed exist in certain countries. Supportive is the possibility, drawn from Chapter 4, that offenders in traditional, primitive, economically underdeveloped societies may kill relatively more out of motives built up over long periods of time and less out of ostensibly superficial motives than is the case in modern, technologically advanced countries.

A valid response is that the data are too crude to be certain about this inference. Until more refined figures become available, however, the inconsistency of Figure 6-1 is useful in expressing the obvious caution that there are many other influences on the reported homicide rate in addition to the presence/absence of firearms and laws controlling them. Thus, a multiple regression on reported criminal homicide as the dependent variable might reasonably begin with a nation's assaultive attack frequency as the leading independent variable, keying to the country's "violent character," if you will—the pressures encouraging violence and the historical processes underlying them. Other important independent variables would include the demand for specific weapons in terms of cost, as well as cultural traditions and daily work needs; the supply of specific weapons in terms of production, licensing, and control; the speed with which an attack can be reported; and the efficiency of medical treatment in preventing an injury from becoming a death.

The data with which to explore such a model are not available, and other independent variables (particularly the rate of reporting) are also at work, but it is instructive to consider the scatter of Figure 6-1 in terms of the 4 independent variables just mentioned. The primitive societies and underdeveloped countries have relatively high reported total homicide rates. The use of firearms appears low, in large part because of the relatively successful regulations discussed earlier. But this is probably balanced by a moderately high frequency of attacks involving more culturally traditional weapons and agriculturally oriented implements that often kill, in spite of reduced lethalness, because of slow and poor medical treatment.

The low total homicide-low firearm homicide cluster can be assessed in terms of effective firearms statutes blocking a weapon more familiar to advanced than primitive societies, efficient medical services, and a relative infrequency of assaultive attacks. In Tokyo, for example, the low attack frequency may reflect minimal ethnic strife, racial homogeneity, an insignificant narcotics problem, full employment, and no slums or ghettos, among other possibly underlying variables.[42] Perhaps the presence of Israel in this cluster reflects a tug-of-war between a relatively higher firearms ownership but a lower attack frequency among Western Jews and assimilated Oriental Jews against a relatively lower firearms ownership but traditional knife-carrying, higher attack frequency among Arabs.[43]

In spite of efficient medical services, the United States has high assault frequencies, traditions receptive to firearms use, and ineffective firearms regulations. Canada, too, has efficient emergency services, ineffective firearms laws, and traditions supportive of firearms possession (although Canada has not had romanticized, southern son-of-a-gun or western cowboy histories comparable to the United States). The intermediate position of Canada and Montreal between the European cluster and the U.S. data points in Figure 6-1 may partially be explained by a lower attack frequency than in the United States. It is possible that this reflects a relative absence of the kind of forces promoting violence in American cities. Because of the considerable ownership of firearms in Canada, it is still possible that the lethalness of the attacks that do occur—as measured by the likelihood of death per 100 attacks—is more nearly the same as in the United States.[44]

Forcible Rape

The United States

Injury in the course of forcible rape was defined as physical harm *in addition to* the sex act itself. Women were injured in 21 percent of the clearances. The figure for non-clearances was the same. Bodily means were almost always used, regardless of the race and age of victim or offender. White rapists hurt their victims more often than blacks. The frequency of physical injury was greater in all-white and black-white than all-black attacks. The chance of being harmed increased with the victim's age, and the likelihood of inflicting injury peaked for offenders between the ages of 21 and 30.[45]

In Washington D.C., Hayman also found that white victims were more often injured than non-whites.[46] Instead of asking whether the victim was hurt, Amir inquired into whether the offender used "force" (roughness, beating, or choking) or "sexually humiliated" the victim (mainly by fellatio, cunnilingus, pederasty, or repeated intercourse). He judged that force was used in 85 percent and sexual humiliation imposed in 27 percent of the Philadelphia cases studied. Force was imposed more in black-black than white-white rapes and more in interracial attacks where the offender was black.[47]

These data seem conflicting, but they are not necessarily inconsistent. At least a working hypothesis can be suggested. The rapist more often than not asserts physical force, but the consequence is not invariably injury; the victim has a good chance of escaping harm or humiliation. Black rapists are relatively more likely to use force, but the possibility of injury or humiliation is relatively greater at the hands of whites. One partial explanation might be that the more force displayed from the onset, the more intimidated becomes the female against fighting back and so enhancing serious injury. White sexual mores accept fellatio, cunnilingus, and pederasty to a greater degree than among blacks according to some sources;[48] if this is true, the likelihood that a white male will introduce such acts is probably greater whether or not intercourse is forced.

Foreign Comparisons

Women were more often hurt in Montreal than urban American rapes (45 percent against 21 percent in American clearances).[49] Yet only 7 percent of the "sexual offenses against women" in England and Wales qualified.[50] Had rapes been separated from the aggregate, a relatively higher frequency could be assumed. The pattern in Denmark was very much like that of the United States.[51] Bodily methods of injury were most often used in all of these countries.

Robbery

The United States

Armed Robbery. Earlier studies have confirmed the comparatively low level of injury to armed robbery victims in the national survey.[52] When there was injury, the weapons used were evenly distributed among blunt instruments, bodily means, firearms, and knives. With certain exceptions, the low degree of injury held—regardless of sex, race, and age of victim or offender—across intra-versus interracial patterns and over the regional aggregates.[53]

The importance of firearms reasserts itself, however, when the perspective is changed slightly and one asks what weapons are used in armed robbery *regardless of* injury to the victim. In 1967, the FBI conducted an investigation into the 117,000 nationally reported armed robberies and found that firearms were present in 63 percent of the cases surveyed.[54] Other studies have registered similar results.[55] In support, one psychiatrist reported to the Eisenhower Violence Commission that robbery appears "infinitely more possible" with a gun. Many offenders, according to this testimony, are so lacking in strength, size, aggresssiveness, and confidence that they could not possibly carry out a robbery without a gun. "Although the men needed a gun to rob, the converse was also true: they needed to rob in order to use a gun . . . it was the gun which provided the power and the opportunity for mastery."[56] However, both Conklin and Normandeau conclude that the expressive use of firearms in robbery, because of psychic needs to feel powerful or assert masculinity, has not been amply demonstrated. Their interpretations are more instrumental; the robber employs a firearm expediently to keep the victim at a distance, to intimidate him, occasionally to make good a threat, and to facilitate escape.[57]

Unarmed Robbery. The important difference between the two varieties of robbery in the national survey was the considerably greater possibility of injury in *unarmed* encounters (28 percent in clearances, 39 percent in non-clearances).[58] Conklin in Boston, Normandeau in Philadelphia, Feeney and Weir in

Oakland, and the D.C. Crime Commission reached similar conclusions.[59] It is safe to think that the kind of male bold enough to yoke and strongarm, without the use of a weapon, not uncommonly has the physical strength to make good his threat. And the victim, at least if male, may be more willing to resist without a gun jammed in his ribs. Thus, as Conklin has concluded,[60] whether or not a robber will resort to violence largely depends on his ability to intimidate the victim.

To this might be added the intuitive, qualifying hypothesis that when injury is incurred the victim is hurt more on the average in armed than unarmed robbery. Yet, interestingly, Normandeau did not find confirming evidence when he used the Sellin-Wolfgang seriousness index as his measure.[61]

White victims of both sexes in unarmed robberies were more often hurt than blacks. Older persons were injured more frequently than younger ones. White unarmed robbers were more dangerous than blacks and offenders 18 to 25 more than those of other ages. As in forcible rape, more injuries were inflicted among whites and in black-on-white unarmed robberies than among blacks. Unarmed robbers were considerably more likely to hurt their victims in the West and North Central areas (54 percent and 44 percent, respectively) than in the South and Northeast (19 percent and 14 percent).[62]

Foreign Comparisons

The proportion of Montreal robberies with injuries to victims (20 percent) was comparable to armed robbery clearances in the urban United States, whereas the figure in London (30 percent) paralleled unarmed clearances in America. However, Canadian robbers almost always used bodily methods of threat and force, which is curious in view of the prevalence of firearms.[63] Encounters in the English metropolis were mostly strong armed or carried out with blunt instruments.[64]

Notes and References

1. See Curtis (1972) for the supporting tables on non-clearances. With certain exceptions, firearms were the most used weapons regardless of the sex, race, or age of the victims in the survey. The same was generally true for offenders. Firearms prevailed in both inter- and intraracial homicide, although relatively greater frequencies of knives and bodily means were present in killings between blacks and whites than in all-black or all-white events. See Curtis (1972) for the supporting tables.

2. Sixty-four percent of the national FBI (1967, p. 7) homicides were with firearms; 20 percent with cutting instruments; 8 percent, bodily means; and 8 percent, other methods.

3. See the FBI *Uniform Crime Reports* for 1962 through 1972. These data are summarized in Curtis (1972).

4. For example, in Houston, about two-thirds of Pokorny's (1965, p. 481) homicides were shootings and one-fourth were stabbings. Forty-one percent of the D.C. Crime Commission's (1965, p. 42) killings were with firearms, and 29 percent were stabbings. In Chicago, Voss and Hepburn (1968, p. 503) found that 50 percent of their victims were shot and 28 percent stabbed; Zimring's (1968, p. 721) percentages were 52 and 30, respectively. In New York, Burnham (1973) found that firearms were used in 47 percent of the killings and knives in 35 percent. In Detroit, 63 percent of the homicides studied involved firearms (Wilt and Bannon, 1974).

5. Wolfgang (1958, p. 84). These results were for clearances. Non-clearances experienced proportionately more beatings and fewer stabbings than clearances. See Wolfgang (1958, p. 293).

6. See Curtis (1972) for tables on the regional breakdowns. The FBI *Uniform Crime Reports* (1967) also break down homicide weapons by region. All reporting areas, urban and rural are included, so the data are not entirely compatible with the survey. In 1967, firearms were most popular in all four regions. However, the regional ranking of firearm popularity from higher to lower percentages was South, North Central, West, and Northeast, which is the same order as in the survey. And, as in the survey, the relative importance of cutting instruments in the *UCR* was much greater in the Northeast than the other regions.

7. In writing this section, the author is grateful for the advice and information received from Dr. William Eckert, Department of Pathology, St. Francis Hospital, Wichita, Kansas and General Chairman, Western Conference on Criminal and Civil Problems.

8. Newton and Zimring (1969, c. 16).

9. All references are to Table 6-2, unless cited otherwise.

10. *Washington Post* (1968).

11. Newton and Zimring (1969, c. 16) and *Washington Post* (1968).

12. *Washington Post* (1968).

13. *Washington Post* (1968).

14. See *Washington Post* (1968) and Table 6-2.

15. Newton and Zimring (1969, c. 16) and Conner (1973, p. 113).

16. Conner (1973, p. 113).

17. Sulzberger (1973).

18. Landau and Drapkin (1968, pp. 33-34).

19. *Washington Post* (1968).

20. *Washington Post* (1968) and Newton and Zimring (1969, c. 16).

21. Mushanga (1970, p. 30).

22. Palmer (1973).

23. Rao (1968, p. 33).

24. Elwin (1943, p. 43).

25. Jayewardene and Ranasinghe (1963, p. 116).

26. Jayewardene and Ranasinghe (1963, p. 116).

27. Ting and Tan (1969).

28. *Washington Post* (1968) and Barth (1971).

29. See Curtis (1972) for the supporting tables.

30. The FBI data (1967, p. 10) are for weapons present *regardless* of injury. Thirty-three percent of the national assaults involved knives or other sharp cutting instruments, 24 percent bodily methods, 22 percent blunt instruments-other weapons-unknown, and 21 percent firearms.

31. Pittman and Handy (1964, p. 465) found the offender to use a knife in 52 percent and a gun in 16 percent of the assaults studied.

32. Pittman and Handy (1964, p. 465).

33. Robert Coles, in a 1966 *New Republic* article, quoted in Morris and Hawkins (1970, p. 68).

34. Berkowitz (1967).

35. Zimring (1972, p. 111).

36. See the FBI *Uniform Crime Reports*, 1964-1972. These data are summarized in Curtis (1972).

37. See Curtis (1972) for the national survey data supporting this paragraph.

38. Tardiff (1966, pp. 33, 38).

39. McClintock (1963a, pp. 51-54).

40. Wolfgang (1958, pp. 82-83).

41. Seitz (1972, p. 597).

42. Barth (1971).

43. This was suggested by Franklin Zimring in a personal communication, 2 July 1970.

44. These comments are based on suggestions in personal correspondence from Franklin Zimring, 2 July 1970, and Andre Normandeau, 30 June 1970.

45. For the supporting tables on non-clearances and the race and age breakdown tables, see Curtis (1972). Rape victims were injured with greater frequency in the South than the other regional aggregates, but the southern sample size was too low for us to be confident about these results.

46. Hayman (1968, p. 1025) found that harm was inflicted in 47 percent of the "definite or probable" rapes of District of Columbia women 18 and over between September 1965 and September 1966, but in 26 percent of the non-white women.

47. Amir (1965, pp. 222, 329, 331). Force was used in 87 percent of the black-black rapes, versus 77 percent in white-white, 85 percent in black-white, and 77 percent in white-black. Victims were humiliated in 25 percent of the black-black rapes, against 34 percent in white-white, 33 percent in black-white, and 29 percent in white-black. In another study, Chappell and Singer (1973, p. 25) found that 15 to 20 percent of the rape victims studied in New York

required some hospital treatment for physical injuries. This compared favorably to the national survey. However, the Seattle Law and Justice Planning Office (1975) reported one victim in three injured, and Giancinti's (1973) figure in Denver was 42 percent.

48. See *Violence, Race and Culture.*

49. Tardiff (1966, p. 33).

50. Radzinowicz (1957, p. 104).

51. Svalastoga (1962, p. 49).

52. For example, the D.C. Crime Commission (1966, p. 64) found that 89 percent of the armed robbery victims in its survey were uninjured, and Normandeau (1968, p. 201) reported that firearms were used to intimidate the victims in 32 percent of his Philadelphia robberies but to harm in only 1 percent.

53. See Curtis (1972).

54. FBI (1967, p. 15). Knives were present in 24 percent of the cases and blunt objects in 13 percent.

55. For example, almost three-fourths of the armed robberies surveyed by the D.C. Crime Commission (1966, p. 64) involved firearms.

56. Newton and Zimring (1969, Appendix E).

57. Conklin (1972, pp. 109, 112), Normandeau (1968, p. 206).

58. See Curtis (1972) for the supporting tables on non-clearances.

59. Conklin (1972, p. 116), Normandeau (1968, p. 201), Feeney and Weir (1973, p. 77), D.C. Crime Commission (1966, p. 64).

60. Conklin (1972, p. 117).

61. Normandeau (1968, p. 357).

62. See Curtis (1972) for the tables supporting this paragraph.

63. Tardiff (1966, p. 33).

64. McClintock and Gibson (1961, p. 34).

7 Spatial Distributions

Onto the steps of front-street leaping
an ashen face portrayed ghetto-agony

Stern-faced children do the boogaloo
Centre Ave. runs through the white-folks

We sit on the Ashy-steps
crying down masturbated days
laughing at City-nuts and friends always broke
riding walking falling we get
no further than these steps
accents on a vulgar history

Resting where the girls go by
old men talking to themselves chant loud women
dressed alone in the passing night
Steps junkie-steps clicking-steps
Steps standing alone

Doorway-steps limping-steps
Wondering what we're doing
tip the last step a green-light at the
corner Beating up each other scared
to death of that white-man

—Charles P. Williams,
From "The Steps"

Introduction

Spatial analysis of crime originated among nineteenth-century European scholars. Crime maps were first used by Guerry and Balbi in 1829, and Quetelet published ecological work shortly thereafter. In 1864, Mayhew came out with his four volume *London Labour and the London Poor*, which included a number of crime and social maps by county of England and Wales.[1] However, ecological research on crime has centered more in the United States during the twentieth century, being given a formulative impetus by the University of Chicago school of criminology.[2]

Chapter 7 is based on several varieties of spatial data. Most important are computer isopleth maps. The prefix "iso" means equal, alike, or similar.

"Isolines" connect points that are equal in value. When the points connected represent ratios or rates for specific areas, they are called "isopleths." Isopleths have been the most useful form of isolines for social science analysis.[3]

The isopleth maps included here are based on the 10 percent sample data in 5 of the 17 cities of the national survey: Boston, Philadelphia, Atlanta, Chicago, and San Francisco. The considerable time and money consumed by the analysis proscribed treatment of all cities. Those chosen offer regional representation, a spectrum of urban environments, and spatially unbiased data.[4]

The use of such maps in ecological research allows presentation of a considerable number of variables that is often more easily comprehensible than in abstract mathematical formulations. In other studies, crime densities have been represented by different shadings of census tracts or zonal gradients, but isolines are methodologically superior. They are a "more reliable, realistic, meaningful, and certainly less arbitrary technique than gradients for developing generalized ecological patterns of crime."[5] Isopleth analysis avoids many of the problems of the more commonly used bounded territorial units (such as placement of boundaries, homogeneity within units, comparability between units, and the restriction of statistical techniques to those appropriate for sets of nominal categories) and provides a more realistic expression of continuous variation.[6] Contour lines are much more successful in conveying the skew of areal distributions—how the crime equivalent of magnetic force fields are arrayed.

Methodology

Before analyzing the maps, the methodology used in their construction should be briefly outlined. In each city, we began with a large, mounted table map that detailed all the streets within city limits. The police reports forming the sample data base gave the place of the crime, the residence address of the offender (if apprehended), and the residence address of the victim. Each of these locations was pin-pointed on the map, and X-Y coordinates referenced to the grid system printed on the map were coded to two decimals. The X-Y data point inputs were used by an IBM 1130 and a 1627 plotter attached online to draw the isopleths via the IBM Numerical Surface Technique and Contour Map Plotting Program.[7]

This system first computed the grid-by-grid centroid values and locations of the crime (offender, victim) input data points for a given city. There was no grid overlapping—that is, the computer scanned each successive, adjacent grid area across the entire map. The centroid Z values represented crimes (offenders, victims) per unit grid land area. In hand-drawn isopleth analysis, the centroid Z's of equal value are connected at this stage. However, the computer program was more precise. A finer grid screen (using predetermined decision rules to insure that gradients could be represented reliably as linear over the distance of one new grid interval) was imposed on each larger grid area. A weighted least squares plane was then fitted to the original centroid Z values. In this way, the Z values of the corners of each of the finer grids were determined. Finally, the isopleths were drawn by computer interpolation between the equal values of these finer Z points.

Hand-drawn and interpolated isopleth analysis has appeared in the criminological literature,[8] and computers have been used to draw crime maps showing density through different shadings of census and police areas,[9] but the maps in Figures 7-1 to 7-12 are one of the first applications of computer isopleths to the ecology of crime. Compared to hand-drawn isopleths, our computer maps are considerably more refined. Imposition of the second grid screen through the weighted least squares plane produces isopleths more sensitive to the gravitational pulls of the data points. The size of the second grid and, therefore, the length of the intervals between isopleths on the maps is determined by formula to avoid either overgeneralization or unwarranted precision. The latter are common problems in isopleth analysis. Similarly, the computer interpolations are more exact than with hand-drawn methods.

To be rigorous, we would have preferred to run separate maps on each of the crimes for which we have data—homicide, assault, rape, armed robbery, and unarmed robbery. However, preliminary runs showed that the 10 percent sample often did not yield enough data points to generate isopleths of any meaning. Therefore, we reluctantly aggregated the crimes that the preliminary assessment suggested best fit together in terms of areal distribution. The outcome was a homicide, assault, and rape aggregate (referred to below as the "assaultive crimes") and an armed plus unarmed robbery aggregate.[10] For each grouping, maps based on crime locations, offender residence locations, and victim residence locations were computer drawn.

To insure data on offenders, maps were run for the cleared-by-arrest data in each city. Crime and victim maps for non-clearances were also drawn for San Francisco to compare with the clearances.

The grey shadings on the maps identify those 1960 census tracts officially labelled poverty areas by the United States Office of Economic Opportunity and the Bureau of the Census. The definition was based on five equally weighted poverty-linked characteristics combined into a "poverty index" by the Census Bureau:

Percent of families with incomes under $3,000 for 1959;

Percent of children under 18 years old not living with both parents;

Percent of males 25 years and over with less than 8 years of school completed;

Percent of unskilled males (laborers and service workers) aged 14 or over in the employed civilian labor force;

Percent of all housing units lacking some or all plumbing facilities or dilapidated.[11]

The index of these elements is a relative one. All the census tracts in all the United States Standard Metropolitan Statistical Areas with a 1960 population of 250,000 or more were ranked according to index score. Tracts in the lowest quartile were designated as "poor" by the Census Bureau.

It would have been prohibitively expensive to publish all 40 of the computer maps originally drawn. The 12 chosen for Chapter 7 are among the most interesting. They serve as a comparative base for references to the unpublished maps, which can be found in the dissertation on which this book is based. If a spatial distribution is not clearly related to an accompanying map in the analysis below, a citation will refer the interested reader to the dissertation.

The isopleths of the maps in Figures 7-1 to 7-12 express crime, offender, and victim locations per unit land area as defined by the grids on the original large table maps.[12] Boggs has demonstrated that, ideally, ecological rates of crime should be probability statements based on the at-risk or target group most appropriate for each type of offense. For example, the crime location rate in burglary of homes might be expressed as the number of homes burglarized in relation to the number of homes that could be burglarized, not the number of persons living in the area.[13]

To conceive the optimum bases, gather the data needed for them in each city, and devise new computer programs would have been far beyond the scope of the study. Besides, there were good arguments for using the area base. One of the main reasons for developing the maps was to observe the degree of "localization"—the extent to which crime, offender and victim concentrations overlapped. A common denominator was therefore required as a base, one that included land area. It was conceptually possible to add other variables to area—the most relevant and traditional being resident population, to produce a population per unit area base. But the packaged computer program used area only, and to replace it would have been unfeasible in terms of time and money.

For the crime locations, especially those in commercial areas or at least not at home, an area base is probably superior to a population per unit area base because the latter can give spuriously high rates in the low population business districts.

Among offender and victim residence locations, it must be acknowledged that the area base cannot distinguish between higher rates due to more people and higher rates due to a higher violence propensity in one population group compared to another. Inferences from the maps will be made with this limitation in mind. However, the strong positive correlation between number of people per unit area and the crime and delinquency propensity of those people is well established in ecological studies.[14] In addition, to provide a check on the absence of the population component in the isopleths, mean distances have been calculated between offender and crime, victim and crime, and offender and victim. These data are summarized in and all textual references refer to Table 7-1. The question of bases does not enter into the computation of means.

The distances are not "beelines," but estimates made with a map measure of the most direct street route between any two points in each city. Differentiating race of offender and race of victim, the means were calculated for the same crime aggregates as the maps. However, the mean for each individual crime was also computed in each city. This will serve as a partial indicator of crime specific variations obscured in the isopleth analysis because of the necessity of aggregating.

Crime locations in all five places fell within city limits—otherwise the reports would not have been on file at the respective city police departments, but rather at other jurisdictions. However, offenders and victims did not necessarily have to live within the city. Frequency distributions were therefore run to find the proportions of offenders living (1) within city limits, (2) out of the city but in the Standard Metropolitan Statistical Area, (3) out of the SMSA but in the state, (4) out of the state, or (5) at addresses unknown. This was also done for victims. For the same reasons as in the analysis of means, the frequency distributions were broken down by race of offender and victim, and the crimes were aggregated as well as identified separately. These figures will allow for a discussion of "regional mobility"—the extent to which the offender or victim lived beyond the city limits.[15]

Analysis

The analysis of these data has two central objectives. The first has already been suggested: an examination of the degree to which crime, offender, and victim isopleths overlap. Past investigators of "crime areas" have often failed to specify the type of location used. Even when this is made clear, the data are often only for one type of area. Thus, Shaw and McKay examined juvenile offender areas, and Wilcox has recently presented flat tone computer mappings of robbery crime locations.[16] Rarely have victim densities been produced, and there has never been a systematic analysis of all three components.

When the crime, offender, and victim patterns are not conterminous, we will be interested in such questions as the degree to which offenders "invade" victim areas, compared to the extent of victims coming into or close to offender neighborhoods and situations when the meeting is on "neutral" ground.

The second objective is to analyze the relative high, medium, and low isopleth concentrations in each city. The anchor points of peaks and plateaus and the skew of their dispersions will be identified. Distinctive features and histories of high intensity areas will be pointed out when the information is available. One salient question will be the validity of the classical concentric zone hypothesis of the Chicago school, in which crime and delinquency rates are said to peak in the central city areas and decline in outward ripples.[17]

Table 7-1
Mean Distances in Miles, by City, Crime Type, and Race, 1967 (Sample Size in Parentheses)

City	Boston (Cleared)			Philadelphia (Cleared)			Atlanta (Cleared)		
Crime Type	Offender Crime	Victim Crime	Offender Victim	Offender Crime	Victim Crime	Offender Victim	Offender Crime	Victim Crime	Offender Victim
Criminal Homicide	1.04 (36)	.96 (38)	1.61 (36)	.74 (57)	.85 (48)	1.30 (59)	1.26 (48)	1.72 (44)	1.89 (48)
Aggravated Assault	1.15 (94)	1.06 (84)	1.46 (83)	.67 (128)	.68 (96)	1.06 (114)	.43 (67)	.53 (76)	.82 (72)
Forcible Rape	1.45 (24)	1.87 (15)	1.97 (16)	1.17 (43)	.78 (30)	1.72 (38)	1.88 (45)	.74 (33)	2.17 (40)
Criminal Homicide, Aggravated Assault, Forcible Rape	1.17 (154)	1.12 (137)	1.56 (135)	.78 (228)	.74 (174)	1.24 (211)	1.09 (160)	.92 (153)	1.48 (160)
Armed Robbery	2.40 (28)	3.18 (15)	4.76 (21)	1.23 (45)	1.57 (35)	2.24 (46)	2.48 (23)	.30 (25)	2.59 (21)
Unarmed Robbery	1.85 (57)	1.31 (30)	1.87 (45)	1.22 (87)	.55 (47)	1.63 (84)	.91 (6)	.79 (5)	2.00 (6)
Armed and Unarmed Robbery	2.04 (85)	1.93 (45)	2.79 (66)	1.22 (132)	.99 (82)	1.85 (130)	2.16 (29)	.38 (30)	2.46 (27)
Criminal Homicide, Aggravated Assault, Forcible Rape: White Offenders White Victims	1.74 (29)	1.23 (28)	1.81 (26)	1.54 (27)	1.33 (24)	2.05 (26)	1.96 (17)	1.65 (17)	2.15 (16)
Criminal Homicide, Aggravated Assault, Forcible Rape: Non-White Offenders Non-White Victims	.97 (93)	.95 (90)	1.26 (89)	.68 (180)	.70 (131)	1.18 (166)	.86 (121)	.85 (121)	1.36 (121)
Armed and Unarmed Robbery: White Offenders White Victims	3.06 (7)	.32 (3)	3.07 (3)	1.42 (17)	.43 (14)	1.68 (18)	2.41 (2)	1.07 (2)	2.16 (2)
Armed and Unarmed Robbery: Non-White Offenders Non-White Victims	1.75 (48)	1.22 (20)	1.96 (37)	.82 (68)	1.10 (43)	1.34 (66)	1.75 (12)	.59 (11)	2.64 (11)
Armed and Unarmed Robbery: Non-White Offenders White Victims	1.04 (16)	1.37 (13)	2.60 (15)	.84 (41)	1.21 (24)	1.63 (39)	0 (0)	0 (0)	0 (0)

City / Crime Type	Chicago (Cleared)			San Francisco (Cleared)			San Francisco (Uncleared)		
	Offender Crime	Victim Crime	Offender Victim	Offender Crime	Victim Crime	Offender Victim	Offender Crime	Victim Crime	Offender Victim
Criminal Homicide	.87 (50)	1.18 (48)	1.60 (51)	2.05 (37)	1.38 (29)	1.48 (36)	— —	.64 (15)	— —
Aggravated Assault	.94 (152)	1.06 (137)	1.46 (151)	1.41 (114)	1.20 (102)	1.76 (100)	— —	.98 (95)	— —
Forcible Rape	1.58 (107)	.99 (98)	1.97 (104)	1.80 (14)	1.62 (19)	2.18 (14)	— —	.77 (23)	— —
Criminal Homicide, Aggravated Assault, Forcible Rape	1.15 (309)	1.06 (283)	1.65 (396)	1.59 (165)	1.29 (150)	1.73 (150)	— —	.91 (133)	— —
Armed Robbery	2.88 (63)	1.66 (42)	4.11 (62)	1.86 (29)	1.27 (18)	3.01 (26)	— —	1.96 (106)	— —
Unarmed Robbery	1.24 (66)	1.35 (34)	2.29 (63)	2.33 (22)	1.56 (10)	2.58 (24)	— —	1.26 (62)	— —
Armed and Unarmed Robbery	2.04 (129)	1.52 (76)	3.19 (125)	2.07 (51)	1.37 (28)	2.80 (50)	— —	1.70 (168)	— —
Criminal Homicide, Aggravated Assault, Forcible Rape: White Offenders White Victims	1.25 (47)	.94 (41)	1.65 (42)	1.54 (45)	1.11 (45)	1.17 (41)	— —	.79 (39)	— —
Criminal Homicide, Aggravated Assault, Forcible Rape: Non-White Offenders White Victims	.90 (226)	.91 (210)	1.47 (229)	1.42 (76)	1.32 (67)	1.79 (66)	— —	.88 (41)	— —
Armed and Unarmed Robbery: White Offenders White Victims	2.09 (17)	1.65 (11)	3.90 (15)	3.90 (11)	1.23 (6)	2.53 (11)	— —	.74 (24)	— —
Armed and Unarmed Robbery: Non-White Offenders Non-White Victims	1.74 (57)	1.07 (35)	2.26 (56)	.49 (8)	.76 (6)	1.10 (8)	— —	2.03 (22)	— —
Armed and Unarmed Robbery: Non-White Offenders White Victims	2.28 (45)	2.70 (27)	4.29 (44)	1.83 (32)	1.57 (17)	3.34 (31)	— —	1.85 (118)	— —

Note: The standard deviations and ranges associated with the means can be found in Curtis (1972).

Boston

The city of Boston was first settled in 1630. The original 700 acres are now included in the central business district. Together with additional acreage gained by leveling hills and filling in parts of the harbor, the area is still known as "Boston" or "Old Boston." The city expanded by annexing nearby communities—East and South Boston, Roxbury, Dorchester, West Roxbury, Brighton, Charlestown, Jamaica Plain, and Roslindale. The 1970 total population was 641,071, an 8 percent decline from 1960. Much of the population loss was due to movement to independent towns—such as Brookline, Dedham, Milton, and Quincy—which surround the city on three sides. Because Boston developed to the south and west, some of the towns across the Charles River on the north, particularly Cambridge, are very close to the central business district located in the vicinity of Washington Street and the Boston Common and Garden.[18]

Figure 7-1 shows that assaultive crime isopleths peaked in the heart of the poverty area around the intersection of Washington Street and Massachusetts Avenue. This is roughly where the South End meets Roxbury and Dorchester, the central ghetto-slums. Offenders and victims generally lived in the same area, although there was a relatively greater skew of residences than crime locations downward into the hearts of Dorchester and Roxbury.[19]

The homicide and assault distances in Table 7-1 were similar and relatively short; rape was somewhat longer. Black-black distances were shorter than white-white distances (the majority of reported assaultive violence being intraracial). Similarly, there was a higher frequency of white than black offenders and victims than black offenders and victims living outside the Boston city limits.[20]

Two robbery crime isopleth peaks are evident in Figure 7-2. The first was in the same Massachusetts Avenue-Washington Street area as the assaultive crime concentration. The other was to the northeast, in the central business vicinity of Washington Street and the Boston Common-Garden area. Figures 7-3 and 7-4 show that few offenders or victims resided in this shopping area. Offender and victim isopleths both tended to anchor back at the Washington Street-Massachusetts Avenue locus. However, the offender dispersion skewed into Back Bay and the extremities of Roxbury. The offender and victim distributions in robbery were also more spread out than in the assaultive crimes.

Armed robbery involved longer distances and more regional mobility than unarmed robbery.[21] Surprisingly, black offenders lived closer to the crime on the average when they robbed whites than blacks, although black victims lived closer to the crime than white victims.

All of this suggests that Washington Street-Massachusetts Avenue may host a relatively great amount of unarmed robberies between neighborhood blacks, combined with interracial muggings of contiguous Back Bay whites coming into the vicinity. Perhaps such action is less rationally planned, less remunerative for the offender, and more drug-related than central business district rip-offs.

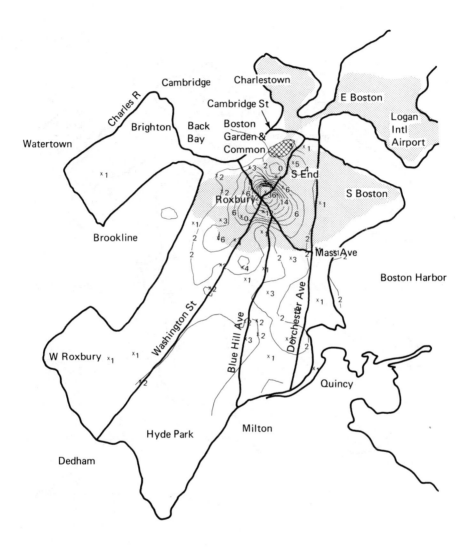

Figure 7-1. Isopleth Map of Criminal Homicide, Forcible Rape, and Aggravated Assault Rates in Boston by Crime Location.

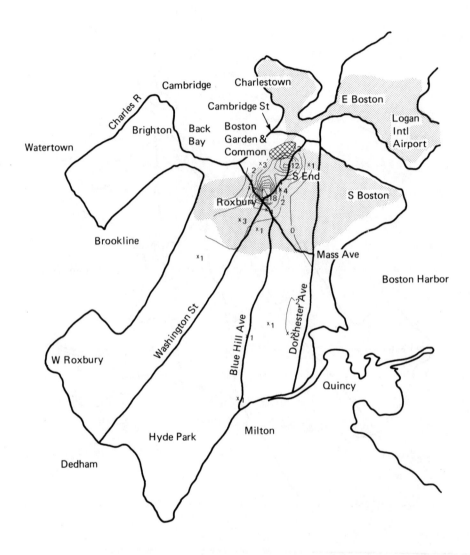

Figure 7-2. Isopleth Map of Armed Robbery and Unarmed Robbery Rates in Boston by Crime Location.

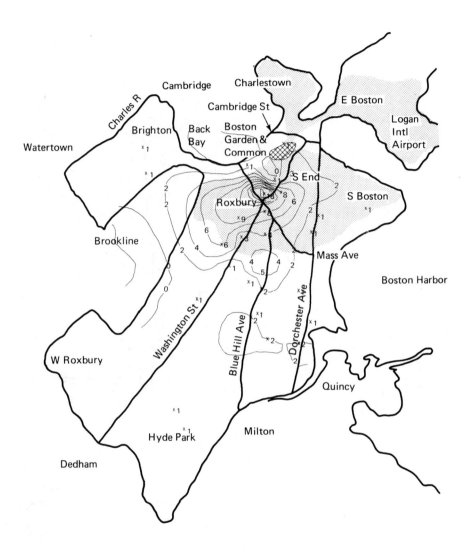

Figure 7-3. Isopleth Map of Armed Robbery and Unarmed Robbery Rates in Boston by Offender Location.

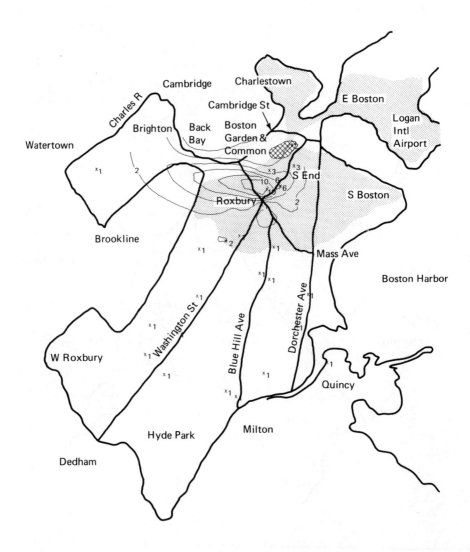

Figure 7-4. Isopleth Map of Armed Robbery and Unarmed Robbery Rates in Boston by Victim Location.

Downtown, there may be a relatively great amount of armed holdups by Roxbury, Dorchester, and South End residents of shops, blacks, and wealthier Back Bay whites who come in to shop, recreate, or work.

In sum, there was a fairly tight correspondence among crime, offender, and victim isopleths in assaultive violence but far more dispersion and mobility in robbery, even though a significant portion of crimes and residences remained anchored in the assaultive neighborhood.

Most of the violence fell in the (greyed) poverty tracts. The non-poverty tracts that experienced significant levels of violence were located in Jamaica Plain and Dorchester. They had high foreign stock but low black percentages. Although above the poverty quartile, these neighborhoods appeared very close to it.[22]

Philadelphia

Unique among the cities examined, Philadelphia was originally set down with a plan. The site chosen in 1682 was on the peninsula between the Delaware and Schuylkill rivers. The original street plan centered on what is now Market, running east and west between the rivers, and Broad, running north and south. It was assumed that the city would develop in from the rivers. But the larger Delaware offered more frontage and navigational advantages, so early settlers preferred to remain near it. Philadelphia's north-south growth was therefore greater than planned.[23]

The area above but near Market, called North Philadelphia, was initially settled by German, Jewish, English, and Irish immigrants in the nineteenth century. After the Second World War, job hungry blacks migrated to North Philadelphia in even greater numbers than during the trend begun 20 years earlier. They settled on the only properties available to them, the former residences of white immigrant stock that had moved to the suburbs. Urban renewal in the 1950s did not disperse blacks, but only increased population density and accelerated formation of the vast present day black ghetto-slum, decaying on the commercial infrastructure of the old Jewish quarter. It was in North Philadelphia that the 1964 race riots took place.[24]

Today, North Philadelphia runs up to white, working-class neighborhoods— such as Torresdale—which are further north. A smaller black ghetto is in South Philadelphia below and close to Market. West Philadelphia is across the Schuylkill. The finest residential areas are in the Main Line suburbs beyond the city limits to the west and northwest. With a 1970 population of just under 2 million, Philadelphia has a commercial and business strip several blocks wide that centers on Market and traverses much of the span from river to river.

On Figure 7-5, the Reading Railroad tracks appeared to form a natural boundary for the area with the highest assaultive crime isopleths, gravitating

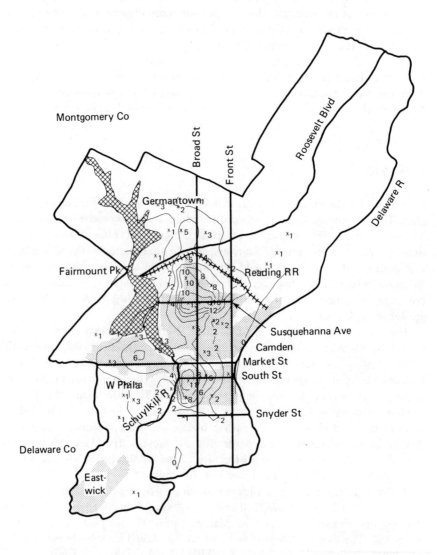

Figure 7-5. Isopleth Map of Criminal Homicide, Forcible Rape, and Aggravated Assault Rates in Philadelphia by Crime Location.

around Susquehanna and Broad Streets in North Philadelphia. The other high crime isopleth locale was in South Philadelphia below South Street. Crime isopleths of medium value centered in West Philadelphia above Market. The offender and victim patterns were anchored at the same points, but with slightly more dispersion, into the working-class areas above North Philadelphia.[25]

Crime-offender, crime-victim, and offender-victim distances were comparable to one another and, on the whole, shorter than for rape in Table 7-1. White-white distances were longer than for black-black encounters. Whereas Boston, with its smaller land area and many independent towns, had a sizeable frequency of offenders living outside the city, this was not the case for Philadelphia.[26]

The robbery crime isopleths of Figure 7-6 were rooted at Susquehanna and Broad, with a northeast skew across the Reading tracks. The other crime concentration was in Center City, gravitating south. Offender and victim residences were most common in the same North Philadelphia area of highest crime isopleths (though the offender skew across the tracks was even more pronounced). Offenders, as well as victims, were clustered in dwellings around South and Broad Streets—but below the corresponding crime location peak.[27] Armed robbery distances were longer than the unarmed distances, but few offenders or victims lived outside of Philadelphia.[28]

Isopleths were also run separately in Philadelphia for black-black and black-white robberies (most reported robberies being one type or the other). Crime locations in all-black robberies peaked only in North Philadelphia, although offender and victim crests were evident in both of the usual, North and South Philadelphia, concentrations. The interracial robberies tended to be perpetrated in North Philadelphia by West and North Philadelphia blacks on whites venturing down from the contiguous working-class neighborhoods. Interracial distances were therefore longer than intraracial ones, but there was little regional mobility.[29]

Thus, a tremendous amount of robbery, localized in the North Philadelphia ghetto, was committed by blacks on working-class whites coming too near or on other blacks and neighborhood shops. North Philadelphia blacks undoubtedly travelled the considerable distance to Center City pickings as well. The South Philadelphia pattern was intermediate; offenders, generally blacks, seemed to slide into Center City temptation opportunities just contiguous to their homes, rather than localize heavily in their residential neighborhood or travel a relatively great distance to rob.

Overall, robbery was again more dispersed than the assaultive crimes. This was consistent with the earlier studies of robbery, rape, and homicide in Philadelphia.[30] Nevertheless, the localization of robbery in the North Philadelphia ghetto slum (turf for the notorious black youth gangs) was not too dissimilar from the assaultive violence pattern.

Most violence fell within the poverty areas. The non-poverty tracts with

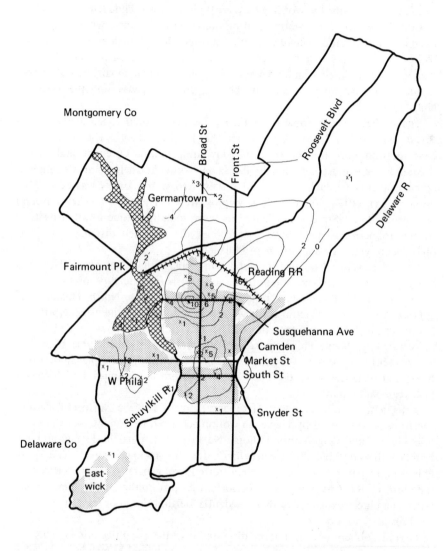

Figure 7-6. Isopleth Map of Armed Robbery and Unarmed Robbery Rates in Philadelphia by Crime Location.

significant violence were very low in percentage black, but the proportion of foreign stock was usually in the 30 to 40 percent range. These tracts were business districts with little resident population, white areas economically close to the poverty quartile and located near the poverty-violence areas, or more affluent white neighborhoods more usually hosting the crime or housing the victim than sheltering the offender.[31]

Atlanta

In the early nineteenth century, Georgia authorized a survey to establish the best terminal point for the state-owned railroad. The site chosen, on the edge of the Appalachians in north central Georgia, grew from the ashes left by Sherman into the commercial, industrial, and financial center of the Southeast.[32]

Economic progress was explosive during the 1960s. Atlanta's sky scrapers sliced into the Georgia sky, its freeways sprawled from suburb to suburb, its big league teams drew great crowds. "Atlanta was . . . the city of the 60s in America," rejoiced former Mayor Ivan Allen. "In an exhilarating period of growth in most cities throughout the nation, Atlanta grew more than any of the others."[33] Reflecting this development, Atlanta was the only urban area of the 5 examined to increase in population from 1960 to 1970 (a 2 percent gain, to 496,973).[34]

The business and political heart of landlocked Atlanta is just northwest of where the South Expressway crosses Memorial Drive on Figures 7-7 and 7-8. In this area are found City Hall; the State Capitol; "five points" at the intersection of Peachtree, Edgewood, and Decateur Streets, which form the center of Atlanta's four quadrants; and the urban renewal area, where all the new buildings and symbols of expansion are centered.

Blacks have shifted across numerous locations in the history of Atlanta. There was a surge from the plantations after Emancipation, which gave rise to many nineteenth- and early twentieth-century shantytowns—places like Darktown, Buttermilk Bottom, Shermantown, Pig Alley, Happy Hollow, the Anthole, Beaver Slide, Hell's Half Acre. By the last decade, the central black ghetto-slum, registering a 20 percent unemployment rate over the dramatic economic growth period and hosting the 1966 riots, had become Summerhill, south and east of the central renewal activity. Today, although the expressways, the new baseball stadium, and the renewal construction have cut into the area and shifted some blacks northward and westward, the poorest and most desperate of Atlanta's blacks still live in and around Summerhill.[35]

Here was where the assaultive crime isopleths were centered—in three adjacent loci generally within the "ring" created by Memorial Drive, the Atlanta, and West Point Railroad tracks and Lee Street (Figure 7-7). Note how the crime peaks sharply declined to negligible levels in the nearby renewal area (distin-

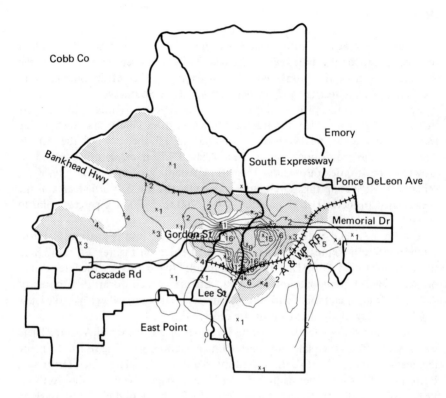

Figure 7-7. Isopleth Map of Criminal Homicide, Forcible Rape, and Aggravated Assault Rates in Atlanta by Crime Location.

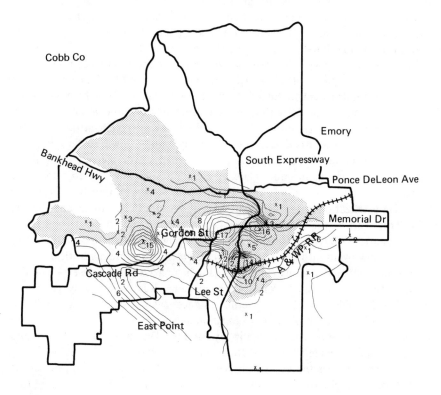

Figure 7-8. Isopleth Map of Criminal Homicide, Forcible Rape, and Aggravated Assault Rates in Atlanta by Offender Location.

guishable on the map as the white non-poverty hole in the center of the grey poverty donut). There was also a crime location plateau of medium intensity to the West, between Cascade Road and Bankhead Highway.

Flat tone maps of crime locations based on 100 percent samples over three other time spans were available from Atlanta Crime and Planning Commission studies. They suggested similar patterns between July 1964 and June 1965 and in 1969, but showed the westerly Cascade Road-Bankhead Highway area gaining in importance by 1970.[36] In part, this may reflect the displacement of people from the southeast into emerging ghetto-slums.

The 1967 survey isolines for victims were almost identical to the crime patterns for that year.[37] Offender isopleths (Figure 7-8) were also anchored in the southeast ring, but there was more skewing—in all directions. Included was a spillover into the renewal area. Why should relatively few crimes occur or victims live in the showplace of New Atlanta, but a noticeable concentration of assaultive offenders remain there? As in the southeast ghetto, the explanation may have something to do with a residual population of more desperate people.

More interesting was another high assaultive offender concentration in the West, above Cascade Road but with ridges extending down to East Point in Figure 7-8. Although the moderate assaultive crime location plateau was near by, generally speaking this offender plateau was not accompanied by corresponding crime and victim concentrations. Here, then, was a divergence from the assaultive localization pattern characteristic of Boston, Philadelphia, and the rest of Atlanta. Part of this assaultive offender area was in poverty tracts, which had black majorities. But the remaining plateau segment and the associated ridges extended downward into non-poverty tracts, which had white majorities.

The distance and regional mobility data help make some sense out of this distribution. The average offender-crime distance was considerably greater in rape than homicide-assault, but victim distances were fairly constant in Table 7-1. Similarly, there was more regional mobility by rape offenders than in homicide-assault, but little variation by victims. Distances were shorter and regional mobility less in all-black than all-white meetings.[38]

What emerged was the usual high degree of localization for homicide-assault (in the southeast ghetto and, to a lesser extent, in the West). This was partly true for rape, yet many rape offenders—probably both black and white—appeared more mobile than their counterparts in homicide and assault.[39] Perhaps they commonly cruised in from the west to pick up and rape strangers in the southeast. The greater mobility of rape offenders in Atlanta, compared to Boston and Philadelphia (and, in fact, to Chicago and San Francisco), might be related to a relatively low average population density in Atlanta.[40]

The results in robbery were uncertain because of small sample sizes. Crime, offender and victim isopleths were mostly anchored in or near the southeast ring, the crime locations being somewhat skewed to the contiguous business-commercial area.[41] The Atlanta Crime and Planning Commission studies, based on 100 percent samples of robbery, produced generally compatible crime location results for the July 1964 to June 1965 period and for 1969 but, as with the assaultive crimes, more of an outward, westerly movement in 1970, particularly between Cascade Road and Bankhead Highway.[42]

The poverty tracts held most of the violence, although there were some exceptions. The non-poverty tracts with significant violence showed the influence of the offender patterns in assaultive violence. They were located in the renewal area (where the population still remaining is black and is close to the poverty quartile), in the white, low-income fringes around the southeast ghetto and in the white, higher-income area to the west.[43]

Chicago

The original settlement of Chicago clustered around the forks of the Chicago River in the early nineteenth century. During the rapid growth of the city, heavy industry developed along the branches of the river. The other major determinant of expansion has been Lake Michigan. The central business district, the Loop (around Madison and State Streets in Figures 7-9 and 7-10) is located near the Lake shore, not in the center of the city. Chicago has radiated inland from the lake, but elliptically, extending like Philadelphia more in a north-south than east-west direction.[44]

The 1970 population was 3,366,975, a 5 percent decline from 1960.[45] Today, blacks have replaced Jews, Poles, Italians, Irish, and Bohemians in the most deteriorated ghetto-slum area, now called the Black Belt, in the Near Southeast Side. There is also a newer black ghetto-slum on the Far West Side.

These were the centers of highest assaultive crime intensity in Figure 7-9. The southeast has the lion's share, with a series of peaks from about E. 43rd Street to the Chicago Skyway, twisting around Hyde Park, Washington Park, and the University of Chicago. Significant downward slopes extend beyond even this extensive area. The Black Belt is packed with tenements and huge federal housing projects, like Robert Taylor Homes, holding about 27,000 blacks in 28 high rises. Wabash, the city's most dangerous police district, is contained in the area. Here one in 71 persons was a victim of homicide, assault, or rape in 1967.[46] It was consequently no surprise to observe the victim and offender isopleths in the Southeast closely converging on the crime locations.[47] Assaultive localization was similar on the West Side, in the Fillmore Street-Garfield Park-Douglas Park area, also saturated with lower-class high rises.

Offender distances were considerably longer for rape than homicide-assault in Table 7-1, although they converged for victims. This resembled Atlanta. There was, however, little regional mobility by offenders or victims for any of the crimes. True to form, offender and victim distances and regional mobility were greater in all-white than all-black homicides, assaults, and rapes.[48]

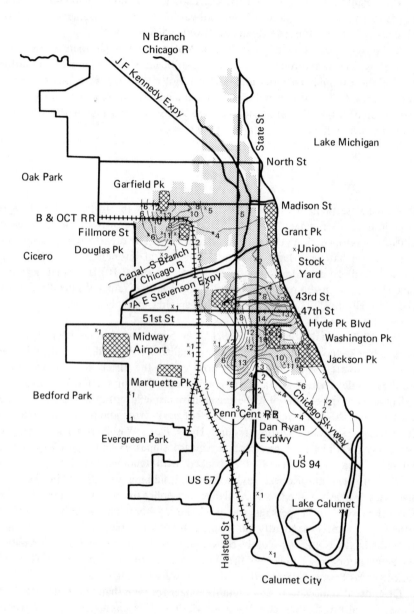

Figure 7-9. Isopleth Map of Criminal Homicide, Forcible Rape, and Aggravated Assault Rates in Chicago by Offender Location.

141

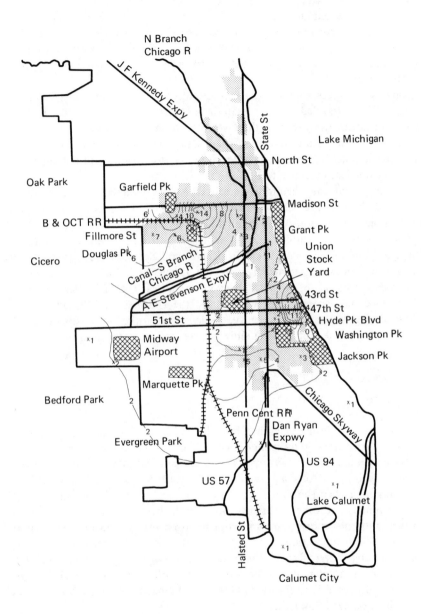

Figure 7-10. Isopleth Map of Armed Robbery and Unarmed Robbery
Rates in Chicago by Offender Location.

Robbery dispersions were rooted in the two ghetto-slums, but there was more skewing than for assaultive violence. In the Near Southeast, offender density (Figure 7-10) peaked in neighborhoods close to the lake, whereas crime and victim patterns were more evenly spread across the Black Belt.[49] On the Far West Side, robbery crime locations were most concentrated west of Douglas Park, but offenders and victims tended to reside northeast of there, around Madison Street.

Robbery distances were longer than assaultive distances, and participants in armed robbery traveled further than in unarmed engagements. Black-black robbery distances were shorter than white-white distances, which were shorter than those in black-white robberies. There was little regional mobility.[50] As in Philadelphia, much of the explanation appeared to lie simply in the large city area, compared, for example, to Boston.

The modal patterns therefore seemed to revolve around blacks victimizing blacks and shops in the ghetto neigbhorhood, as well as blacks robbing blacks, whites, shops, and institutions in contiguous environs.

Most violence fell within poverty tracts. Several of the non-poverty tracts with significant violence were in the Bridgeport and New City sections just north and east of the stock yards. This is the tough, high foreign stock, white working-class Chicago of Richard Daley's youth, near the Black Belt. Another high-violence, non-poverty area was around the University of Chicago, where considerable victimization of faculty, students, and other university residents apparently occurred, not uncommonly by persons from the nearby southeast ghetto.[51]

San Francisco

At the tip of a peninsula extending into the ocean and bay, San Francisco owes its sixteenth-century discovery and much of its history to Portuguese, English, and Spanish explorers. It developed as a trade and distribution center and was the westerly outpost for many sailing vessels. Rule passed from the Spanish to Americans in 1846. The Great Gold Rush of '48 produced not only a large influx of miners and other transients, but also the beginnings of a cosmopolitan lifestyle, with newcomers arriving from all over the world. Its sailors' port atmosphere and international heritage, coupled with a predominance of young people, among other factors, have created today a highly individualistic, independent, and tolerant city in one of the world's most beautiful settings. With a 1970 population of over 700,000, San Francisco is the largest complex within the urbanized Bay Area.[52]

As in Boston, there are relatively few blacks (10 percent in 1970), but many are clustered in the ghetto-slum on both sides of Fillmore Street. Smaller in size but equally black is Hunter's Point, near the Navy Shipyard, where some residents work. Here a number of people are still living in shanty dwellings erected as "temporary" housing during World War II.[53]

Much of San Francisco's fascination lies in its diversity of neighborhoods over a small land area. One section blends into another much more quickly than in, say, Chicago or Philadelphia. Among the places most relevant to the ecology of violence, Haight-Ashbury, near Golden Gate Park, is racially mixed. Civic Center includes City Hall, federal and state office buildings, and the Civic Auditorium. The Tenderloin district runs very roughly from Golden Gate and Market Streets through Union Square and up to about California Street. It is a major tourist attraction, heavy in topless joints, bars, restaurants, dope sellers, male and female prostitutes. The lower part of the Tenderloin contains many run down hotels, boarding houses, and apartments—home to large concentrations of pensioned senior citizens and drug-using young people. Above the Tenderloin is Chinatown and then upper-middle class Telegraph Hill. Below is the South of Market skid row and the Mission District, a stable working-class community with a substantial Spanish-speaking population.[54]

The central array of cleared assaultive crime isopleths in Figure 7-11 ran in a northeasterly belt. There were peaks near Haight-Ashbury, around Fillmore and on Van Ness between California and Geary. A ridge of high intensity extended along the upper Tenderloin. The main offender and victim patterns spread across the same area, but peaked only in Fillmore and the upper Tenderloin.[55]

Social changes during the late 1960s are of crucial importance in appraising the assaultive violence centering around Haight-Ashbury. The isopleths represent crimes committed in 1967. This was the Summer of Love in Hashbury, the blossoming of peaceful flower child society, paisley-painted buses, tribal gatherings led by Ginsberg and Leary, H.I.P. (Haight Independent Proprietor) stores, rock musicians, poster artists, spiritual gurus. Pot was everywhere, but LSD better defined the lifestyle. The acid culture was populated not uncommonly by middle-class, successful individuals of above average intelligence, "into mysticism, universal love and total non-violence, often to the point of refusing to eat meat."[56]

Yet that same year the great worldwide publicity attracted a new, diverse, transient, and more disturbed population that persuaded many of the original flower children to leave and took over the Haight like an occupying army by 1969. Included were older alcoholics of all races from Skid Row, black delinquents from Fillmore, and Hell's Angels as well as other bikers. The new population preferred opiates, barbituates, and amphetamines to pot or acid. It was also more violent.[57]

Violence, Race and Culture considers how assaultive violence can break out between heroin pushers and users, especially when the latter think they have been cheated. Yet addicts are more likely to rip off in support of their habits, with any injury to victims more of an incidental means to the end of theft. Conversely, assaults, rapes, and killings are more often ends in themselves for

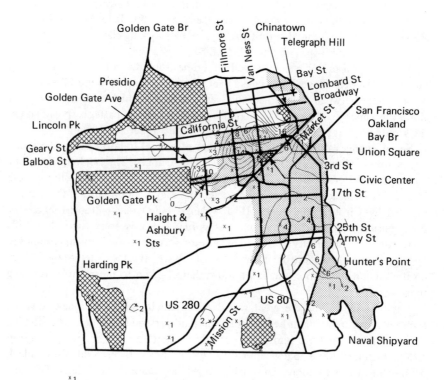

Figure 7-11. Isopleth Map of Criminal Homicide, Forcible Rape, and Aggravated Assault Rates in San Francisco by Crime Location.

speed freaks. The induced behavior is "violent, hostile and hyperactive," said the medical director of the Haight-Ashbury Medical Clinic, which by 1969 frequently treated injuries caused by violence—"suppurating abrasions, knife and razor slashes, damaged genitalia, and other types of traumatic injuries."[58]

It appears that the level of violence has subsided in the 1970s,[59] but the 1967 assaultive isoline concentration in Haight-Ashbury apparently reflected the influx of the criminal, heroin-speed group.

Compared to the Haight, the background literature useful for understanding the other high assaultive crime peaks in Figure 7-11 is meager. The heaviest concentration of all and the most localization of violence was in the Fillmore ghetto. Second in concentration and localization was the upper Tenderloin, where assaultive violence in 1967 partially may have reflected hustling and drug-related activities. The Van Ness high crime (but not offender or victim) intensity neighborhood was commercial, with many car dealerships and hotels. A pool hall in the area was then reputed to be a center for heroin dealing.[60] Although its isopleths were not as dense as over the main belt of peaks, Hunter's Point also hosted a concentration of assaultive crime.

Overall, a high degree of assaultive localization existed in San Fransisco, even though there was at least as much in-city mobility as, say, Atlanta.

For comparative purposes, San Francisco crime and victim location isolines were also computer-drawn for uncleared events.[61] Here, Fillmore and the upper Tenderloin were more uniquely the center of assaultive violence. The diminished importance of Hashbury in the non-clearances may suggest that assaultive violence there has a relatively higher visibility than other areas, more likely leading to arrests. Another possible interpretation is that assaultive violence is more out of police control (so that many offenders get away) in Fillmore and the upper Tenderloin than elsewhere.

The cleared robbery maps were disappointing because of low sample size.[62] Crimes centered in Fillmore and the upper Tenderloin. Offenders lived in Fillmore, but close to the Haight, and in the section of the Tenderloin inhabited by young drug users. Robbery motivated by the need for drug money thus seemed to correlate with these patterns. Other offenders lived in Hunter's Point. No clear victim concentrations could be discerned.

The uncleared robbery isopleths were very rich, giving more detailed information than any other robbery maps in the chapter (unsurprisingly, given low robbery clearance rates in the 5 cities). The uncleared robbery crime location isopleths form Figure 7-12. As in the cleared robbery crime location map, Fillmore and Hunter's Point concentrations were present. But, unlike the case for clearances, this figure has a non-cleared robbery crime location concentration that extended itself from the top of the Tenderloin through Chinatown and up along wealthy Telegraph Hill. This area and the Fillmore ghetto (with extensions into the Mission District) housed most victims in uncleared robbery.[63] The great majority of uncleared robberies consisted of non-white offenders and white victims, according to Table 7-1.[64]

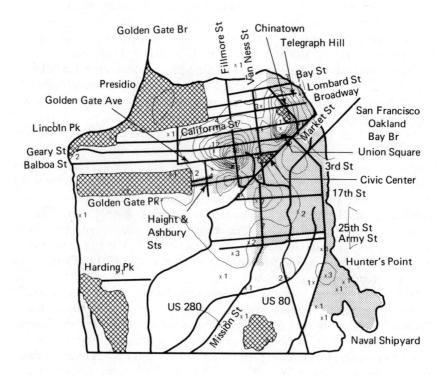

Figure 7-12. Isopleth Map of Uncleared Armed Robbery and Unarmed Robbery Rates in San Francisco by Crime Location.

Together, the cleared and uncleared robbery data suggested a large amount of robbery localized by crime-offender-victim in the Fillmore and Hunter's Point ghetto slums, plus an "invasion" by robbers and robber-addicts from Fillmore, Hunter's Point, and the lower Tenderloin into areas like Telegraph Hill, Chinatown, and the upper Tenderloin, where the crime occurred and the victim often lived. This pattern of offenders entering victim residence areas to rob seemed more pronounced than in the other cities examined in the chapter. One might speculate on a higher than average rate of interracial robberies somehow related to the city's remissiveness. But less debatable is the probability that the many small and rapidly changing neighborhoods offer rapid access to temptation opportunities and egress to sheltering locales.

Relatively few robbers resided in Chinatown, even though robberies were often committed there on residents. The configuration was also observable for the assaultive crimes, although frequencies were lower. The traditional portrait of a section whose inhabitants are noted for their social quiescence and honesty was thus confirmed, even though there has been some increase in violence attributed to Chinese youth groups in the early 1970s.[65]

All in all, robbery again showed more dispersion than assaultive violence, but there were common anchor points in Fillmore, the Tenderloin, and Hunter's Point. The exercise of comparing cleared with uncleared ecological patterns confirmed that uncleared spatial data do have certain biases. The divergence seemed somewhat greater than between clearances and non-clearances for the other variables, discussed in earlier chapters.

Most of the violent crime in San Francisco occurred in poverty census tracts, yet there was also a considerable amount in non-poverty areas. A large portion spilled over into neighborhoods adjacent to Chinatown, Fillmore, and Haight-Ashbury, which had poverty profiles not much above the lowest quartile. Most of the rest seemed to be associated with robbery occurring in wealthier areas, especially Telegraph Hill, where the victims lived.[66]

Summary and Discussion

Homicide and assault consistently showed the highest degree of localization and robbery the least among the 5 cities. Rape was in between, but mobility patterns for the crime were probably closer to homicide-assault than robbery. Thus, the extent of spatial similarity and dissimilarity among the four major violent crimes lines up in very much the same way as the pattern for the other variables discussed in the study.

Ecological studies by others on the same cities examined here have reached compatible results. Relevant work in other cities—most notably Washington D.C., Indianapolis, St. Louis, Houston, Seattle, Montreal, and London—also heads in the same direction. One departure has been Boggs' finding in St. Louis of even more mobility in rape vis-à-vis homicide and assault than was evident for the cities analyzed in this chapter.[67]

There was reason to believe that armed robbers traveled proportionately longer distances than unarmed robbers. Perhaps this was bound up with greater planning, more rationality and larger heists by the armed thieves. As could be expected from the reality of residential housing segregation, interracial robberies had longer offender-crime, victim-crime, and offender-victim distances than interracial encounters. There were instances of offenders attracted to contiguous neighborhoods, but the somewhat more distant central business district was also a target for North Philadelphia and Roxbury-Dorchester robbers. With the possible exception of the University of Chicago vicinity in Chicago, San Francisco was the only city with a significant "invasion" by black robbers into wealthier white neighborhoods, as opposed to "neutral" business areas or black communities. In spite of the overall mobility of robbers, it should be remembered that a considerable amount of robbery remained in areas that were also centers of assaultive localization.

The isopleths reveal the crudeness, at least for the major violent crimes, of the Chicago school's zonal gradient hypothesis of rates declining from a central business district peak. Boston and Atlanta most closely approximated the theory, yet the computer contoured a number of central peaks. Philadelphia and Chicago consistently had two and San Francisco more. The results reinforced Schmid's observation that "characteristically, in comparison to one mile zonal gradients, most of the gradients constructed from isopleth maps reveal much higher central peaks, more precipitous declines and lower and broader minima in peripheral areas."[68] The available trend data suggested that the peaks shift over time—for example in Atlanta, with renewal activity. Isopleth studies would therefore appear to be of considerable use in tracing the impact of intervention strategies over a number of years.

High violence and poverty coincided spatially for the most part. Non-poverty areas with significant violence were usually on the fringes of high violence poverty areas or better-off neighborhoods that robbers entered to victimize residents.

A Concluding Note on Poverty, Race, and Violence

As an outgrowth of the main analysis, the data assembled in this chapter allow for a very preliminary examination of the often made assertion that the disproportionately high rates of many violent crimes by blacks in comparison to whites in the United States would vanish if socioeconomic status were held constant.

The inquiry is limited to the OEO poverty census tracts greyed-in on the maps, as discussed earlier. By exploring the relationship between race and violence within these tracts in the 5 cities with isoline data, we were able to very roughly control for income, education, employment status, family size, and housing (the poverty index variables). For each city, the percent black in each of these poverty tracts was correlated with an aggregate score based on the isolines for homicide, assault, rape, and robbery.

The method by which the aggregate violence score was determined requires some explanation. The basic idea was to distinguish among the relative peaks or plateaus, the downslopes or lower peaks-plateaus, and the areas with little or no isopleth elevation for the violent crime aggregates in each city. After an assessment of the range and frequency of isopleth values over crime locations on the Boston cleared homicide-assault-rape map, it was decided to judge poverty tracts with isopleth values of 0 to 3 as low in violence, 4 to 7 as medium, and 8 and above as high. Each Boston poverty tract was classified into one of the three categories—high, medium, or low crime location density. Then a second scan was made of each tract using the same decision rules, but for the cleared homicide-assault-rape offender isopleths. A third scan used the victim isopleths. The same was done for the crime, offender and victim maps on robbery clearances (although the minimum isopleth values for the medium and high designations were lowered because the sample size for robbery clearances was smaller than for the assaultive maps). Thus, each Boston poverty census tract was scored for degree of violence 6 times—for 2 crime groupings times 3 types of location. The average score was the overall designation (high = 3, medium = 2, or low = 1) that was related to percent black. Because the data were based on a 10 percent sample, often spread across a large land area, a more refined sealing system was judged infeasible. It would have introduced a degree of precision with which we could not have been confident.

Each poverty tract in the other cities was scored in a similar way.[69]

It might be argued that only offender maps should have been used in determining a violence score. It has been traditional in American crime ecology, from the Chicago school on, to relate areal socioeconomic characteristics mostly to offender rates. The assumption has been that environmental explanations of why an offense occurs logically begin with influences on the offender who commits it. But Chapter 5 showed that the victim often shares responsibility, at least in homicide and assault. This implies that a search for environmental correlates should not leave out the victim's neighborhood. There is also usually some element of opportunity associated with the crime location. Thus, ghetto bars, poolhalls, and corners are congregating attractions where altercations can break out. Institutions and shoppers in commercial areas can offer temptation opportunities to robbers.

Because of their environmental importance, all three locations were therefore used for the joint violence score. In turn, the assaultive and robbery results were averaged together because of the relatively small robbery sample size (so that the composite violence score may give a somewhat better picture of assaultive crime than robbery).

Collapsed from the continuous variation of the isolines into three intervals, the violence data scores were less than metric, whereas the census data on percent black was, of course, metric. The Pearsonian r was chosen as the measure of association between these two scales for several reasons. It is robust to moderate violations of normality and homoscadacity. There is a long precedent for using r in ecological research—e.g., Shaw and McKay, Lander, Schmid, and Boggs.[70] More information was available than required in non-parametric tests. Computations for Kendall's Tau and Spearman's r are often more tedious than the calculation of the Pearsonian r when considerable data are at hand (the present case). In the computation of partials, even Kendall's Tau, among the methods of rank order correlation, becomes theoretically questionable if the number of ties is great, as here.[71] Although all the assumptions for using Pearson's r have not been met, and although certain criticisms have been raised against ecological correlations,[72] they remain "a useful method for investigating relationships that can be checked by alternative methods of analysis."[73]

The hypothesis that disproportionately higher rates of violence associated with blacks in comparison to whites would disappear if socioeconomic status were held constant predicts no significant correlation between percent black and violence score within the OEO poverty tracts. Table 7-2 shows that this was true for Boston, Atlanta, and San Francisco,[74] but not for Chicago and Philadelphia.[75]

It might be contended that disproportionate violence by poor blacks in

Table 7-2

Correlation between Violence Score and Percent Black within OEO-Defined Poverty Tracts

	Zero Order Correlation[a] r_{12}	First Order Partial Correlation[a] $r_{12.3}$
Boston	+.21	+.05
Philadelphia	+.32[b]	+.35[b]
Atlanta	+.22	−.01
Chicago	+.67[b]	+.63[b]
San Francisco	+.13	+.17

[a]1 = Violence score 1967, from isoline maps in Curtis (1972). 2 = Percent black, 1960, from U.S. Census. 3 = Rank within poverty quartile, 1960, from U.S. Census Bureau. In 1960, the number of officially defined poverty census tracts was 67 in Boston, 96 in Philadelphia, 50 in Atlanta, 248 in Chicago, and 42 in San Francisco.

[b]Significant at .05 level.

Chicago and Philadelphia is simply a function of relatively greater poverty by blacks than whites *even within the poverty quartile.* Consequently, partial correlations of violence score and percent black were run controlling for Census Bureau poverty rank by tract within the poverty quartile.[76] Table 7-2 shows that the hypothesis must be rejected. The significant Chicago and Philadelphia partials remained about the same as the zero orders.

These findings, only meant to be exploratory, are clearly very crude. Future research must survey a greater number of cities and employ a more refined index of violence. The influence of many other variables not controlled by the OEO poverty index would also have to be systematically examined. Leading examples are age distributions, sex distributions, and in-migration. Violent offenders tend to be young and male. The tracts with higher violence may have had disproportionate representations of these groups. Ferdinand, among others, has related urban migration to violent crime increases.[77]

The promise of such research is that it might uncover city-level variables to explain why poor blacks possibly remain violent disproportionate to poor whites even after all the logical controls are applied. Thus, among our 5 cities, the degree of segregation and the proportion of blacks out of a city's total population do not appear to be indices that uniquely set apart Chicago and Philadelphia from the rest.[78] Conversely, the absolute number of blacks in Chicago and Philadelphia is much greater than in Atlanta and especially Boston and San Francisco.[79] Thus, one hypothesis suggested by this very preliminary analysis and worth testing in a more sophisticated follow-up would relate disproportionate violence by poor blacks to a very large black population, say in excess of 500,000. We are particularly interested in this possibility because it is consistent with the hypothesis raised in *Violence, Race and Culture* that intervening cultural variables related to violence committed by poor blacks require a critical black population mass before their effect is felt.

Notes and References

1. Levin and Lindesmith (1937).

2. See, for example, Shaw and McKay (1969 Edition).

3. Schmid (1954, p. 212).

4. Spatially unbiased data were not assured in all cities. For example, in Washington, the 10 percent robbery sample had to be collected on a precinct-by-precinct basis, and the data on some precincts were unavailable. The precincts available were sampled so as to minimize the likelihood of biases in most variables—for example, racial proportion—but obviously this could not be done with regard to area.

5. Schmid (1960b, p. 666).

6. Hoiberg and Cloyd (1971, p. 65).

7. See International Business Machines Corporation (1967).

8. See, for example, Schmid (1960).

9. See, for example, St. Louis Police Department (1966), Atlanta Commission on Crime and Delinquency (1966), Atlanta Region Metropolitan Planning Commission (1971), and Wilcox (1973).

10. In the homicide-assault-rape maps, the N's for assault were usually greatest, but the distribution was reasonably equal for armed and unarmed robbery.

11. See U.S. Census Bureau (1966).

12. The size of the grid printed on the large table maps varied:

	X and Y Values of Grid in Miles	Unit of Land Area for Isopleth Analysis in Square Miles
Boston	.600 × .600	.360
Philadelphia	1.044 × 1.017	1.062
Atlanta	.963 × 1.161	1.118
Chicago	1.100 × 1.100	1.210
San Francisco	.712 × .656	.467

The numbers printed by the computer on the maps are the numbers of crimes (offenders, victims) per unit land area. Thus, for example, isopleths in Figure 7-1, of Boston, which are identified with the number 2 refer to 2 assaultive crimes per .360 square miles of Boston at that point based on the 10 percent sample of clearances. Similarly, in Figure 7-6, of Philadelphia, isopleths identified with the number 4 refer to 4 robbery crime locations per 1.062 square miles of Philadelphia at that point, based on the 10 percent sample of clearances. The different land area base made comparisons of isopleth values among cities hazardous, but our concern was with variation within a given city. Isopleths are based on ratios or rates. We should be clear on the definitions of these terms and their precise meaning in the present context. In his widely cited introduction to demographic research procedures, Barclay (1958, p. 2) defines a ratio as "a single term indicating the relative size of two numbers." "Density" is defined as one kind of ratio—that "of the number of people to the area of land that they occupy." A rate is a special kind of ratio, the crucial distinction being that a rate incorporates time and change, whereas a ratio does not. Customarily, the unit time period associated with a rate is one year. "Thus, vital rates answer the question, 'how much per unit of ___ per year?' " The isopleths in Figures 7-1 to 7-12 refer to numbers of people (offenders or victims) or numbers of crime per unit land area, so, by Barclay, we are dealing with density ratios. (Strictly speaking, the numbers on the maps are only the numerators of ratios and not the numbers computed by dividing numerator by denominator.) However, because the police data come from a discrete time period, the year 1967, we do in fact have rates, according to Barclay's definition. Overall, then, the numbers on the maps are numerators of density ratios that technically can be considered as rates.

13. Boggs (1965).

14. See, for example, Lander (1954).

15. The frequency distribution tables on regional mobility are found in Curtis (1972) but not reproduced here. Discussions of these data in the text are cited to Curtis (1972). The great majority of offenders and victims lived inside the city, as will become clear. Because of this—along with (1) the difficulty of finding precise enough street maps for entire regional areas, (2) the problems that would have resulted in reducing isopleth drawings of regional areas to a printed page of reasonable detail, and (3) the possible distortion that a few very long distances could have had on the computed means—the offender and victim isopleths were based only on persons living within city limits. In the map analysis, distance analysis, and regional mobility analysis, "institution" was left in as a "victim" in robbery whenever race was not specified. When race was specified, only the "white" and "non-white" categories were used and "institution" was dropped. ("Institution" was never tabulated, of course, in homicide, rape, and assault.) Although the maps and distances were run for "non-whites," the dominant non-white crime population in each city was black.

16. See Shaw and McKay (1969 Edition) and Wilcox (1973).

17. See Shaw and McKay (1969 Edition).

18. From Shaw and McKay (1969 Edition, pp. 244-5) and U.S. 1970 census data.

19. See Curtis (1972) for the offender and victim maps.

20. For the regional data, see Curtis (1972).

21. For the regional data, see Curtis (1972).

22. See Curtis (1972) for these data.

23. Shaw and McKay (1969 Edition, p. 194).

24. Bernson (1966, pp. 23-26).

25. See Curtis (1972) for the offender and victim maps.

26. For the regional data, see Curtis (1972).

27. See Curtis (1972) for the offender and victim maps.

28. For the regional data, see Curtis (1972).

29. For the maps on these data and the regional figures, see Curtis (1972).

30. See Normandeau (1968, pp. 270-1), Amir (1965, p. 194), and Wolfgang (1958, p. 387). Using "mobility triangle" analysis, Normandeau found that only 14 percent of his robbery cases involved a "crime neighborhood triangle" (offense, offender, and victim in the same census tract). Only 18 percent were involved when the unit of analysis was expanded to the same tract or adjacent ones. But Amir found that 68 percent of his rape cases involved a "crime neighborhood triangle," based on a 5-block unit area. The percent would have been even greater if the unit were a census tract. Wolfgang's areal analysis of homicide was limited to a map cluster of crime locations. Most fell in two dense places, North and South Philadelphia.

31. See Curtis (1972) for these data.

32. See Allen (1971) and Arrow Street Guide to Atlanta, *Atlanta and Vicinity*.

33. *New Republic* (21-28 August 1971, p. 24).

34. U.S. 1970 census data.

35. Allen (1971, p. 179) and *Atlanta Magazine* (1972, pp. 120, 152, 154).

36. See Atlanta Commission on Crime and Juvenile Delinquency (1966) and Atlanta Region Metropolitan Planning Commission (1971).

37. See Curtis (1972) for the victim map.

38. For the regional data, see Curtis (1972).

39. Average distances were much shorter but N's much greater for black than white offenders in Table 7-1. Thus, even if only a very small proportion of the total black offenders traveled a considerable distance, the number of blacks traveling considerable distances could well be comparable to the number of whites.

40. The 1960 U.S. Census gave these population per square mile figures for the 5 cities: Boston, 15,157; Philadelphia, 15,584; Atlanta, 3,587; Chicago, 16,014; San Francisco, 16,307.

41. See Curtis (1972) for the crime, offender, and victim maps.

42. See Atlanta Commission on Crime and Juvenile Delinquency (1966) and Atlanta Region Metropolitan Planning Commission (1971). Armed robbery offenders lived further away and showed more regional mobility than offenders in the assaultive crimes. Robbery victim-crime distances were generally short. This fact, combined with the rape results, may suggest a unique Atlanta pattern. When localization was not present in the other cities (in rape and robbery, to different degrees), *both* victim and offender were mobile. In Atlanta, the emphasis was much more on the offender. For the regional data, see Curtis (1972).

43. See Curtis (1972) for these data.

44. Shaw and McKay (1969 Edition, pp. 22-27).

45. U.S. census data for 1970.

46. *Chicago Daily News* (15 and 16 July, 1968).

47. See Curtis (1972) for the offender and victim maps.

48. For the regional data, see Curtis (1972).

49. See Curtis (1972) for the crime and victim maps.

50. For the regional data, see Curtis (1972).

51. See Curtis (1972) for these data.

52. Becker and Horowitz (1970); Arrow Street Guide, *San Francisco*; U.S. 1970 Census.

53. Little (1966) and Hippler (1970).

54. See Little (1966) and Marat et al. (1967). Some of this information was also supplied in a personal communication from Stephan M. Pittel, Director, Haight-Ashbury Research Project, 1 November, 1971.

55. See Curtis (1972) for the offender and victim maps. In the distance analysis, rape distances were longer than in homicide and assault. All-white distances were roughly the same as all-black. There was little regional mobility by victims in these crimes (88 to 100 percent living in the city). The results were similar for offenders, except in rape, where 24 percent resided outside the city but in the SMSA. (However, the sample size was small, N = 21. See Curtis (1972) for the regional data.)

56. Smith et al. (1970) and *Washington Post* (14 September, 1969).

57. Smith et al. (1970) and *Washington Post* (14 September, 1969).

58. Smith et al. (1970).

59. Personal communication from Stephan M. Pittel, Director, Haight-Ashbury Research Project, 14 October, 1971.

60. Personal communication from Stephan M. Pittel, 1 November, 1971.

61. See Curtis (1972) for the crime and victim maps. It should be remembered that, up to now, all data in Chapter 7 have been cleared. An uncleared *offender* density map was not possible, of course, because addresses of offenders who have not been arrested are seldom available. Uncleared victim-crime distances in assaultive crimes were all shorter than cleared ones. This was surprising because it obliquely undermines the traditional assumption that closer proximity leads to greater likelihood of arrest. (Obliquely because the assumption is more oriented to offenders, and no uncleared offender distances were available.) No significant differences in regional mobility could be discerned between uncleared and cleared assaultive data. See Curtis (1972) for the regional figures.

62. See Curtis (1972) for the crime, offender, and victim maps.

63. See Curtis (1972) for the victim map.

64. Cleared and uncleared robbery distances were longer than their assaultive counterparts in Table 7-1, but there was considerable regional mobility, like Boston, and probably for the same reasons—a small city land area with many other communities near by. See Curtis (1972) for the regional data.

65. Lyman (1970).

66. See Curtis (1972) for these data.

67. In Washington, D.C., the FBI did a special study of index crimes cleared by arrest in October and November 1964. More homicide, assault and rape victims resided in the community of the crime than robbery victims, but localization was about the same in robbery. See FBI (1965, p. 25). Also, in an unpublished manuscript on homicide and rape that extends his analysis of all index crimes in the D.C. Crime Commission Report (1966), Sussman found that offenses, offenders, and victims were in the same precinct in 56 percent of the homicide cases but 42 percent of the rapes. (The data were from different periods in the 1960s.)

In Indianapolis, White (1932) found these distances for 1931 crimes (N's in parenthesis):

Manslaughter	.11 miles (9);
Assault & Battery	.91 miles (16);
Forcible Rape	1.52 miles (11);
Robbery	2.14 miles (20).

In St. Louis, Boggs (1965) considered, among other index crimes, homicide-assault (aggregated together), forcible rape, business robbery (probably closer to this survey's category of armed robbery), and highway and miscellaneous robbery (probably closer to this survey's category of unarmed robbery). Police data on clearances for 1960 were used and rates were computed for offenders (using population as the base for all crimes) and for offenses (using the number of pairs of persons as the base in homicide-assault, the number of resident females in rape, a business-residential land use ratio in business robbery, the number of square feet of streets in highway robbery, and the resident population in miscellaneous robbery). As measured by the correlation between offender and offense rates, localization was considerable in homicide-assault (r = .889), moderate in highway robbery and miscellaneous robbery (r = .591 and .500, respectively), but not present in forcible rape (r = .018) or business robbery (r = .099). Mobility in business robbery was explained by temptation opportunities in areas close to where offenders reside, but no explanation was ventured for rape.

In Houston, the Bullock (1955) study of 489 homicides in 1945-49 and the Pokorny (1965) study of 360 homicides in 1958-61 pointed to very short distances (even though Houston is very spread out):

Percent of Cases

Distance in Miles	Victim-Offender 1945-49	Victim-Offender 1958-61	Offender-Crime 1945-49	Offender-Victim 1945-49
0 to .9	57.5	72.8	67.0	75.3
1.0 to 1.9	12.7	7.8	7.2	12.1
2+	29.8	19.4	25.8	12.6
Total	100.0	100.0	100.0	100.0

In Seattle between 1949 and 1951, Schmid (1960) showed more localization for offenders in homicide-assault and rape than in robbery. Also, Reiss' (1966) comparison of rape, robbery, and assault offense locations and offender residences in Seattle showed assault to be most localized, followed by robbery and then rape. The N was very low in rape, however.

Tardiff's (1966, pp. 135-6) maps, shaded by Montreal police district, indicated roughly similar inner city high intensity crime location areas for homicide and assault. Rape was more evenly distributed across a wider territory.

Robbery locations peaked, but covered somewhat different territory than the other crimes. Separate maps were drawn for victims and offenders, but all four crimes were aggregated. There was a considerable inner city victim, offender, and crime location overlap, but victims also lived in certain outlying areas.

McClintock's (1963, p. 40) "crimes of violence"—mostly aggravated assaults—tended to the clubs, cafes, and streets of the Picadilly-Soho heart of London and the "poor neighborhoods among people living in overcrowded tenement houses or under slum conditions." Most victims and offenders lived in or near the crime areas, and a gradient declining to outer London could be discerned.

68. Schmid (1960, p. 669).

69. With the interest in relative intensities in each city, the high-, medium-, and low-range values were adjusted slightly for each aggregate according to the range and intensity of isoline values. The race-specific maps were not used in Philadelphia. In San Francisco, the non-clearances had the same range values as the clearances in the two respective aggregates.

70. Shaw and McKay (1969 Edition); Lander (1954); Schmid (1960); Boggs (1965).

71. See, for example, Blalock (1960, p. 336).

72. See, for example, Robinson (1950).

73. Boggs (1965, p. 902).

74. In the correlation for San Francisco poverty tracts, mean violence scores were determined from the uncleared data plus the cleared assaultive data. The uncleared robbery data were removed because preliminary analysis of their ecological distribution suggested that they might produce very different violence scores on many poverty tracts. Averaging in such data with the rest might result in figures very difficult to interpret. Accordingly, we computed correlations separately for the uncleared robbery data. However, our initial concern proved unfounded because the r here was very close to the one in Table 7-2 for the rest of the San Francisco data.

75. Note that the isoline violent crime data are from 1967 and the census poverty tract percent black data are from 1960. The poverty tracts are determined every 10 years. Thus, it would have been better to use 1970 rather than 1960 poverty tracts and their percents black, because 1970 is closer to 1967 than is 1960. However, at this writing, the 1970 poverty tracts are not yet available. The Census Bureau has assured the writer by personal communication that most of the 1960 tracts defined as poor can be expected to retain their status in 1970, so that minimal bias is assumed from using earlier figures.

76. Thanks are extended to Dr. Herman Miller, Chief, Population Division, Bureau of the Census, and Mr. Donald Fowles of the Census Poverty Statistics Program for supplying the unpublished poverty rank for each Census tract in the cities examined, so that the partial correlations could be computed.

77. Ferdinand (1969).

78. City breakdowns of these variables are as follows:

	Index of Residential Segregation, 1960 (*Source:* Tauber and Tauber, 1965, p. 30)	Percent Negro in City (*Source:* U.S. Census Bureau)	
		1960	1970
Boston	83.9	9.1	16.3
Philadelphia	87.1	26.4	33.6
Atlanta	93.6	38.3	51.3
Chicago	92.6	22.9	32.7
San Francisco	69.3	10.0	13.4

79. Black population size for the cities examined here is as follows:

	1960	1970
Boston	63,165	104,707
Philadelphia	529,240	653,791
Atlanta	186,464	255,051
Chicago	812,637	1,102,620
San Francisco	74,383	96,078

A Summary, and Some Implications for Research and Policy

"Let us sit on this log by the roadside," says I, "and forget the inhumanity and ribaldry of the poets. It is in the glorious columns of ascertained facts and legalized measures that beauty is to be found. . . ."

"Go on, Mr. Pratt," says Mrs. Sampson. "Them ideas is so original and soothing. I think statistics are just as lovely as they can be."

—O. Henry,
The Handbook of Hymen

Summary[1]

Criminal Violence is an integrative, descriptive sourcebook of information derived from police offense and arrest reports, the first study of its kind to embrace all four major violent crimes and a sample of national dimensions. Set in the middle of a dramatic 10-year uptrend in reported criminal violence that refused to trail off like group disorders, the 17-city data from 1967 are examined for significant patterns. Unlike most other comparable studies, clearances are compared to non-clearances, and there is a flexibility that allows the most appropriate unit of analysis (interaction, case, or offender and victim separately) to be used for any given variable. The national aggregate is broken into regional groupings and, when possible, trends over time are followed. Perspective is added by systematic comparisons to many domestic and foreign studies.

Although there are always variations in individual areas, reported criminal homicide and aggravated assault in the aggregated "national city" most frequently involve black offenders and victims. Typically, the participants are black males in their teens and twenties victimizing other black males of the same age or older—friends, acquaintances, or strangers living in close proximity to the offender and attacked in the course of relatively trivial altercations. Or, somewhat less frequently, the episode involves black husbands and wives, other family-member combinations, or males and females in less formal relationships caught up in domestic quarrels and altercations. The ultimate victim may very well bring on his or her own demise, and one or both parties often are drinking, commonly on a weekend night, before the fatal attack is facilitated by a gun (used relatively more in homicide) or a knife (used relatively more in assault). Drug use—amphetamines and barbituates more than opiates, halucinogens, and cannabis—is another more than occasional correlate, although alcohol plays a

159

considerably more prominent role. The next most frequently reported racial patterns in the national aggregate are white offenders on white victims and black offenders on white victims, respectively.

Some killers in the United States may be more determined than assaulters, so that they choose a more lethal weapon, particularly a gun over a knife. (And perhaps this is more so in underdeveloped countries, with relatively high proportions of killings based on motives built up over long periods of time.) But the facts better support an accessibility interpretation: American homicides and assaults are very similar in circumstance, structure, intent, and motivational background, with the difference in their seriousness explained in no small part by killers happening to have more deadly weapons at hand.

The largely intraracial nature of American homicide and assault is upheld cross-culturally. One of the few crime patterns examined that transcends national boundaries is the intragroup (race, ethnicity, caste, and so forth) character of homicide.

As in American homicides and assaults, the great majority of killers are males in countries throughout the world, and the percentage of females among victims is usually higher than among offenders. Although local institutions and customs vary, the preponderance of men in these crimes is related to socially and culturally defined roles such as aggressor, provider and leader; to the greater social pressures exerted by these positions; and to the greater frequency of external contacts. There is some tendency for the homicide rate by female offenders to approach the male rate in countries where females have relatively greater freedom and equality.

Comparisons between the United States and other countries show that homicide and assault are driven by deep social and cultural undercurrents. This suggests the incompleteness of Von Hentig's concentration on the interpersonal "dyad." Unique institutions, roles and expectations that develop in a country over time (like the degree and kind of family cohesiveness and female subservience) become crucial in understanding the interpersonal relationships between offender and victim characterizing the country. Beneath such generalized statements, it is difficult to identify a unifying order to cross-national relationship configurations. However, it is possible to suggest with qualification that there may be a relatively greater proportion of strangers committing impersonal killings in urban areas, a pattern imposed upon a more universal locus of homicide and assault among the friends and intimates one can love and therefore hate.

The kinds of "immediate" conflicts that most frequently characterize American homicides and assaults—the trivial altercations and "little ol' arguments over nothing at all"—appear somewhat more consistently in homicides committed in Western and technologically advanced countries. Forms of revenge arising out of long, drawn out hostilities seem to be more consistently relevant to the non-West and to populations less advanced technologically. This coarse dichotomy thus balances more superficial motives set in an impersonal, hostile, complex modern urban environment against motives of retribution built up over long periods of time in more traditional, family and friend oriented cultures— where, for example, it is more difficult to get rid of undesirable family members by desertion, where an inheritance of property or money has a relatively greater economic and social impact and can accordingly arouse more jealousy, where the tight social network makes more difficult the satisfaction of sexual desire outside of marriage and where breaks with family and ethnic solidarity causes more resentment.

In cross-national perspective, the weapons used in homicide are largely a function of their availability and the culture-technology's tradition of implements for work and protection. Although the relationship is not completely clear, the proportion of killings with firearms is generally higher where no gun controls or weak, ineffective ones exist in a country, and it is usually lower or negligible under rigid and strongly enforced interdicts. However, the homicide rate in any given country is based on many other factors besides the supply of various weapons (as measured by production, licensing, and control). Other elements include the nation's assaultive attack frequency (reflecting the whole complex of forces encouraging violence and the historical process underlying them), the demand for specific weapons in terms of cost, tradition, and daily work needs; the speed with which an incident can be reported; and the efficiency and sophistication of medical treatment in preventing an injury from becoming a death.

The most frequent American rape pattern at the aggregated 17-city level has blacks as offenders and victims, both in their teens or the women in her teens and the man older. The typical incident occurs on a weekend night, with an assailant previously unknown to the victim being slightly more likely than a friend or previous acquaintance. Unlike Amir, the national data suggests a very low level of provocation by the victim. It is also possible that the more force and intimidation displayed by a rapist at the onset, the less likely the victim is to resist and therefore be injured. The other leading racial patterns are white-on-white and black-on-white, respectively, although the latter, interracial, attacks form a much higher proportion in some places, compared to the "national city" total.

Unique among the major violent crimes, robbery has higher interracial than intraracial frequencies at the 17-city aggregate level. Commonly, younger black males, not previously known to their victims and often in groups, rob older white males or institutions. Except for the victimization of institutions, similar age, sex, interpersonal, and multiple offender relationships hold in the second most frequent variety, by blacks on other blacks. Many robbers are supporting drug habits. The relatively greater frequency of armed robbery in colder months can be partially explained by the greater economic privation experienced then by the poor, at least in some parts of the country, and the expansion of nighttime hours, with their protective cloak. The increased volume of business and shopping activity centered around Christmas also offers more opportunities. An important difference between armed and unarmed robbery is the considerably greater possibility of injury in the latter. The victim may be less intimidated and therefore more likely to resist, whereas the thief who yokes or mugs without the crutch of a weapon often has the physical strength to make good his threat.

As measured by the national survey variables, homicide and assault are almost identical, except for final outcome; robbery is quite distinct and rape falls somewhere in between. For example, use of alcohol, the presence of multiple offenders, and the degree of spatial localization are highest for homicide and assault, lower for rape and lower still for robbery. In addition, the popularly conceptualized fear that violent attack will come from a stranger on the street in the United States is justified for robbery and relevant for rape, but relatively less valid for assault and homicide (although the role of strangers in homicide and assault seems to be increasing over time). More generally, the percentage of non-primary group relationships steadily rises from homicide to robbery, whereas the frequency of family and other primary group relationships uniformly declines. One partial exception to this relative ordering of the major violent crimes may be victim precipitation, which appears not uncommon for homicide and assault (a finding with some cross-cultural validation), less frequent but still empirically noteworthy for robbery and perhaps least relevant for rape.

The concept of victim precipitation has a rather unique potential for use both by those who resist change and defend the established order (like males who blame women for their own rape) as well as by those who criticize the status quo and see offenders as encouraging by their acts further victimization of themselves by accelerated repression from the system whose inequalities promoted the crime in the first place.

Some cities in the American West appear to have higher proportions of criminal violence by blacks on whites than a number of other cities throughout the country. The reported rates per 100,000 population of violent crime for each race combination seem to have increased in most cities over the last decade, and it is possible that black-white rates have increased the fastest in many places.

The Chicago school of criminology's zonal gradient hypothesis, of crime rates declining from a central city business peak, is very crude when tested by computer isolines. Ecologically, crime peaks and plateaus appear to shift somewhat over time.

Most urban criminal violence can be related geographically to poverty areas. Non-poverty areas with significant violence are usually on the fringes of high violence poverty tracts or better off neighborhoods that robbers enter to victimize residents and businesses.

There is some reason to speculate that city-level demographic characteristics, like the absolute number of blacks, are associated with violent crime rates by poor blacks that remain disproportionate to violent crime rates by whites who are also poor.

The failure of homicide, assault, and rape rates to be dramatically and significantly higher during the summer than other seasons suggests that the "thermic law of delinquency," postulating that warmer months and climates are associated with higher crime rates against persons and cooler months and climates with higher rates against property, is not as strongly operative in the United States for serious violence as nineteenth-century observers of Europe believed. Today, the "law" does not even seem to hold in Europe or many African and Asian sites.

Research

Combined with the results of other studies, the national survey has supplied more than enough information on the similarities and dissimilarities among homicide, assault, rape, and robbery to fulfill the objective, stated in Chapter 1, of locating the relative positions of these criminal systems in behavioral space.

Replicative work covering the same crimes and variables will still be needed to supply trend information and profile individual localities, but thoughtful analysts should now proceed beyond the contemporary first generation of such studies—illustrated by Wolfgang, Pittman and Handy, Amir, Normandeau, and the national survey. Second and future generations of research on individual criminal behavior systems in the United States would profit from triangulating within the same research design victimization studies, other survey research and participant observation in the general population with clinical interviewing and projective testing of offenders and victims. A dynamic, perhaps Markovian, analysis of a single criminal behavior system must begin in the community and seek to differentiate persons who do and do not become offenders or victims. Comparisons of persons who, faced with an offender, escape victimization to those who succumb may yield valuable insights, for instance, on the merits of aggressiveness by women against sexual assaulters. Offender and victim interviews are necessary because police information is so limited. Conklin[2] should be commended for doing just this in his study of robbery. Police data (clearances compared to non-clearances) should continue to be tapped, because they cover essential information on the criminal event. But other useful insights on offenders and victims are potentially available from the courts and correctional institutions (depending on local records keeping, diagnostic capability, and the like), and a dynamic analysis will have to follow through all the contingencies of the criminal justice system.

A more ambitious, second-generation research design also needs to be multicity, so that criminal justice idiosyncrasies can be placed in clearer perspective, along with regional and city-specific (especially demographic) variables relating to true incidence.

Because it has been understudied in the past, because of the interest and activism of feminists, and because of a receptive posture by many funding sources, forcible rape, more than any of the other major violent crimes, is likely to be the object of such research. Beyond better documenting the apparently increasing role of strangers in sudden encounters recorded by several cities, one line of inquiry consonant with the kind of second generational effort just suggested would be to focus empirically on the very ill-defined process by which encounters with non-strangers, often in social or quasi-social circumstances, escalate into reports of rape. A well-triangulated design might include the following kinds of illustrative questions, asked in interviews with rape victims:

1. Right before the incident, were you with the offender, near him, or wasn't he around at all?

IF WITH OR NEAR HIM:

2. Were you talking to him?
3. Why were you with him or near him—were you at home, at work, on a date, or what?
4. Did he try to build up to intercourse by his words and actions, or did he immediately rape you?

IF HE TRIED TO BUILD UP:

5. What did he do or say?
6. Did he actually ask you to have intercourse?

IF YES:

7. What did you say?
8. Did you immediately say no to his advances or wait a while before saying no?

IF WAITED A WHILE:

9. Why did you wait a while?
10. Do you think that there was anything you said or did that might have encouraged the offenders?
11. Do you think that there was anything you could have done to prevent or avoid the incident?

The roles played by each party, the course of communication (or lack thereof), victim participation, offender motive and intent, the impact of social circumstance are all threads intertwined in the transactional build up to forced intercourse. In addressing these matters, and rape generally, feminist analysts might be more responsive analytically to the national predominance of reported black-black rape encounters and the possibility of different racial patterns. For example, *Violence, Race and Culture* suggests that young black males may more often verbally request intercourse, whereas young white males may be relatively more prone to esculate silently. Feminists have often failed to consider race specifics or implicitly assumed interpersonal processes possibly more relevant to whites than blacks.

Similar questions should be administered to incarcerated rape offenders. The perspectives of offenders—with all their biases—are needed to avoid becoming locked into the perceptions of victims alone. The current flood of studies on rape victims runs the risk of biasing the analysis for or against the victim simply because she is relatively more available to be interviewed than the offender. The new emphasis on victimology and the emerging interest in rape: their convergence should not unduly channel research and policy primarily on the victim side of the rape encounter. A full understanding of rape and the social and law enforcement strategies that may be possible to reduce or control it must inquire much more carefully into the motivations, intents, perceptions, and techniques of the offender.[3]

This is not to diminish the importance of policy-oriented rape victim research. In fact, the writer has been engaged in such research with the New York City Police Department. This inquiry—and the others like it now being undertaken—addresses questions of more fair, understanding, and efficient treatment of victims (like whether female investigating detectives are preferable to males). The anticipated answers are likely to imply relatively straightforward, rapidly implementable policy responses. But, as much as such action is needed to right undeniable wrongs that have been perpetuated by a sexist criminal justice system far too long, the much more complex problem of researching rapists with an eye to longer run policy action should be kept in sight. Notwithstanding feminist advice on how to avoid rape, an emphasis on victims will be a difficult if not impossible means to affect what many believe to be the ultimate research-action goal: reducing the real rate of rape. Research on why rapes occur and how they might occur less must assess the offender, over his developmental history and as he faces the victim, particularly if Chapter 5 is correct in suggesting that the victim's role in the genesis of rape is less than popularly imagined.

Together, police, victim, and offender data promise to generate a more realistic typology of the participants in and circumstances of rape. By improving our understanding of the phenomenon, such typologies have direct policy implications. For example, what if the most typical combinations of offender type-victim type-circumstance type in attempted rapes are significantly different from those in rapes actually completed? Herein might lie the germ of a public education campaign in which women are instructed how to recognize, avoid, and, at worse, cope with, certain types of potential offenders in certain circumstances.

Independent of their contributions to the understanding of specific criminal behavior systems, several of the national survey variables deserve more study in their own right, across many varieties of deviance. Victim precipitation is the most obvious example. Replication studies are needed to validate the extent of precipitation as defined here for the violent crimes—especially in the less researched areas of rape and robbery. New definitions ought to be considered and extensions made to other acts against person and property. Chapter 5 has already proposed standardization of a more refined scale combining offender intent with victim involvement; triangulation of offender, victim, and researcher definitions of precipitation, possibly leading to Delphi explorations of consensus; pursuit of the developmental history of any prior relationship; and application of the concept to theories of political marginality and social deviance. Without considerably more work of this kind, victim compensation programs will continue to lack sufficient guidance on denial of funds as a function of victim culpability.

It is also highly respectable to engage in their own right the distance, spatial, and demographic variables discussed in Chapter 7. A promising development of distance analysis can be found in the work of Fabrikant, who is building an economic-location theory of crime in which offender area and offense area are analyzed via an analog to international trade. He is seeking to partition urban areas into discrete socioeconomic communities and to clarify them in terms of the degree to which they export or import crime.[4] A more rigorous analysis in a large number of cities that builds on Chapter 7 to see which demographic variables may influence relative rates of violence by poor blacks versus poor whites will help validate or refute concepts like "agglomention effects" and "cultural takeoff," which *Violence, Race and Culture* speculatively raises when interpreting violence by blacks in cities where their numbers are very large.

Finally, cross-cultural studies, both first generation replications and work headed towards the second generation, should be encouaged in all of these topical areas because of the depth and understanding that they have added to American patterns in the foregoing chapters. The surface of cross-national inquiry has barely been scratched, particularly for assault, rape, and robbery.

Policy

Much of the above research is action oriented, and so the realm of policy has already been unavoidably entered. What follows is a continuation that reviews some of the more direct policy implications leading from the national survey findings. The reader is again reminded that the data presented in Chapters 2 through 7 are not etiological; in and of themselves, they do not trace causal processes. As a result, the policy implications that can be drawn from them are more related to instruments of social control, mainly in the criminal justice system. From the writer's perspective, such policies are more or less short-run holding actions that respond to symptoms rather than longer run strategies sensitive to ultimate causes. Nonetheless, it would be remiss to discourage criminal justice policies that can increase the short-run safety of the population, particularly in the ghetto, with its locus of all-black violence.

Edward Banfield's book, *The Unheavenly City*,[5] is a convenient point of departure for an appraisal of how the national survey findings can be applied to questions of social control. In what is probably the least distinguished part of that study (it is hard to decide), Banfield isolates personal and environmental propensity and incentive factors behind criminal patterns, tying them together with the assumption, complementary to Fleisher and other economists, of rational cost-benefit behavior by the offender. The consequent policy ordered up consists mainly of deterrence, target hardening, increases in the risks of apprehension, and similar threats to the strategically thinking crook.

However, the national survey findings force an awareness, which Banfield does not seem to have, that only certain varieties of serious criminal violence fit his rationality assumption and are therefore likely to respond to his policy. Was the offender a stranger, did the crime occur outside or at least in some public location, was there a degree of planning? Here is a partial index upon which to predict the utility of control instruments against personal violence. Robbery receives high scores. Some homicides, assaults, and rapes fit, but as a rule the crimes lower in incidence but greater in seriousness are much more likely to fail on at least one of the criteria. Much homicide and assault occurs in private and interior settings among protagonists who are anything but unfamiliar to one another. We have seen that it is common for those homicides and assaults that do happen outside and among strangers (or at least among persons not well acquainted) to be spur of the moment outbursts that defy deterrence—unless a police officer is on the spot. Rape frequently catches the fringe of social engagements like parties and dates. Rapists not previously known by the girl may pick her up outside, but the attacks usually take place indoors.

It is with an understanding of these facts that now commonplace public control measures (such as improved police command and control efficiency, use of footpatrols, installation of bright sodium arc lights, institution of restrooms accessible only by keys possessed by legitimate personnel, and so forth) should be pursued, and devices discouraging robbery (such as television cameras in banks, credit cards difficult to use when stolen, sliding barriers between drivers and passengers in taxicabs, scrip on public transportation vehicles, and so forth) should be promoted.

The related bag of mixed potential is to encourage private individuals to alter their behavior, and make themselves harder targets. The pervasive fear of crime and violence has in fact raised the consciousness of citizens. The lock and alarm business has flourished. Residences have been fortified, and the safety afforded by distance from the inner city is prized. Yet this strategy has only marginal impact on those who need protection most. However careful poor non-whites are, they remain highly impregnable as long as they must live in a high risk environment and because they lack the resources with which suburban whites can harden themselves as targets.

The survey data on victim precipitation in homicide, assault, and robbery point to a greater potential for the criminal justice system in controlling the latter crime than the former two. The high degree of emotion and irrationality in many homicides and assaults would seem to make warnings against precipitating attack rather futile. In spite of the seemingly lower prevalence of precipitation in robbery, a public response, in terms of greater personal care and public and private target hardening, is more feasible. As for rape, if the low percentage of provocation found here is upheld in validation studies, further momentum is added to efforts that seek to counteract criminal justice operations implicitly or explicitly assuming a bias against victims.

One still promising innovation evolving out of the control perspective is the police-based "domestic quarrel team" or "family crisis intervention unit" on twenty-four-hour call to defuse conflict situations that might lead to outcomes like homicide and assault among friends and intimates. The national survey has documented the continuing large proportion of such encounters, in spite of the apparent rise in homicide and assault by strangers. In Bard's well known evaluation of the concept in a West Harlem precinct,[6] police officers learned to express respect for combatants, avoid show of force (except when absolutely necessary for self defense), deescalate anger through informality, listen and discuss with sympathy the arguments of both sides, concede explicitly a man's masculinity, permit antagonists to talk out their problems at length, and suggest alternative solutions. It is a sad commentary on the strategy of innovating non-hardware programs to learn that in spite of the project's high evaluation, it was not retained by the New York City Police, apparently because of failure to muster sufficient administrative and political allies. But this does not prevent other departments from implementing the idea.

Along related lines, minor criminal cases arising from neighborhood and family disputes are screened by the local prosecutor's office in Columbus, Ohio and referred to trained hearing officers for mediation at times convenient for the disputants. The mediation in this experimental program is geared to searching for lasting solutions to interpersonal problems, not to establishing a judgment of right or wrong.[7] Preliminary evaluations suggest that the approach is promising.

To really be effective, however, mediation must be anteceded with an intervention system that does in fact catch minor conflicts before they escalate into assault or homicide. Yet, short of a cop or television camera in every house, it is impossible for the police themselves to pick up on the majority of incipient and potentially dangerous domestic conflicts. Perhaps the best that can be hoped for is a well-publicized emergency telephone system that screens calls initiated by participants—or friends, neighbors, and relatives who are aware of the conflict—and directs them to police and social service specialists cast in the domestic quarrel team model. The team's response, in turn, must be rapid as well as sensitive. If, as the national survey data suggests is likely, the call originates from blacks or other non-whites, team members should be prepared to respond to the unique perceptions, attitudes, values, behavior, and coping mechanisms of these groups. Of course, such a system cannot be effective against many other incidents that end in homicide and assault, like those characterized by sudden encounters, minor altercations with no past history, and stranger-to-stranger confrontations.

The notion of specially trained crisis intervention specialists is applicable to the treatment of rape victims as well. Bard and Ellison[8] have shown how knowledgeable use of crisis theory (originally developed by Lindemann's work with the survivors of the Cocoanut Grove fire in 1942) by police rape investigators can greatly help the victim to preserve her psychological integrity and therefore better assist detectives in the apprehension of offenders and prosecutors in the preparation of court cases.

The national survey data also offer several arguments for stronger controls on the possession of handguns. The first argument relies on the positive, if qualified, association between the proportion of firearms in homicide and the kind of control enforced. Add to this the conclusions that homicide and assault are similar, except for final outcome, and that firearms are more frequent in killings but knives in assaults. The fatality rate for firearm attacks is approximately five times as high as for knives. Thus, "a rough approximation would suggest that the use of knives instead of guns might cause four-fifths, or 80 percent, fewer fatalities."[9] Effective handgun control would not reduce the motivation or desire to kill, but it would necessitate the use of less efficient and more deadly weapons. Thus, relatively fewer homicides and more aggravated assaults might be expected to occur.

Second, guns predominate as the weapon used in armed robbery. There is every reason to believe that the gun is often essential for the armed robber and that without it, many would be unable ro produce the threat of force needed to carry out such a crime.[10] In addition, the fataility rate for armed robberies involving firearms is approximately four times as great as that for other armed robberies.[11]

Third, consider the common practice of keeping firearms in the home for purposes of self-defense. There is an assumption here that a great deal of violence is by strangers intruding into the home and that firearms are an efficient defense. Yet criminal homicide, while often occurring at home, is not preoccupied with strangers. Aggravated assault has proportionately more strangers, but it also occurs outside more often. Even for the relatively few homicides and assaults where strangers penetrate a home, existing evidence indicates that the element of surprise substantially limits the effectiveness of personal defense.[12] Robbery occurs between strangers most of the time, yet it rarely happens in the home; even when it does, the element of surprise exists. Burglary has a much higher incidence rate than the four major violent crimes, is the most common type of intrusion by a stranger, and causes the greatest property loss. Yet burglary rarely threatens the homeowner's life.

Not only do the facts show the limits of firearms as protective devices, but they also suggest that guns are often hazardous in the home. In the heat of an altercation, family quarrel, or jealous rage, guns stored for protection against strangers can be used on friends and loved ones. Nor does the shooting need to be criminal; a substantial number of the 23,000 annual firearms accidents in the country occur in the home.[13]

Social Indicators

Ultimately, the longest-staying and most far-reaching use of the national survey data, the studies compared to it in this volume, and the many investigations like it that are now being produced is as an assembly of factual social indicators to guide policy formation, program evaluation and the construction of theories of criminal violence. The Office of Management and Budget recognized this function by graphing much of the national survey data into its *Social Indicators, 1973* report. Similarly, the Law Enforcement Assistance Administration included our data in the 1973 *Sourcebook of Criminal Justice Statistics.* Yet the United States still does not have an annual social indicators report (the OMB work remains preliminary and experimental), and the only national survey variables found each year for all four violent crimes in the one relevant annual crime publication that is now available, the FBI *Uniform Crime Reports*, are monthly variation patterns.[14] These are perhaps the least valuable of all the survey variables. The annual figures now being generated by the Law Enforcement Assistance Administration and the U.S. Census Bureau in their National Crime Panel may begin to partially fill the void.

At this time, national survey type data are now routinely produced and applied to help shape operations in many enlightened criminal justice planning agencies and local police departments. For example, the Law Enforcement Assistance Administration's National Impact Cities program, aimed at street crime, chose Atlanta, Baltimore, Cleveland, Dallas, Denver, Newark, Portland, and St. Louis as target cities in part because they all had a high incidence of stranger-to-stranger felonies.[15] Conversely, the Police Foundation-funded project on homicide and assault with the Detroit Police Department is aimed at developing policy against non-stranger attacks that have evolved from a history of interpersonal conflicts.[16] The New York City Police and the criminal justice planning agencies in cities like Denver, Portland, and Seattle are all accumulating baseline, national survey-like data on rape to provide information for future experiments and policy innovations.[17] The Kansas City Police are exploring multivariate techniques for making better use of their data on homicide and assault.[18] The St. Louis police use computer maps to help supervisors plan the allocation of patrol resources.[19] More broadly, computer isoline mapping can be applied to evaluation research on the impact of intervention strategies by plotting the extent to which programs areally displace rather than absolutely reduce crime. Such analysis need not be static. Changes over time can be traced on film, as part of the development of kinostatistics as social indicators.[20]

Do high and increasing rates of black-on-white criminal violence in certain places reflect black outrage and hostility toward whites? Or—or in addition—do the figures indicate pockets of more integrated society, where growing inter-action between the races means that black-white violence is another manifesta-tion of intragroup aggression, rather than an exception to it? This is only one isolated example of the theoretical and speculative thought encouraged by the national survey profile. The nonetiological nature of these data should not for a moment impede their use as a base in the construction of interpretive concepts and causal explanations. They provide one empirical framework whose contours theory might partially follow. Such is the fate of the national survey variables in the companion volume to this study, *Violence, Race and Culture.*

Notes and References

1. The summarized material on location, temporal patterns, and multiple offenders comes from Appendix A. References to alcohol and drug use are based on the literature review in *Violence, Race and Culture.* These variables were coded in the national survey, but unknowns were prohibitively high to allow use of the data.

2. Conklin (1972).

3. As Conklin (1972) found for robbery, interviews of incarcerated rapists will have to overcome many problems. For example, ideally, one would like to interview a sample of *all* rape offenders. But it is difficult if not impossible to interview offenders in (1) rapes not reported, (2) rapes reported but not cleared by arrest, and even (3) rapes where an arrest has been made. Incarcerated rapists, then, are a very small and unique group out of the total set of all rapists. Nonetheless, Conklin's sample suggests that careful, qualified analysis of inter-views from this group can yield extremely valuable information.

4. Fabrikant (1973).

5. Banfield (1970).

6. Bard (1970).

7. Law Enforcement Assistance Administration (1974).

8. Bard and Ellison (1974).

9. Newton and Zimring (1969, p. 42).

10. See Chapter 6.

11. Newton and Zimring (1969, p. 47).

12. Newton and Zimring (1969, p. 64).

13. Newton and Zimring (1969, p. 20).

14. Arrest volumes (not rates) by race, sex, and age are published for each of

the major violent crimes in the *Uniform Crime Reports*, but with a few exceptions, only offender characteristics are recorded, and there are no data expressions linking offender to victim.

15. U.S. Department of Justice (1974).

16. Wilt and Bannon (1974).

17. Cottell (1973), Giancinti (1973), Seattle Law and Planning Office (1975).

18. Sawtell (1974).

19. St. Louis Police Department (1966).

20. Biderman (1971).

Appendices

Appendix A:
Location, Temporal Patterns,
and Multiple Offenders

Appendix A presents national survey data and comparative findings on location (of the actual crime, rather than initial contact), temporal patterns, and multiple offenders. Usually included in earlier, single-city studies, these variables were not considered important enough to be treated as chapters. Some of the findings have been tapped at appropriate points in the text, however.

Location

Summary of the National Survey

Table A-1 shows locations for cleared events. Cleared homicides experienced a fairly even distribution among outside, home, and other inside locations. The results were similar for non-clearances. Indoor and outdoor places were almost equal in assault clearances, with the outside percentage somewhat higher for non-clearances. There is more room for escape out-of-doors, and perhaps witnesses don't get as close a look. Outside places had a lower frequency (34 percent) in cleared rapes than any of the other crimes, although non-clearances rose to 46 percent. Half the clearances and 40 percent of the non-clearances were committed in residences. Cleared and uncleared armed heists were outside about half the time, even though the inside frequencies for places other than the home were higher than for any of the other crimes, pointing to the many commercial targets. Victims of unarmed robbers had the most justification for fearing outside locations (69 percent in clearances and 72 percent in non-clearances).[1]

One of the more significant regional patterns was a higher frequency of homicides and assaults at home in the West. This correlates with the higher proportion of western family homicides and assaults discussed in Chapter 3.[2]

Criminal Homicide

The United States. In other U.S. studies, Wolfgang reported a higher percentage of clearances in the home than the national survey, Washington, D.C. had a greater proportion of residential killings, and New York a higher percentage of street homicides. Houston and Florida paralleled the national survey.[3]

Within the home, the three major locations in the national survey were the living room, where family members and friends probably come into contact with

Table A-1

Location by Type of Crime, 17 American Cities, 1967, Clearances (Percent)

Major Violent Crime Type Location	Criminal Homicide	Aggravated Assault	Forcible Rape	Armed Robbery	Unarmed Robbery
Bedroom	10.7	2.8	35.5	0.8	3.2
Kitchen	3.2	2.4	0.1	0.4	0
Living Room Den, Study	12.5	17.1	9.4	2.1	2.4
Hall, Stair, Elevator	6.4	5.7	4.6	4.4	11.5
Basement, Garage	1.8	0.2	3.9	0	1.5
Total: Home	34.6	28.2	53.5	7.7	18.6
Service Station	0.7	1.1	0	4.0	0.9
Chain Store	0	0.5	0	1.8	0
Bank	0	0	0	2.5	0
Other Commercial Establishment	2.9	3.4	1.4	21.8	5.9
Bar, Tavern, Taproom, Lounge	7.8	3.1	0.4	2.4	0
Place of Entertainment Other than Bar, etc.	1.0	1.0	0.4	0	0
Any Other Inside Location	14.1	11.9	9.8	3.8	5.6
Total: Other Inside Location	26.5	21.0	12.0	36.3	12.4
Immediate Area Around Residence	4.2	5.8	2.2	2.9	5.2
Street	24.2	34.8	4.2	37.9	48.9
Alley	1.1	1.3	6.6	1.8	2.5
Park, Playground	0.4	1.7	2.1	0.6	3.7
Lot	2.6	0.8	3.0	2.0	1.4
Private Transport Vehicle	2.3	0.9	11.3	4.0	4.3
Public transport Vehicle	.4	1.1	0	4.0	2.4
Any Other Outside Location	1.1	1.8	4.2	2.1	0.4
Total: Outside Location	36.3	48.3	33.6	55.6	69.0
Total Unknown	2.6	2.6	0.8	0.6	0
Grand Total	100.0 (608)	100.0 (1238)	100.0 (522)	100.0 (310)	100.0 (288)

Total number of cases = 2966.

Note: Frequencies weighted according to total reported violent crimes for 1967, by type in the 17 cities surveyed. Column figures may not add up exactly to 100.0 percent because of rounding.

one another more than in any other single place; the bedroom, where the close proximity of intimates may encourage unresolved conflicts to flare up; and halls, stairways, and elevators—places of transition where the victim may be caught by his adversary after moving from a scene of conflict.[4]

Homicides in inside places other than the home were mainly distributed between miscellaneous indoor locations and bars or taverns. Most outside killings occurred on the streets.[5]

Regardless of race, higher percentages of female than male victims and offenders were evident in home killings.[6] Women spend a greater proportion of work and leisure hours at home, and their more common primary group experience in homicide also favors residences. The relative outside orientation of men is associated with their greater use of the streets at night, during the hours and on the days of the week when homicide peaks. Groups of young males often move from one place of amusement to another late at night; but when a woman is out, she more likely has a male companion, who escorts her home but then, if he leaves her, makes his way alone.

Locational distributions were nearly the same for interracial versus intraracial homicides in the national survey. Reasonably, primary group homicides tended to occur inside and non-primary killings outside.[7]

Foreign Comparisons. Table A-2 summarizes some of the results in other countries. The data from Poland were comparable to the national survey, but more killings (81 percent) occurred outside in Montreal.

The distribution of homicides among Jews in Israel was almost identical to that in urban America, yet the majority of non-Jewish killings were outside. Rather than being based on ethnic differences, the explanation was set in the Jewish gravitation to urban life, compared to the preponderance of Arabs in rural places. More personal contacts, especially those related to working activities, took place outside buildings in rural settlements.[8]

There was a nearly equal split between inside and outside murders in Delhi, but the rural Indian findings from the Maria tribe were difficult to evaluate because of a high unknown proportion. Fully 80 percent of the homicides in the Southern Province of Ceylon happened out-of-doors. About a third, however, occurred in the "environs of buildings," which in Ceylon are places of entertainment integral to the home. If this figure is added to the inside percentage, the results become more compatible with the United States.

Overall, there appears some tendency for the West and more advanced industrial societies to have a greater proportion of inside killings than the non-West and less advanced countries. The Israeli results, however, may offer the key; urban centers have an abundance of enclosed places and inside activity relative to rural settlements.

Aggravated Assault

The United States. There were some variations, but earlier work roughly converged on the 50-50 split in the national survey between inside and outside

Table A-2
Location, by Crime and Country (Percent)

Crime & Country / Location	United States Urban (17 City Survey, Clearances) 1967	Canada[1] Urban (Montreal) 1964	Poland[2] Entire Country 1955-1961	Israel[3] Entire Country (Jewish Pop. 2/3 Urban, Non-Jewish Pop. Rural) 1950-1964			India[4] Urban (Delhi) 1962-1964	India[5] Rural (Maria tribe) 1921-1941	Ceylon[6] Southern Province (Both Urban & Rural Areas) 1960
				Jews	Non-Jews	Total			
Inside	61.1	81.2	63.1	57.0	43.0	51.0	47.0	39.0	20.5
(Home)	34.6	47.9	50.4	–	–	–	34.0	33.0	14.8
(Other Inside)	26.5	33.3	12.7	–	–	–	13.0	6.0	5.7
Outside	36.6	18.8	36.9	43.0	57.0	49.0	53.0	27.0	79.5
(Street)	24.2	16.0	21.8	–	–	–	–	–	–
Unknown	2.6	0	0	0	0	0	0	34.0	0
Total	100.0 (608)	100.0 (48)	100.0 (942)	100.0 (150)	100.0 (110)	100.0 (260)	100.0 (147)	100.0 (100)	100.0 (88)

Criminal Homicide

Crime & Country	Aggravated Assault		Forcible Rape			Robbery				
	United States Urban (17 City Survey, Clearances) 1967	Canada[7] Urban (Montreal) 1964	United States Urban (17 City Survey Clearances) 1967	Canada[8] Urban (Montreal) 1964	Denmark[9] Entire Country (Mostly Rural Areas & Provincial Cities) 1946-1958	United States Urban (17 City Survey Clearances) 1967 Armed Robbery	United States Urban (17 City Survey Clearances) 1967 Unarmed Robbery	Canada[10] Urban (Montreal) 1964	England[11] Urban (London) 1950	England[11] Urban (London) 1957
Inside	49.2	51.2	65.5	64.6	24.0	44.0	31.0	47.9	41.1	36.6
(Home)	28.2	36.1	53.5	60.2	–	7.7	18.6	12.3	–	–
(Other Inside)	21.0	15.1	12.0	4.4	–	36.3	12.4	35.6	–	–
Outside	48.3	48.0	33.6	33.6	76.0	55.6	69.0	50.5	58.9	63.4
(Street)	34.8	43.7	4.2	8.0	–	37.9	48.9	50.0	–	–
Unknown	2.6	0.8	0.8	1.8	0	0.6	0	1.6	0	0
Total	100.0 (1238)	100.0 (119)	100.0 (522)	100.0 (113)	100.0 (141)	100.0 (310)	100.0 (288)	100.0 (202)	100.0 (287)	100.0 (462)

Note: A dash ("—") means data for the particular category are not available.

References: [1]Tardiff (1966, p. 50); [2]Holyst (1967, p. 34); [3]Landau and Drapkin (1968, Table 8); [4]Rao (1968, Table 9); [5]Elwin (1943, tabulation from Appendix); [6]Jayewardene and Ranasinghe (1963, p. 61. The low proportion of inside killings may be qualified by the fact that many "outside" homicides were in the environs of a building.); [7]Tardiff (1966, p. 50); [8]Tardiff (1966, p. 50); [9]Svalastoga (1962, p. 49); [10]Tardiff (1966, p. 50); [11]McClintock and Gibson (1961, Tables 6 and 7).

locations.[9] Aggravated assaults in the home were most likely to happen in the living room and outside attacks on the street.

The national survey data showed that women of both races were more commonly assault victims or offenders in the home. Men more often participated in outside brawls.[10] Primary group assaults mostly took place indoors, whereas non-primary group combatants tended to fight outside.[11] The patterns resembled homicide, though one departure was an intraracial assault skew inside and an interracial dispersion outside.[12]

Foreign Comparisons. The assault data from Montreal in Table A-2 follow the same basic pattern as in the urban United States.

Forcible Rape

The United States. Other U.S. studies confirm the leading role of residences as places where the crime actually occurs. They also concur with the national survey that outside locations grow in importance for uncleared data relative to cleared data.[13]

Cars, alleys, and only then the street were the ranking outdoor locations in the national survey. Regardless of where and how men may first approach women who are subsequently raped, the discernible pattern is to find a more intimate, non-public place, even if it is only the back seat of an automobile.

There was little variation between all-black and all-white contexts in the national survey, but intraracial rapes happened outside less frequently than black-white attacks. The home was prominent in incest and for other primary group relationships. Outside locations grew in use when the relationship was non-primary.[14]

Foreign Comparisons. Table A-2 shows that rapes in Montreal followed the same pattern as the urban United States. Yet 70 percent of the events studied in Denmark between 1946 and 1958 were *outside*. The most likely victims were women walking or bicycling home late at night, either alone or with casual male acquaintances.[15] The Danish figures, however, were from the entire country rather than just from urban centers, and this resulted in a heavy representation of rural locales and provincial towns. In U.S. cities (and probably also in Montreal) the victim was very often picked up outside but eventually raped inside, presumably reflecting a desire by the offender(s) for greater seclusion in an area of high population density proliferating with accessible inside places. This may not have been necessary or convenient in the non-urban environ of the typical Danish rape studied by Svalastoga.

Rapists among urban Bantus living in Port Elizabeth, South Africa, also tended to attack outside, according to Laubscher. Offenders were usually "idle delinquent youths who rape[d] single girls or women in dark streets or out-of-the-way places."[16]

Robbery

The United States. Commercial establishments and outside locations also absorbed most armed robberies in earlier studies.[17]

The tendency for more female victimization indoors and male victimization outside, regardless of race, held for armed robbery in the national survey. All-black and black-white armed robberies were usually outside, but the few white-white encounters gravitated to "other indoor" locations.[18]

A more noticeable portion (about one-sixth) of unarmed than armed robberies in the national survey took place in the home. Without a weapon, robbers seldom chose commercial establishments. Three-quarters of all unarmed jobs were outside, primarily on the street.

The sex-race distributions of the two forms of robbery differed, but non-primary group relationships were usually the rule.[19]

Foreign Comparisons. The locational profile in Montreal and London very much resembled U.S. cities (Table A-2).

Temporal Patterns

Summary of the National Survey

The temporal aspects of crime—the month of year, day of week, hour of day—have been intensively studied throughout the last two centuries. Guerry and Quetelet related French crimes against the person to places where warmer weather is prevalent. Levi's survey in England reached a similar conclusion. Georg von Mayr's reference to the "influence of nature," Enrico Ferri and William Douglas Morrison's "cosmic" consideration of crime, Meyer's "tellurionic" interpretations, and Gaedeken's speculation about the "physicochemical influence of meteorologic agents" on crime motivated a number of studies on the relationship between crime and specific weeks, months, seasons, and climate.[20]

Today, the cosmic and tellurionic have been discarded. Temporal patterns, like locations and certain other variables, are seen not so much as causal imperatives as situational correlates.

There was little important monthly variation in the national aggregate of survey clearances, except for a lower occurrence of armed robbery in the summer months relative to the rest of the year. The homicide, assault, and rape frequencies were highest in July-August, but other consecutive two-month spans also sustained numerous attacks. Friday through Sunday set the weekly interval standing out in homicide and assault. A crime peak on Saturday-Sunday was more singularly prevalent in forcible rape, and the Thursday-Saturday period contained the majority of armed and unarmed robberies. The time between 4 p.m. and 4 a.m. hosted the most homicides and assaults. Rape peaked more narrowly, between 8 p.m. and 4 a.m. This interval was also highest for armed robbery, but events between noon and 8 p.m. were not far behind. Early evening and afternoon hours were even more attractive in unarmed robberies.[21]

The crystalization of armed robbery in colder months can be partially explained by the greater economic privation experienced then by the poor, at least in some parts of the country, and the expansion of nighttime hours, with their protective cloak. In addition, the increased volume of business and shopping activity centered around Christmas offers more opportunities. The failure of homicide, assault, and rape to be dramatically and significantly higher during the summer suggests that Quetelet's "thermic law of delinquency," postulating that warmer months and climates are associated with higher crime rates against person and cooler months and climates with higher rates against property, is not as strongly operative, at least in this country for serious violence, as early observers believed.

The loading of serious violent crimes on weekends is an intuitively reasonable tendency in an economic society committed to a five-day work week followed by a Saturday and Sunday of leisure, a traditional time of letting off steam and engaging in more remissive behavior. Opportunities for personal contacts between friends and relatives are more abundant from Friday evening to Sunday evening. Alcohol is often present when these crimes, as well as rape, occur (see *Violence, Race and Culture*), and weekend nights are receptive to social imbibing and drunken sprees. The unravelling of leisure time offers more social contexts potentially leading to rape by friends or acquaintances and situations where strangers have easier access to women. Friday is payday, and so a relationship can be hypothesized with some confidence between robbery, the greater accumulation of money in commercial establishments and the increased circulation of money generally. To do one's thing is to spend, especially in the ghetto, where *Violence, Race and Culture* suggests that the ephemeral nostrum of immediate gratification may often have as its only alternative no gratification at all. Temptation opportunities created by careless behavior with money are manifest on Friday and Saturday more than during the rest of the week.

In the same way, social engagements, personal encounters between friends and intimates, drinking and temptation opportunities are more common to night life than to daytime activity. It is no wonder that weekend nights are generally the most prone to aggressive violence, and the abundance of early morning interludes is recurrently traceable to behavior set into motion the previous night. Nocturnal commission of robbery, as well as many of the aggressive crimes occurring outdoors, is facilitated by darkness. The business hours of commercial establishments and the increased chance of encountering people in charge of money and goods or in recent receipt of wages or bank withdrawals suggest why robbery uniquely extends into the daylight hours.

There were some divergences, but on balance the survey's national urban findings were consistent with annual variation by month published for all reporting areas by the FBI[22] and with monthly, daily, and hourly frequencies recorded in single-city investigations.[23]

Regional temporal patterns more likely than not gravitated to the national profile, especially by hour of day. Among the exceptions, armed robbery did not peak during the winter in the southern cities, and there were high western frequencies of homicide and assault between January and March and of robbery at the beginning of the work week.[24]

Foreign Comparisons

Month. Rejected by the national survey data, the "thermic law" was built largely upon nineteenth-century European homicide information.[25] But, among more recent foreign examinations, only the results from the Maria tribe in India showed a strong relation between the hot season and a high frequency of homicide.[26] The studies in Montreal, Florence, Israel, Africa, Delhi, Ceylon, and Singapore did not bring out any obvious correlation.[27]

The one source of comparable assault data—Montreal—showed no clear monthly trend.[28] As with homicide, the earlier European literature on rape (and sexual offenses generally) reported some rise in the warmer months.[29] In two of the more recent seasonal accounts, Montreal evidenced no consistent pattern, but Denmark did have a summer high..[30] In his summary of the literature, Amir concluded that "the association between season and forcible rape does exist but it is not a strong and consistent one."[31] Only Canadian results were found for robbery, and they revealed the winter-high, summer-low tendency characteristic of American armed robberies.[32]

Day. The modal American weekend homicide and the accompanying perspectives on leisure time, greater remissiveness and the relief of tensions accumulated over the past five working days were broadly applicable to Montreal, England and Wales, Finland, and Delhi.[33]

Yet there was little variation in the Southern Province of Ceylon, Tuesday having the greatest homicide frequency. Jayewardene and Ranasinghe observe that in a country with high employment, homicide is reasonable on weekends—for the reasons discussed earlier. But, at the time of the study, there was high unemployment, so that the weekend explanation had less applicability.[34] In addition, agrarian life in developing countries is not conditioned to a regular post-week reprise from work, and alcohol, often homemade, must be consumed a short time after being prepared.

There was little weekly homicide variation in Israel as well. But everyone works who wants to. Jews and Arabs belong to non-drinking cultures, so the absence of alcoholic catalysts during weekend leisure-time activities, combined, of course, with the shutdown of activity on the Saturday Sabbath, may partially explain Israel's lack of conformity to weekend concentrations in other nations with full employment.[35]

The weekend skew of assaults in Montreal followed the American urban experience.[36] Earlier European observations on rape did not depart from the U.S. Saturday-Sunday loading,[37] and this was similarly the case in the more recent data from Montreal and Denmark.[38] Robbery was highest from Thursday to Saturday in Montreal and London,[39] as in American cities, presumably for like reasons: the end-of-the-week pay and the business and personal temptation opportunities generated by more rapidly circulating money.

Hour. Hours of work, leisure and sleep vary a bit among countries, but like the United States, homicides in Canada, England and Wales, Finland, Delhi, and the Southern Province of Ceylon,[40] as well as assaults in Canada,[41] normally reached a low point during the early morning hours when most people are asleep and peaked after work, when, in Jayewardene and Ranasinghe's words:

The individual, freed from the burden of occupational routine, has time to contemplate and discuss his grievances with others;
his occupational frustrations, removed from the context of his occupation, assume a different flavour;
the mental and physical fatigue is greatest; and
he is made acutely aware of the domestic needs that he cannot successfully meet.[42]

Israel again refused to fit the mold, however, with no period of the day having an especially high frequency of killing.[43]

The earlier European studies[44] and later publications from Denmark and Finland[45] underscored the American tendency for rape to be somewhat more concentrated later at night than homicide and assault (although the time intervals used were too broad to be sure in Montreal[46]). Afternoon robbery in Montreal was less apparent than in the United States.[47] This was also true of London in 1950, but the 1957 results were more in accord with the American frequency of daylight events.[48]

Multiple Offenders

Summary of the National Survey

The police report data in the national survey did not consistently specify whether gang activity was suspected or confirmed. All that could be coded with certainty was the number of offenders. The frequency of two or more offenders in the national aggregate of clearances rose from 8 percent in homicide and 14 percent for assault to 21 percent in rape and 58 percent in both armed and unarmed robbery[49] (Table A-3).

It is likely that a sizeable proportion of the multiple offender armed robberies in the national survey indicate a process of "mobbing up" to achieve a number optimal for a given job. Although the complexity of some professional heists demands a division of labor spread over more than one partner, there is also evidence that careful planning seeks to keep the size as small as possible. This ensures a bigger cut per person but is also done to minimize the risk of apprehension after a successful robbery. A professional is more often caught by police being tipped off than by his failing en flagrante or being traced through imaginative, independent detective work.[50]

Among the single-city studies, results on multiple offenders were comparable to the national survey in Philadelphia and Houston homicides, but Burnham's later New York data show a higher proportion of multiple offenders. Pittman and Handy's St. Louis assaults and Normandeau's Philadelphia robberies showed relatively lower percentages of two or more offenders. Frequencies of rape multiples were higher in Philadelphia but roughly the same in New York and Denver.[51]

The most noticeable variations when race-specific breakdowns were made on the survey national aggregates showed higher percentages of multiple offenders in black-on-white than intraracial homicides and armed robberies.[52] There was a relatively lower proportion of western forcible rapes with three or more offenders and a relatively higher frequency of northeastern armed robberies with three or more.[53]

Foreign Comparisons

Homicides in Montreal, England and Wales, Scotland, Denmark, Western Uganda, rural India, and among Jews in Israel more or less held to the single offender tendency in the United States (Tables A-3 and A-4).[54] But victims of multiple offender killings fell with increased frequency in Delhi, Ceylon, and among Arabs in Israel. Are group and gangs legitimately indicated, or do the figures only show how zealous the police are in rounding up suspects? Most Ceylenese cases of multiple offenders, at least, revolved about members of opposing family groups, and gang activity was discounted.[55]

Multiples operated more in Montreal assaults than in U.S. cities. Domestic assaults usually came singly in London, but multiples were more abundant in pub, cafe, and street assaults. The Canadian and Danish rape figures were not inconsistent with American cities, where two or more offenders participated in 21 percent of the clearances. In his impressionistic account of Port Elizabeth Bantu rapes, Laubscher ventures that, "the typical pattern is for several persons to blindfold and put a cloth into the victim's mouth while others hold her legs

Table A-3
The Number of Arrested Offenders, by Crime and Country (Percent)

Crime & Country / Number of Offenders	Criminal Homicide							Aggravated Assault
	United States Urban (17 City Survey Clearances)	Denmark[1] Entire Country 1934-1939 and	Israel[2] Entire Country (Jewish Pop. 2/3 urban, Non-Jewish Pop. rural) 1950-1964				Ceylon[3] Southern Province (Both Urban and Rural Areas)	United States Urban (17 City Survey, Clearances)
			Western Jews	Oriental Jews	Non-Jews	Total		
	1967	1946-1951					1960	
One	92.5	97.2	85.0	76.0	59.0	71.0	52.3	86.4
Two or More	7.5	2.8	15.0	24.0	41.0	29.0	42.5	13.6
Unknown or Miscellaneous	0	0	0	0	0	0	5.2	0
Total	100.0 (608)	100.0 (177)	100.0 (66)	100.0 (90)	100.0 (117)	100.0 (273)	100.0 (88)	100.0 (1238)

Crime & Country / Number of Offenders	Aggravated Assault — England[4] Urban (London) 1957		Forcible Rape		Robbery			
			United States Urban (17 City Survey Clearances) 1967	Denmark[5] Entire Country (Mostly Rural Areas & Provincial Cities) 1946-1958	United States Urban (17 City Survey, Clearances) 1967		England[6] Urban (London)	
	Domestic Assaults	Assault in Pubs, Cafes, on Streets, etc.			Armed Robbery	Unarmed Robbery	1950	1957
One	82.5	60.3	78.8	84.0	41.6	41.8	39.0	35.5
Two or More	17.5	39.7	21.2	16.0	58.4	58.4	54.4	60.0
Unknown or Miscellaneous	0	0	0	0	0	0	6.6	4.5
Total	100.0 (600)	100.0 (908)	100.0 (522)	100.0 (141)	100.0 (310)	100.0 (288)	100.0 (287)	100.0 (462)

References: [1] Svalastoga (1956); [2] Landau and Drapkin (1968, p. 38); [3] Jayewardene and Ranasinghe (1963, p. 83); [4] McClintock (1963a, p. 48); [5] Svalastoga (1962, p. 49); [6] McClintock and Gibson (1961, p. 24).

Table A-4
Ratio of Number of Arrested Offenders to Number of Cleared Cases, by Crime and Country

Crime and Country	Criminal Homicide							
	United States Urban (17 City Survey, Clearances) 1967	Canada[1] Urban (Montreal) 1964	England and Wales[2] Entire Country 1967	Scotland[3] Entire Country 1967	Italy[4] Urban (Florence) 1951-1963	Western Uganda[5] Rural 1955-1968	India[6] Urban (Delhi) 1963	India[7] Rural (Maria Tribe) 1921-1941
Ratio	1.1	1.3	1.2	1.4	1.2	1.2	2.0	1.1

Crime and Country	Aggravated Assault		Forcible Rape		Robbery		
	United States Urban (17 City Survey, Clearances) 1967	Canada[8] Urban (Montreal) 1964	United States Urban (17 City Survey, Clearances) 1967	Canada[9] Urban (Montreal) 1964	United States Urban (17 City Survey, Clearances) 1967 Armed Robbery / Unarmed Robbery		Canada[10] Urban (Montreal) 1964
Ratio	1.2	1.6	1.2	1.1	1.6	1.7	2.1

References: [1] Tardiff (1966, p. 83); [2] Gibson and Klein (1969, p. 15); [3] Gibson and Klein (1969, p. 81); [4] Simondi (1970); [5] Mushanga (1970); [6] Rao (1968, p. 19); [7] Elwin (1943, p. 39); [8] Tardiff (1966, p. 83); [9] Tardiff (1966, p. 83); [10] Tardiff (1966, p. 83).

apart and take their turn."[56] Robbery in Canada and England and Wales did not depart from the American profile.

The penchant was therefore roughly upheld: within the confines of available cross-cultural information, robberies appear to more frequently involve multiple offenders than the other serious violent crimes.

The inferential leap (made in *Violence, Race and Culture*) that groups and gangs are therefore more likely to be engaged in acquisitive action when they turn to violence at all is more difficult to make from the international than the American data. Few of the foreign studies discuss the relationship between multiple offenders and gangs, the foreign gang literature is undeveloped in the main and the composition of violent gang activity is rarely specified.

The facts at hand do allow the assertion that at various times since the Second World War, youthful groups and gangs have emerged abroad, with interests criminal as well as political. Consider the Teddy-boys, rockers, and skinheads of England, the Halbstarken (half-strong) of West Germany and Austria, the Skinnknutte (leather jackets) of Sweden, the blousons noirs (black jackets) of France, the stilyagi (style boys) of Russia, the taiyozoku (children of the sun) of Japan, and the bodgies of Australia.[57] There is undoubtedly some association between these aggregates and post-war increases in the incidence and seriousness of youth and juvenile deviance throughout the world.[58]

Notes and References

1. For the data on non-clearances, see Curtis (1972). No trend figures on place of occurrence for any of the crimes are available. It should be reiterated that the national survey data are frequency distributions for a sample of crimes, not incidence figures per 100,000 population. Table A-1 does not give the probability of victimization (an incidence figure) inside or outside. It states that *when or if* someone is killed the location is more likely to be inside than outside and *when or if* a person is robbed the location is more likely to be outside than inside. If we do integrate in rates, the probability of being victimized on the street is much greater in robbery and assault than in rape and homicide becuase of the higher incidence as well as the higher outside proportions in the first two crimes.

2. See Curtis (1972).

3. Fifty-one percent of Wolfgang's (1958, pp. 123, 294) clearances were in the home, although 58 percent of the non-clearances occurred on streets. The D.C. Crime Commission (1966, p. 42) reported almost two-thirds of the homicides studied to be at the residence of victim, offender, or an acquaintance of either. Twenty-eight percent happened on the street. Burnham (1973, p. 1) found that 38 percent of the New York homicides studied occurred on the street. In Chicago, Voss and Hepburn (1968, p. 504) found more homicides in

the home than any other single location. Schafer (1965, p. 159) recorded 44 percent of his Florida killings in the home and 35 percent outside. Forty-two percent of the homicides Pokorny (1965, pp. 481-2) studied in Houston were at home and 26 percent on public streets, alleys, or fields.

4. Wolfgang's (1958, p. 124) ranking was bedroom, living room, kitchen and stair-hall.

5. Wolfgang's (1958, p. 124) figures were similar.

6. Wolfgang's (1958, p. 124) results in Philadelphia and Voss and Hepburn's (1968, p. 505) findings in Chicago were consistent.

7. See Curtis (1972). Mate slayings, in particular, were likely to be at home. Husbands were killed in the kitchen about twice as often as wives. As a frequent family meeting place, especially among the lower classes, where frustrations accumulated during the day may be released, where questions about the family budget are raised, where women spend much of their time, and as a place where deadly weapons are handy, the kitchen is not an unexpected setting for wives who kill their husbands. Wolfgang (1958, p. 215) also found the leading husband-wife homicide location pattern to be in the home. But fully 85 percent of his Philadelphia cases occurred in the home (compared to 49 percent in the national survey). He concurred that the percentage of husbands killed in the kitchen by their wives was about twice as high as the husband-wife percentage.

8. Landau and Drapkin (1968, p. 26).

9. In St. Louis, 46 percent of Pittman and Handy's (1964, p. 464) cases occurred on public streets and 38 percent in residences. Slightly less than half of the Washington assaults reported by the D.C. Crime Commission (1966, p. 79) happened in the home and more than a third on the street. In Chicago, Reiss (1967, pp. 111-2) found that the "most common premises for persons to be victimized in all major assaults against persons with a dangerous weapon are the private residence and public premises." The location varied considerably according to race, sex, and type of assault, however. For example, for all persons victimized by white male offenders with guns, the most common location was the street, but black men and women most commonly victimized one another in a gun assault when they were in a private residence. Nearly a third of Schafer's (1965, p. 159) Florida assaults occurred in the home, and a similar proportion was found for outside locations.

10. In the same vein, Pittman and Handy (1964, p. 464) found that females committed assault more indoors and males outdoors.

11. Pittman and Handy (1964, p. 464) observed a comparable pattern.

12. See Curtis (1972).

13. Fifty-six percent of Amir's (1965, pp. 300, 576) Philadelphia clearances were at the residence of one of the participants, but the frequency of open-space rapes was much greater for non-clearances. In New York, Chappell and Singer (1973, p. 61) found that the greatest proportion of rape (47 percent) happened inside apartments. Fifty-eight percent of the rapes MacDonald (1971, p. 33) and

Giacinti (1973, p. 32) observed in Denver were indoors or in residences. In Chicago, Reiss (1967, pp. 103-4) found that a majority of rape victims were victimized in residences. "What is also surprising is how few of the offenses of forcible rape occur in what might be called public places such as school property, parks, alleys or streets."

14. See Curtis (1972).

15. Svalastoga (1962, p. 50).

16. Laubscher (1965, p. 246).

17. In Philadelphia, Normandeau (1968, p. 244) found more than half of his armed plus unarmed robberies to be on the street, 21 percent in commercial establishments, and only 7 percent in private residences. Armed and unarmed robberies were most likely to occur on the street or in a business setting in Reiss' (1967, p. 108) Chicago study. Less than 4 percent of the Washington (armed plus unarmed) robberies tabulated by the D.C. Crime Commission (1966, p. 66) happened in a home; 80 percent were on the street. The thefts with violence reported by Schafer (1965, p. 159) in Florida happened mostly in shops or stores (45 percent) or outside (30 percent).

18. See Curtis (1972).

19. See Curtis (1972).

20. Schafer (1968, p. 85).

21. The national survey tables on temporal patterns have not been reproduced here. They can be found in Curtis (1972).

22. See FBI (1967, pp. 21-22) for the 1963 to 1967 moving average.

23. Wolfgang (1958, pp. 99, 106, 108) found "a slight but insignificant association between seasons and the number of criminal homicides." The most frequent days in Philadelphia were Saturday (32 percent), Friday (17 percent), and Sunday (17 percent), with much lower percentages for the rest of the week. The most lethal hours were clearly 8:00 p.m. to 1:59 a.m. (50 percent), followed by 2:00 p.m. to 7:59 p.m. (25 percent), 2:00 a.m. to 7:59 a.m. (16 percent) and 8:00 a.m. to 1:59 p.m. (9 percent).

The winter and summer months were relatively equal in Chicago homicide events for Voss and Hepburn (1968, pp. 503-4). Most killings were on the weekend, with Saturday highest. The hours of greatest frequency were 8 p.m. to midnight.

Pokorny (1965, p. 481) observed no clear monthly homicide pattern in Houston. Killings were most frequent on Saturday, Sunday and Friday respectively. About half the cases occurred between 8:00 p.m. and 2:00 a.m., while the 2:00 a.m. to 2:00 p.m. span accounted for only a quarter.

The St. Louis aggravated assaults studied by Pittman and Handy (1964, pp. 463-4) showed no pronounced monthly variation. The most frequent days were Saturday (30 percent), Friday (18 percent), and Sunday (14 percent). Forty-four percent of all assaults occurred between 6:00 p.m. and midnight, with the midnight to 6:00 a.m. span second.

In Washington, the differential between the month with most assaults (July) and the lowest month (January) was only 2 percent according to the D.C. Crime Commission (1966, pp. 67-68). Sixty-five percent of the events studied happened on Saturday, Sunday, or Friday, respectively. "In 1961-1965 the 3-hour period from midnight to 3:00 a.m. accounted for 19 percent of all aggravated assaults while the 6-hour period from 6:00 p.m. to midnight accounted for 43 percent."

Although Amir (1965, pp. 597-8) found Philadelphia rapes to increase somewhat during the hot summer months, "there was no significant association either with the season or with the month of the year." Rape was significantly associated with certain days of the week. The highest concentration (53 percent) was on weekends, with Saturday the peak day. The top risk hours were between 8:00 p.m. and 2:00 a.m.; almost half of all events occurred weekends between 8:00 p.m. and midnight.

April and July through September were the months of greatest danger to women in MacDonald's (1971, pp. 29-30) Denver rape study. Over half of the attacks came between 10 p.m. and 4 a.m., with Saturday night-Sunday morning leading the week.

In Washington, rape was not a markedly seasonal crime, although more occurred in July and August (a 20 percent total) and fewer in October and December (a 13 percent total). The most common days reported by the D.C. Crime Commission (1966, pp. 48-49) were Saturday (20 percent) and Sunday (15 percent). "The period from 6:00 p.m. to 3:00 a.m. accounted for 59 percent of all rape offenses."

In New York, Chappell and Singer (1973, p. 10) found no clear seasonal rape pattern. There were weekend and 8:00 p.m. to 2:00 a.m. peaks.

Agopian et al. (1972) found the highest percentage of rapes (33 percent) in Oakland to occur in the summer.

Normandeau (1968, pp. 211-7) found a significant association between the winter season and the number of robberies (armed and unarmed) in Philadelphia. The winter (November-February) frequency was 43 percent; the spring-autumn (March, April, September, October) frequency, 29 percent; and the summer (May-August) frequency, 28 percent. About 45 percent of the robberies occurred on Friday and Saturday. "There is no build up to this Friday-Saturday high, for the frequency during the remaining days of the week varies only slightly." The most dangerous hours were between 8:00 p.m. and 2:00 a.m. (38 percent), followed by 2:00 p.m. to 8:00 p.m. (34 percent), 8:00 a.m. to 2:00 p.m. (17 percent) and 2:00 a.m. to 8:00 a.m. (11 percent).

The D.C. Crime Commission (1966, p. 55) reported that more robberies (armed and unarmed combined) occurred in the winter than in any other season in Washington. December and January alone accounted for 22 percent. Forty-three percent were committed on Friday or Saturday. The time intervals most associated with robbery were 6:00 p.m. to midnight (52 percent) and noon to 6:00 p.m. (20 percent).

24. See Curtis (1972).

25. This earlier material is reviewed in Wolfgang (1958, p. 97).

26. Even Elwin (1943, p. 42) adds some qualifications, however:

There is a definite increase in the hottest months of the year, April and May, and a corresponding increase in September and October, which are also hot and enervating. On the other hand these variations may not be due entirely to climatic causes. The figure for June and July, for example, is only half that of the figure for September and October, but June and July are the months during which everybody is hard at work in their fields. June, in which only 3 murders occurred, is the busiest month of the year and sees the breaking of the monsoon. April and October, which show a heavy incidence of homicides, are festival periods, which are not only occasions for heavy drinking, but, by providing opportunities for people to meet together, make it possible for disputes to arise and old grievances to be remembered. Yet the influence of festivals must not be exaggerated.

27. In Montreal, Tardiff (1966, p. 41) reported that August was the month of greatest frequency, yet July had the lowest. Simondi (1970) found homicides were highest in Florence during the months of December, September, April, and March, respectively. Landau and Drapkin (1968, p. 17) reported slight peaks in March-April and August-September, but a slight trough in June-July. No correlations between month and homicide frequency were present among the Luyia in Africa, according to Bohannon (1960, p. 161). Among the Tiv in Africa, the slight monthly variation was related to factors other than the temperature peaks in Bohannon (1960, p. 34):

Arrangement of the homicides by month of the year reveals that killings are most numerous in February, March, and April, the months of the late dry season. When the hunting accidents are deducted—most of them occur at this season—there is still a slight increase in killings in those months. No single pattern accounts for the increase, which is a general one. This period is the one in which Tiv have the largest amounts of food, perform the most ceremonies, and give the most parties. The period from May to December, which shows a slightly lower incidence of homicide, is the time of heaviest agricultural labor, tasks in which mainly small family groups take part. In any case, the differences by time of year are small, and seem to be of less importance than they are in Europe or America.

In Western Uganda, Mushanga (1970, p. 95) could not verify the hypothesis that homicide varies by season and climate. In Delhi, Rao (1968, p. 10) observed that the most homicides occurred over the April-June period, but there were almost as many in January-March and July-September, so it was "difficult to accept that climatic conditions . . . have any influence on the trends of homicide." In Ceylon, Jayewardene and Ranasinghe (1963, p. 69) found that the highest homicide frequency was in February-March, then June-July; the lowest was in May. In Singapore, Ting and Tan (1969, pp. 243, 247) concluded that "there did not seem to be any time of the year when homicide was more rife."

28. Tardiff (1966, p. 41).

29. For example, consider this summary by Amir (1965, p. 169):

Lombroso, on the basis of statistical figures in England, France, and Italy, showed that forcible rape was most prevalent in the warm weather season, from June to September, and also, that the crime of rape increases in the "hot years."

And Von Hentig, (1948, p. 349) concluded from European data:

Then there is another peak on the Spring and early Summer. At this time the crimes of violence and sex crimes reach a maximum; they rise again, but less vehemently in September or October.

See also Falk (1952).

30. In Canada, Tardiff (1966, p. 41) saw the peak come in April and the trough in November, with little other variation.

In Denmark, the rape frequency was lowest over December-March, according to Svalastoga (1962, p. 2).

31. Amir (1965, p. 175).

32. Tardiff (1966, p. 41).

33. In Canada, Tardiff (1966, p. 45) found that Saturday dominated, although the Friday figure was not high and the Sunday percentage negligible. Studying a select group of 208 murderers sentenced to death in England and Wales between 1886 and 1905, McDonald (1911, p. 95) found the greatest number was on Saturday (although the lowest was on Sunday). In Finland, Verkko (1951, p. 82), reported that the worst homicide day was Sunday, with Saturday and Monday close behind. In Delhi, Rao (1968, Table 7), disclosed that Sunday dominated, and there was little variation among the other days.

34. Jayewardene and Ranasinghe (1963, pp. 73-74).

35. Landau and Drapkin (1968, p. 22).

36. Assaults in Montreal peaked from Friday to Sunday, with Saturday the highest, according to Tardiff (1966, p. 45).

37. For example, Amir (1965, p. 180) makes the following observations:

Bonger reports that in Europe most of the crimes of violence, including rape, are committed on Saturday and Sunday and are related to the consumption of alcohol on these days. Falk, who summarizes the early European studies, says that for Italy, France and Germany, weekends and especially Saturday are the high incidence days.

Von Hentig maintains that crimes of violence and serious sex crimes culminate on Saturday and Sunday. He, however, warns against placing an absolute reliance on figures obtained in such data. He says that often "the hour . . . is not established with absolute safety." Thus, some Saturday rapes really take place on Sunday. Later he adds that this Saturday night criminality is "obviously caused by alcoholic and other excesses."

38. In Montreal, Tardiff (1966, p. 45) found that rapes reached a peak on Friday. In Denmark, rapes were highest on Sunday, according to Svalastoga

(1962, p. 49). LeMaire's earlier investigation (1946) concluded the peak was Saturday-Sunday.

39. Tardiff (1966, p. 45) and McClintock and Gibson (1961, p. 132).

40. In Montreal, Tardiff (1966, p. 48) observed that the 4 p.m.-midnight and midnight-8 a.m. periods dominated (although it was assumed that the frequency fell off during the latter part of the second interval). In his study of murderers sentenced to death in England and Wales between 1886 and 1905, MacDonald (1911, p. 95) found that about one-fifth were committed between 10 p.m. and midnight and nearly half between 8 p.m. and 2 a.m. In Finland, homicide and assault occurred mainly during the late evening hours in Verkko's (1951, p. 82) study. In Delhi, Rao (1968, Table 8) found 65 percent of the murders to be committed between 6 p.m. and 6 a.m., although it was assumed that the frequency fell off during the later hours. In Ceylon, Jayewardene and Rana-singhe (1963, p. 75) concluded that the least number of homicides occurred between 2 a.m. and 6 a.m. when most people were in bed and the most, between 6 p.m. and 10 p.m.

41. The 4 p.m.-midnight period had the highest assault frequency, according to Tardiff (1966, p. 45).

42. Jayewardene and Ranasinghe (1963, p. 75).

43. Landau and Drapkin (1968, p. 23).

44. For example, consider Amir (1965, p. 184):

Falk, in summarizing the early European studies, concludes that most of them indicate that rape is prevalent in the late evening hours, the peak being the two hours before midnight. He attributes this fact to the consumption of alcohol in the evening, especially on weekends.

45. In Denmark, Svalastoga (1962, p. 49) found two-thirds of all rapes occurred between 10 p.m. and 2 a.m., and LeMaire (1946) concluded that the peak time was midnight to 6 a.m. In Finland, rape occurred mainly during the late evening hours, according to Verkko (1951, p. 82).

46. Eight-hour intervals were used; 4 p.m.-midnight had the highest frequency, with midnight-8 a.m. a close second in Tardiff (1966, p. 45).

47. In Montreal, Tardiff (1966, p. 45) found the 4 p.m.-midnight period to dominate.

48. In London, McClintock and Gibson (1961, p. 131) reported 55 percent of the robberies in 1950 were between 9 p.m. and 3 a.m., with 30 percent between noon and 9 p.m. In 1957, the figures were 48 percent and 45 percent, respectively.

49. It was not possible to obtain row totals from Table A-3—that is, to ask what percent of major violent crime involving three or more offenders was homicide, what percent assault, and so forth. The weighting system applied to the data allows displays of a given variable (or cross-tabulated set of variables) for any one crime but does not permit frequencies to be added across crimes. (See Appendix B.)

50. DeBaun (1950, p. 71).

51. Wolfgang (1958, p. 27) found 550 victims and 621 known offenders in Philadelphia homicide clearances. There were 425 victims and 430 offenders in Pokorny's (1965, p. 479) Houston homicides. In New York, Burnham (1971) found that 76 percent of the homicides had single offenders. Of Pittman and Handy's (1964, p. 467) 241 St. Louis assault cases, 219 were one-on-one. Amir (1965, p. 413) showed that 57 percent of his Philadelphia rapes were single offender attacks; 16 percent involved two offenders; and 27 percent, three or more. Chappell and Singer (1973, p. 72) found that 77 percent of the rapes studied in New York had one offender. In Denver, 81 percent of MacDonald's (1971, p. 160) victims were raped by one male, 8 percent by two and 11 percent by three or more. Giacinti's (1973) later Denver findings were similar. Only 33 percent of Normandeau's (1968, p. 171) Philadelphia robberies involved two or more offenders. The number of uncleared homicides with two or more offenders in the survey was much greater, however (36 percent, although only a relatively small proportion of all homicides are not solved). Frequencies for two or more offenders were slightly higher for assault and unarmed robbery non-clearances than clearances, but almost identical patterns prevailed in rape and armed robbery.

52. See Curtis (1972).

53. See Curtis (1972).

54. The two different data formats in Tables A-3 and A-4 respond to the different ways information on multiple offenders was shown in the respective foreign studies.

55. Jayewardene and Ranasinghe (1963, p. 90).

56. Laubscher (1965, p. 246).

57. Fyvel (1962, c. 2).

58. Fyvel (1962, c. 2).

Appendix B:
Methodology

Appendix B describes the data collection, processing, analysis, and basic methodology of the national survey.

Collection and Sampling

Precise distributional criteria were not applied, but the 17 cities in the national survey were chosen to represent all sections of the country. Only cities of 250,000 or more were selected because they form the major locus of violent crime.

A local advisor was first established by the Violence Commission in each city (see Preface). Advisors were usually university social scientists. Some were professionals in government. Each advisor received a description of the survey and its sampling requirements. The Commission then contacted the Police Chief in each city, with the kind and valuable aid of an introductory letter by Mr. Quinn Tamm, Executive Director, International Association of Chiefs of Police. After the Commission's needs were explained to the police and a person within the force was assigned to implement the project (see Preface), the local advisor was brought in to supervise the sampling.

A 10 percent sample of police offense and, if suspects were apprehended, attached arrest reports from 1967 was requested for homicide, assault, rape, and robbery. The sample size was qualified by asking for no fewer than 50 nor more than 200 reports for any city-crime type. The lower bound was set to insure a statistically meaningful contribution (in a few instances, where less than 50 reports over the entire year were filed for a city-crime type, all reports were sent). The upper bound was required mainly because of New York, Detroit, Chicago, and Los Angeles, where the volumes for certain of the crimes (usually robbery or assault) were so great that a 10 percent sample would have been unmanageable for the Commission to code and process during the time available.

Advisors used systematic or random samples. Overall, the sampling was excellent. (Through no fault of the local advisor, New Orleans was the main exception—see below.) Once drawn, the reports were Xeroxed and sent to the Commission. Each advisor also submitted to the Commission a summary of his experience.

Coding and Verification

Students—mostly in law and some in the behavioral sciences—were hired in Washington to read the offense-arrest reports and record information on coding sheets, from which punchcards were made via an optical scanner.

A number of variables recorded on the coding sheets are not presented in the text or Appendix A. Social context and marital relationship added little to what could be said through victim-offender relationship. Information on alcohol presence, drug presence, offender occupation, victim occupation and prior arrests was rarely available on the police reports. (Earlier, single-city studies usually were able to report on items like alcohol presence or arrest record because the investigators were on the spot and able to dig more deeply into records.)

Definitions were initially reviewed verbally with the coders, who then filled out sample coding sheets under supervision and fed back any problems that arose. Thereafter, with the coders more on their own, the instruction was to contact the survey director whenever definitional questions or other ambiguities emerged. When a coder finished a city-crime type, the assistant survey director randomly sampled a small percentage of the police reports and verified the coding sheets for every item. Mistakes were corrected, and if any systematic error pattern was discerned, the coder was called in and the problem discussed and rectified. At the extreme, this resulted in one city-crime type being completely redone. A control sheet was filed for each city-crime type after this checking procedure was successfully completed.

When the coding sheets were run through the optical scanner, those with certain mechanical mistakes were rejected and corrections made. After conversion into punchcards, a more elaborate computer consistency-logic-range check was programmed and rejects were again corrected. The data were massaged to a state of arousal where diminishing marginal benefits were superseded by increasing marginal costs.

Analytical Bases

The police offense and arrest reports describe situations that may or may not involve multiple victims and offenders. There is usually just one of each in homicide, but multiples, especially of offenders, increasingly appear in the other crimes. How should they have been accounted for in describing the behavior patterns of interest? Statements could be made about victims and offenders separately: "Half of all mates killed were female and most robbers were male." Multiples could be avoided by talking about the case: "One third of the homicide cases occurred in the home." Or, the "interaction" between each offender and each individual victimized could be used as the basic unit of analysis. Say a report includes two offenders and one victim. There is just one case, but two victim-offender relationships, i.e., interactions.

It was decided to use whatever base seemed most appropriate for a given variable. (Previous work has been based on cases or victims and offenders treated separately.) The practical result was emphasis on the interaction. The discussions of race, sex, and age relationships, interpersonal relationships, motive, victim precipitation, offender weapon, and victim injury all address face-offs between each offender and his particular victim(s). An interaction base was accordingly deemed most sensitive to the informational demands. The considerations of location, temporal patterns and multiple offenders have a contextual objective that is above particular transactions. Here we only wanted to know where the event as an entity took place, when it happened or how many offenders played a role. The more encompassing case was therefore selected as the unit of analysis. The areal chapter plots victim, offender and crime locations separately and also computes distances between victim and offender, victim and crime, and offender and crime.

Each coding sheet contains the characteristics of and relationships between one offender and one victim. Each coding sheet, and the card punched from it, therefore represented one interaction. But interactions in the same case were given the same Violence Commission Identification Number, allowing just the cases to be run for location, temporal patterns, and multiple offenders. Similarly, victims and offenders could be picked out separately.

Note that if two offenders attacked one victim, two coding sheets were made out. Each sheet had the characteristics of a separate offender. But each recorded for the *same* victim. Thus, the presence of multiple offenders meant that victims were double counted (or triple counted, and so forth). This was negligible in homicide, but common in assault, rape, and robbery.

One interpretation of the procedure would be to see it as biased toward the victim. But it was really an intentional effort to give greater weight to victims attacked by more than one offender. Much more important, the positive features of the interaction vis-à-vis the alternative bases greatly outweighed the negative features (if one sees the victim double counting as a liability). Thus, treating victims and offenders separately precluded making "dynamic" interactional statements like "in x percent of all incidents a white victimized a white," which are particularly crucial in the analysis of race. And the case was too general a measuring rod in seeking relationships between specific victims and offenders.

As a test of the possible biases introduced by using interactions versus cases, the interaction-based interpersonal relationship data were comparatively run by case[1] and the case-based locational data by interaction. The data are presented in the original dissertation. It might be contended that an attack by more than one offender has a greater likelihood of occurring when the offenders are strangers to the victim or have some non-primary group relationship. Thus, it can be hypothesized that interaction based relationship figures will yield significantly higher non-primary group percentages and lower primary group frequencies than data based on cases. Because of the association between non-primary relationships and outdoor locations, it can be similarly hypothesized that interactions will yield significantly lower indoor percentages and higher outdoor frequencies than cases. These postulated results held in almost all instances; however, the disparities were small and the inferences that could be made from the case versus interaction data forms were the same.[2]

Data Processing

The total number of Xeroxed offense-arrest reports received from police was generally in close compliance with the sample size requested, although there were some departures for individual city-crime types. As the data were processed there was some attrition in the sample size. Outside of the loss of some cases because they proved unfounded or because they defied correction after consistency check rejection, the attrition was mostly for two reasons.

First, only clearances were sent by 4 of the cities. But the rest sent clearances plus non-clearances, in proportions reflecting local clearance rates. This meant that when it came to running just the clearances for the 17 cities aggregated together, the 4 mavericks would have been overrepresented, especially for crimes like robbery and assault with relatively low clearance rates. To adjust, enough clearances were randomly sampled out and discarded in the 4 cities to make the volume remaining equal to what would have been expected. (The expected clearance volume was the sample size requested times the clearance rate.)

Second, there were more problems involving one of the cities—New Orleans—which sent clearances only. A complicated set of restrictions and poor filing procedures made scientific sampling difficult if not impossible to attain. The sample was most doubtful for assault, and so it was decided to withhold all 128 reports sent to the Commission. Homicide, rape, and armed robbery clearances were accepted, however. (No unarmed robberies were made available.)

The Weighting System

One of the interests in the survey was to analyze clearances and non-clearances separately, to see whether the patterns were any different. Comparisons made in the text are based on the complete tabular analysis in the original dissertation.

It was not feasible to ask for separate 10 percent samples of clearances and non-clearances because, among other reasons, some police departments filed clearances and non-clearances together. It would have been prohibitive to divide them and then draw reports. The samples were simply drawn across the total number of cleared and uncleared reports considered together (except, of course, for the 4 cities not sending clearances). The relative proportions of cleared and uncleared reports received from each city thus were dependent upon police clearance rates, which varied greatly among departments, to say nothing of crime types. This meant that, for example, even though 10 percent of city A's crime produced a much larger volume of reports than 10 percent of city B's, it was possible to receive more cleared cases from B—if its clearance rates were sufficiently larger than A's.

Thus, if for the moment we consider the 17-city aggregate for clearances only, the result was that the sample size became a function of both the volume of crime in each city and the reported efficiency of police (as reflected in their clearance rates).

The situation was unsatisfactory from the perspective of what the relative influence of each city would be in the cleared "national city" composite. Say, for example, that the national aggregate had been composed of only two cities. If the volume of a certain kind of crime in A were twice B, and if all the interactions in A had offenders using Weapon 1, whereas all offenders in B used Weapon 2, then we would want the national sample to produce a percentage distribution having twice as many interactions with Weapon 1 than 2. But if the clearance rate in B were twice A, then the national weapons split would be 50-50. The percentages would be considered spurious because they partially reflected police efficiency, which has absolutely nothing to do with the basic characteristics of and relationships between victims and offenders—the information being sought. Rather, it would have been much closer to reality if the relative influence of each city in the cleared sample were only a function of that city's total volume crime-by-crime vis-à-vis the other cities.

A weighting system was devised to have just this effect. The matrix of weights is presented in the original dissertation and not reproduced here. In computing the weights, we began with the official total number of "offenses known" published in the FBI *Uniform Crime Reports* for each crime in each city for the year 1967.[3] FBI procedures are such that the number of "offenses known" is in effect the number of victims. Although it would have been preferable to use cases or interactions, the FBI does not report in such units: the most comprehensive totals published are these "offenses known" = victims figures, which therefore had to form the base of the weighting system.

For each crime, the total number of "offenses known" = victims in all 17 cities was calculated. The percentage for each city out of the total was then computed. Next, the same was done for the reports coded in the survey sample. For each crime, the total number of victims in the sample in all 17 cities was calculated. The percentage for each city out of the total was than computed.

After this was done, the weight computed for any particular crime in any particular city was simply that value which, when multiplied times the survey sample percent, produced the FBI "offenses known" percent.[4]

The same procedure was used for each city-crime type. Separate weights could not be computed for armed and unarmed robbery because the necessary *UCR* data for "offenses known" do not make the distinction. The same general robbery weight therefore had to be used for both armed and unarmed events.

Another weighting system was devised in the same way for the non-clearances.[5] With non-clearances missing from 4 of the cities, the "national city" aggregate here was composed of only 13 areas. Generalizability was correspondingly diminished.

The cleared weights were then multiplied times the cleared, processed Ns for each city-crime type, the bases being either cases or interactions, according to the variable. In the same way, the uncleared weights were multiplied times the uncleared, processed Ns. The aggregates formed the statistical number of cleared and uncleared interactions or cases listed in Table 1-1. These are the Ns upon which most tables in the text and appendices are based. (Some tables have fewer Ns because unknowns are eliminated.) The race-by-race, sex-by-sex and age-by-age tables only include interactions where the relevant characteristics are known for both victim and offender.

The weighted, statistical numbers thus eliminated the influence of clearance rates and were the basis of frequency distributions for the variables in which the relative importance of each city reflected the total volume of crime reported in that city.

Note that the weights had to be derived from volumes and proportions of victims ("offenses known"), but that they were then applied to interactions or cases to produce the statistical numbers.

With regard to interactions, the number of victims need not equal the number of interactions, especially in assault, rape, and robbery. In addition, the victim-offender ratio need not be constant among cities; the average number of interactions in a typical crime event can vary from city to city. And here is an important point. The victim-based weighting system that had to be used made the volume of cleared or uncleared interactions reflect the total volume of victims in the city, but at the same time kept any differential victim-offender ratios intact. In other words, the statistical readjustment in no way changed the average number of interactions in a typical crime event for any one city.[6]

With regard to cases, the number of victims similarly need not equal the number of cases. However, the case base does not have the nicely double-jointed quality of interactions, where victim weighting can be applied while not affecting offenders. Here a full-blown, apples-oranges problem existed—of applying victims to cases. There was no way to get around it—except to assume only one victim per case. Thus, when a weight of 2 was applied to a case-based city-crime type variable, the number of cases was doubled. Yet the resulting bias need not be considered a major difficulty, for single victims were more the rule than single offenders. More crucially, it turned out that case bases were appropriate only for the less important variables, and even there, the case distributions still proved roughly the same as the interaction frequencies.[7]

While eliminating the influence of clearance rates, the weighting systems also conveniently reinstated the relatively great importance that cities like New York, in particular, had in crimes such as assault and robbery—where the cutoff point of 200 meant that sample sizes were considerably less than 10 percent. Unsurprisingly, the cleared and uncleared weights assigned to New York assaults and robberies, among others, were well above 1.

One concern with the weighting systems was that very small and unrepre-sentative samples might be greatly magnified in influence by very large weights. However, as a rule, when weights considerably expanded the relative influence of a city-crime type vis-à-vis the rest of the aggregate, the original sample was reasonably large. When it was not, the magnification did not create a statistical number that proved influential in the aggregate.

The weighting system had to accept at face value the "offenses known" reported from each police department, and so any inaccurate reporting—by definitional quirk or by conscious plan—violated the integrity of the results. Nonetheless, it was unlikely that gross influences fell the wrong way. Regardless of reporting inaccuracies, for example, it would be inconceivable not to expect the New York robbery volume to vastly exceed Minneapolis.

In retrospect, methodological compromises had to be made at times and the best available second-best solutions converged upon in cleaning and processing the data. "One can be so much afraid of violating assumptions that he refuses to use any statistical techniques at all," writes Blalock. "Especially in a discipline characterized by exploratory studies and relatively imprecise scientific tech-niques, it is necessary to make compromises with reality."[8] The final output remained burdened by the impreciseness of the police report input, but the broadest patterns that have been inferred are for the most part defensible, particularly as they have been complemented by other work.

Notes and References

1. For multiple offenders, the victim-offender relationship among the major-ity was associated with the case. In the rare instances where other were ties, the case was not coded.

2. See Curtis (1972).

3. These and the FBI data for the other cities were taken from Table 57 of the 1967 *UCR*.

4. For more details, see Curtis (1972).

5. See Curtis (1972) for the matrix of weights for non-clearances.

6. For more details, see Curtis (1972).

7. See Curtis (1972).

8. Blalock (1960, p. 111).

Bibliography

Bibliography

Abelson, R.P. and J.W. Tukey. 1959. "Efficient Conversion of Non-Metric Information into Metric Information." *Proceedings, Social Statistics Section, American Statistical Association*, pp. 226-30.

Agopian, M., D. Chappell, and G. Geis. 1972. "Interracial Forcible Rape in a North American City." Paper presented at American Society of Criminology Conference, Caracas, November.

Allen, I., Jr. 1971. *Mayor: Notes on the Sixties.* New York: Simon and Schuster.

Allen, V.L., ed. 1970. *Psychological Factors in Poverty.* Chicago: Markham.

Amir, M. 1965. "Patterns in Forcible Rape." Ph.D. Dissertation. University of Pennsylvania.

————. 1971. *Patterns in Forcible Rape.* Chicago: University of Chicago Press.

Anderson, J. 1971. "The Victims of Rape." *San Francisco Chronicle*, June 17, p. 26.

Arnold, M.R. 1971. "The Silent Murders." *The National Observer*, September 6, p. 1.

Atlanta Commission on Crime and Delinquency. 1966. *Opportunity for Urban Excellence*, Atlanta, February.

Atlanta Magazine. 1972. "History of Black Atlanta."

Atlanta Region Metropolitan Planning Commission. 1971. *Safe Streets in '72*, Atlanta, September.

Avison, N.H. 1973. "Victims of Homicide." Paper presented at the First International Symposium on Victimology, Jerusalem, Israel, September 2-6.

Banfield, E. 1970. *The Unheavenly City: The Nature and Future of Our Urban Crisis.* Boston: Little, Brown & Co.

Bannon, J. 1974. "Social Conflict Assaults: Detroit, Michigan." Draft manuscript, March 18, Washington, D.C., The Police Foundation.

Baratz, J. and S. Baratz. 1972. "Black Culture on Black Terms: Rejection of the Social Pathology Model." In T. Kochman, ed., *Rappin' and Stylin' Out.* Urbana: University of Illinois Press.

Barclay, G.W. 1958. *Techniques of Population Analysis.* New York: Wiley. 1970.

Bard, M. 1970. "Training Police as Specialists in Family Crisis Intervention." Washington, D.C.: LEAA Institute Publication PR 70-1, May.

————and K. Ellison. 1974. "Crisis Intervention and Investigation of Forcible Rape." *The Police Chief*, May, pp. 68-73.

Barth, A. 1971. "Tokyo—The Lowest Crime Rate." *Washington Post*, November 23, p. A 18.

Batten, J.K. 1970. "You Must Be Out of Your Mind to be Out Alone in a Neighborhood Like This." *New York Times Magazine*, March 22, pp. 22, 23, 60.

Bayer, M. 1968. "A Comparative Study of Some Types of Property Crimes in Yugoslavia, Austria, and Poland." Mimeo, Institute of Criminology, Faculty of Law, University of Ljubijana, Yugoslavia, April.

Becker, H.S. and I.L. Horowitz. 1970. "The Culture of Civility." *Transaction* VII, pp. 12-19.

Berkowitz, L. 1967. "Experiments on Automation and Intent in Human Aggression." In C. Clemente and D. Lindsley, eds., *Aggression and Defense: Neural Mechanisms and Social Patterns.* Los Angeles: University of California Press.

Berson, L.E. 1966. "Case Study of a Riot: The Philadelphia Story." American Jewish Committee Pamphlet Series Number 7. New York: Institute of Human Relations Press.

Biderman, A.D. 1967. "Surveys of Population Samples for Estimating Crime Incidence." *The Annals* V. 374, pp. 16-33.

_____. 1971. "Kinostatistics for Social Indicators." *Educational Broadcasting Review* 5/5, pp. 13-19.

_____. 1973. "When Does Interpersonal Violence Become Crime? Theory and Methods for Statistical Surveys." Paper presented for a meeting on "Access to Law," Research Committee on the Sociology of Law, International Sociological Association, Guitor College, Cambridge, England.

_____ and A.J. Reiss. 1967. "On Exploring the Dark Figure of Crime." *The Annals* V. 374 pp. 1-15.

Black, D.J. 1971. "The Social Organization of Arrest." *Stanford Law Review* 23, pp. 1087-1111.

Blalock, H.M. 1960. *Social Statistics.* New York: McGraw-Hill.

Blassingame, J. 1972. *The Slave Community.* London: Oxford University Press.

Boggs, S.L. 1965. "Urban Crime Patterns." *American Sociological Review* 30, pp. 899-907.

Bohannon, P. 1969. "Cross Cultural Comparison of Aggression and Violence." In D. Mulvihill and M. Tumin, with L. Curtis, *Crimes of Violence.* Task Force Report on Individual Acts of Violence, National Commission on the Causes and Prevention of Violence. Washington, D.C.: Government Printing Office.

_____, ed. 1960. *African Homicide and Suicide.* Princeton: Princeton University Press.

Bongier, W.A. 1916. *Criminality and Economic Conditions.* Boston: Little, Brown & Co.

Bordewich, F.M. 1973. "Where Women Are an Annoyance That Disturbs the Symmetry of Life." *New York Times*, December 9, Section 10, p. 1.

Borgatta, E.F., ed. 1969. *Sociological Methodology 1969.* San Francisco: Jossey-Bass.

Brearley, H.C. 1932. *Homicide in the United States.* Chapel Hill: University of North Carolina Press.

Brown, M.J., J.W. McCulloch, and J. Hiscox. 1972. "Criminal Offenses in an

Urban Area and their Associated Social Variables." *British Journal of Criminology* 12/3, pp. 250-68.

Bullock, H. 1955. "Urban Homicide in Theory and Fact." *Journal of Criminal Law, Crime and Police Science* 45, pp. 565-75.

Burnham, D. 1973. "Black Murder Victims in the City Outnumber White Victims 8 to 1." *New York Times*, August 5, p. 1.

_____ . 1974. "Federal Surveys to Gauge Crime Levels in Big Cities." *New York Times*, January 27, p. 1.

Camp, G.M. 1967. "Bank Robbery." Unpublished Ph.D. dissertation, Yale University.

Caruso, L.J., Director, Research and Planning Division, New Orleans Police Department. 1974. Personal communication, March 22.

Cassidy, J. 1941. "Personality Study of 200 Murderers." *Journal of Criminal Psychopathology* 2, pp. 296-304.

Cavan, R.S. 1962. *Juvenile Delinquency*. Philadelphia: Lippincott.

Chappell, D., G. Geis, S. Schafer, and L. Siegel. 1972. "Forcible Rape: A Comparative Study of Offenses Known to the Police in Boston and Los Angeles." In L. Curtis *Criminal Violence: Inquiries into National Patterns and Behavior*. Ph.D. dissertation, University of Pennsylvania.

Chappell, D., G. Geis, and F. Fogarty. 1974. "Forcible Rape: Bibliography." *Journal of Criminal Law and Criminology* 65, pp. 248-63.

Chappell, D., and Singer, S. 1973. "Rape in New York City: A Study of Material in the Police Files and Its Meaning." Unpublished paper.

Clinard, M.B. 1963. *Sociology of Deviant Behavior*. Rev. Ed. New York: Holt, Rinehart and Winston.

_____ and R. Quinney. 1967. *Criminal Behavior Systems: A Typology*. New York: Holt, Rinehart and Winston.

_____ , ed. 1964. *Anomie and Deviant Behavior: A Discussion and Critique*. New York: The Free Press.

Cohen, B. 1968. "Internecine Violence: A Sociological Investigation of 199 Delinquent Gangs and Groups." Unpublished Ph.D. dissertation, University of Pennsylvania.

Cohen, J. 1941. "The Geography of Crime." *The Annals of the American Academy of Political and Social Science* 217, pp. 33-34.

Cohen, T. 1961. "Geography of Crime." In J.S. Roucek, ed., *Sociology of Crime*. New York: Philosophical Library.

Conklin, J.E. 1972. *Robbery and the Criminal Justice System*. Philadelphia: Lippincott.

Connor, W.D. 1973. "Criminal Homicide, U.S.A./U.S.S.R.: Reflections on Soviet Data in a Comparative Framework." *Journal of Criminal Law and Criminology* 64/1, pp. 111-7.

Cook, F.J. 1971. "Chance Killings, or Deeper Problem." *New York Times*, August 29.

Cottell, L. 1973. "New York Police Rape Project." Proposal submitted to the Police Foundation, Washington, D.C., February.

Csida, J.B. and J. Csida. 1974. *Rape: How to Avoid It and What to do if You Can't.* Chatsworth, California: Books for Better Living.

Curtis, L. 1971. Book Review of *The Unheavenly City*, by E.C. Banfield. *Issues in Criminology* 6, pp. 117-9.

_____. 1972. "Criminal Violence: Inquiries Into National Patterns and Behavior." Philadelphia: University of Pennsylvania Ph.D. dissertation.

_____. 1974. "Towards a Cultural Interpretation of Forcible Rape by American Blacks." Paper presented at Eighth World Sociology Congress, Toronto.

_____. 1974. "Victim Precipitation and Violent Crime." *Social Problems* 21, pp. 594-605.

DeBaun, E. 1950. "The Heist: The Theory and Practice of Armed Robbery." *Harper's* 200, pp. 69-77.

Delaney, P. 1973. "Census Millions Missed." *New York Times*, "News of the Week in Review," April 29, p. 3.

Demarest, D.P. and L.S. Lamdin, eds. 1970. *The Ghetto Reader.* New York: Random House.

Drapkin, I. and E. Viano. 1974. *Victimology.* Lexington, Mass.: Lexington Books. D.C. Heath and Company.

Driver, E. 1961. "Interaction and Criminal Homicide in India." *Social Forces* 40, pp. 153-8.

Durkheim, E. 1950. *Rules of Sociological Method.* Eighth Ed. Glencoe: The Free Press.

Einstadter, W.J. 1969. "The Social Organization of Armed Robbery." *Social Problems* 17, pp. 64-83.

Elwin, V. 1943. *Maria Murder and Suicide.* London: Oxford University Press.

Ennis, P.H. 1967. *Criminal Victimization in the United States: A Report of A National Survey.* Field Surveys II, President's Commission on Law Enforcement and Administration of Justice. Washington, D.C.: Government Printing Office.

Eralason, D.A. 1946. "The Scene of Sex Offenses," *Journal of Criminal Law and Crime* 31, pp. 339-40.

Erikson, K. 1966. *Wayward Puritans.* New York: Wiley.

Fabrikant, R. 1973. "A Location Model of Criminal Behavior." Dissertation Proposal Abstract, Department of Economics, University of California, Santa Barbara.

Falk, G.J. 1952. "The Influence of Season on the Crime Rate." *Journal of Criminal Law, Criminology and Police Science* 43, pp. 199-213.

Feder, L.H., Director, Bureau of Criminal Information, San Francisco Police Department. 1974. Personal communication, March 27.

Federal Bureau of Investigation. 1959-1974. *Crime in the United States:*

Uniform Crime Reports–1958-1973. Washington, D.C.: Government Printing Office.

———. 1965. "Profile of a Bank Robber." *FBI Law Enforcement Bulletin* 34, pp. 22-25.

Feeney, F. and A. Weir, eds. 1973. *The Prevention and Control of Robbery.* Five Vols. Davis, California: The Center on Administration of Criminal Justice, University of California.

Ferdinand, T. 1969. "Reported Index Crime Increases Between 1950 and 1965 Due to Urbanization and Changes in the Age Structure of the Population Alone." In D. Mulvihill and M. Tumin, with L. Curtis, *Crimes of Violence.* Task Force on Individual Acts of Violence, National Commission on the Causes and Prevention of Violence. Washington, D.C.: Government Printing Office.

Freed, L.F. 1973. "A Victimological Assessment of the Problem of Crime in The Republic of South Africa." Paper presented at the First International Symposium on Victimology, Jerusalem, Israel, September 2-6.

Frenkel, H. 1930. "The Murderer Who Is Not Motivated by Personal Gain." *Social Science Abstracts.* 2, p. 947.

Fry, M. 1951. *Arms of the Law.* London: Victor Gollancz.

Fyvel, T.R. 1962. *Troublemakers.* New York: Schoken Books.

Geis, G. and D. Chappell. 1971. "Forcible Rape by Multiple Offenders." *Abstracts in Criminology and Penology.* A.E. Kluwer: Deventer, Netherlands 11, pp. 431-6.

Giacinti, T.A. 1973. "Forcible Rape: The Offender and His Victim." Unpublished Masters' Thesis, Southern Illinois University.

Gibbs, J.P. and S. Labovitz. 1964. "Urbanization, Technology and the Division of Labor: Further Evidence." *Pacific Sociological Review* 7, pp. 3-9.

Gibson, E. and S. Klein. 1969. "Murder." Home Office Studies in the Causes of Delinquency and the Treatment of Offenders, No. 4. London: H.M.S.O.

———. "Murder 1957-1968." 1969. Home Office Research Studies, No. 3. London: H.M.S.O.

Gibson, W.B. 1966. *The Fine Art of Robbery.* New York: Grosett and Dunlop.

Gilles, H. 1965. "Murder in the West of Scotland." *British Journal of Psychology* 3, pp. 1089-94.

Gillin, J.L. 1946. *The Wisconsin Prisoner.* Madison: University of Wisconsin Press.

Goffman, E. 1963. *Stigma.* Englewood Cliffs, New Jersey: Prentice-Hall.

Goldner, N.S. 1972. "Rape as a Heinous but Understudied Offense." *Journal Of Criminal Law, Criminology and Police Science* 63/3, pp. 402-7.

Goode, W. 1969. "Violence Among Inmates." In D. Mulvihill and M. Tumin, with L. Curtis, *Crimes of Violence.* Task Force Report on Individual Acts of Violence, National Commission on the Causes and Prevention of Violence. Washington, D.C.: Government Printing Office.

Goodman, L.A. and W.H. Kruskal. 1954. "Measures of Association for Cross Clarifications." *Journal of the American Statistical Association* 49, pp. 732-63.

Gordon, R.A. 1967. "Issues in the Ecological Study of Delinquency." *American Sociological Review* 32, pp. 927-44.

Graham, H.D. and T.R. Gurr. 1969. *Violence in America: Historical and Comparative Perspectives.* Task Force on Historical and Comparative Perspectives, National Commission on the Causes and Prevention of Violence. Washington, D.C.: Government Printing Office.

Greene, J.E. 1948. "Motivations of a Murderer." *Journal of Abnormal Social Psychology* 43, pp. 526-31.

Greider, W. 1971. "A Long, Hot Summer: Why Was It So Cool." *Washington Post*, September 12, p. A1.

Guy, R. 1972. "Black Perspective: On Harlem's State of Mind." *New York Times Magazine*, April 10, pp. 74, 80.

Hackney, S. 1969. "Southern Violence." In H. Graham and T. Gurr, eds., *Violence in America.* Task Force on Historical and Comparative Perspectives, National Commission on the Causes and Prevention of Violence. Washington, D.C.: Government Printing Office.

Halleck, L. 1967. "Emotional Effects of Victimization." In R. Slovenko, ed., *Sexual Behavior and the Law.* Springfield: Charles C. Thomas.

Harlan, H. 1950. "Five Hundred Homicides." *Journal of Criminal Law, Criminology and Police Science* 40, pp. 736-52.

Harpold, J. 1973. "Rape in Kansas City." Kansas City Police Department, Mimeo.

Harries, K.D. 1971. "Geography of American Crime." *Journal of Geography* 70, pp. 204-13.

Hayman, C. 1971. "Comment." *Sexual Behavior* 1, p. 33.

_____ and C. Lanza. 1971. "Sexual Assaults on Women and Girls." *American Journal of Obstetrics and Gynecology* 109, pp. 480-6.

_____ et al. 1968. "Sexual Assault on Women and Children in the District of Columbia." *Public Health Reports* 83, pp. 1021-8.

_____ et al. 1971. "Rape in the District of Columbia." Paper presented to the American Public Health Association, October 12.

Hayner, N.S. 1946. "Criminogenic Zones in Mexico City." *American Sociological Review* 11, pp. 428-38.

Herron, J.C., Inspector, Computer Division, Philadelphia Police Department. 1974. Personal communication, March 29.

Hibley, R. 1973. "The Trial of a Rape Case: An Advocate's Analysis of Corroboration, Consent and Character." *The American Criminal Law Review* 11, pp. 309-34.

Hippler, E. 1970. "The Game of Black and White at Hunter's Point." *Transaction* 7, pp. 56-63.

Hoiberg, E.O. and J.S. Cloyd. 1971. "Definition and Measurement of Continuous Variation in Ecological Analysis." *American Sociological Review* 36, pp. 65-74.

Holmstrom, L. and A. Burgess. 1973. "Rape: The Victim and the Criminal Justice System." Paper presented at First International Symposium on Victimology, Jerusalem, September 2-6.

Holyst, B. 1967. *Detection of Criminal Homicides.* Warsaw: Juridical Edition.

_____. 1969. "Factors Connected with Homicides and Their Importance in Investigations." *International Criminal Police Review* 226, pp. 78-80.

Iceberg Slim. 1969. *Pimp: The Story of My Life.* Los Angeles: Holloway House.

International Business Machines Corporation. 1967. "1130 Numerical Surface Techniques and Contour Map Plotting (1130-CX-11X) Programmer's Manual." White Plains, New York: IBM Corporation.

Iowa Law Review. 1960. "Armed Robbery—Use of a Dangerous Weapon Subsequent to the Taking," pp. 151-4.

Jayewardene, C.H.S. 1960. "Criminal Homicide: A Study in Culture Conflict." Unpublished Ph.D. dissertation, University of Pennsylvania.

_____. 1964. "Criminal Homicide in Ceylon." *Probation and Child Care Journal* 3, pp. 15-30.

_____ and H. Ranasinghe. 1963. *Criminal Homicide in the Southern Province.* Colombo: The Colombo Apothecaries Company.

Jones, A. 1971. "In Roxbury You Can't Even Sit on Your Steps These Days." *Boston Globe*, September 1, p. 17.

Kifner, J. 1973. "The Boston Murders: Racial Hate or Random Slaying." *New York Times*, "News of the Week in Review," October 7, p. 2.

Labovitz, S. 1965. "Territorial Differentiation and Social Change." *Pacific Sociological Review* 8, pp. 70-75.

Ladd, F.C. 1970. "Black Youths and their Environment: Neighborhood Maps." *Environment and Behavior* 2, pp. 74-99.

Landau, S. and I. Drapkin. 1968. "Ethnic Patterns of Criminal Homicide in Israel." Mimeo, the Hebrew University of Jerusalem, Faculty of Law, Institute of Criminology.

Lander, B. 1954. *Towards an Understanding of Juvenile Delinquency.* New York: Columbia University Press.

Laubscher, J.F. 1965. "Sex in a Pagan Culture." In R. Slovenko, ed., *Sexual Behavior and the Law.* Springfield, Illinois: Charles C. Thomas.

Law Enforcement Assistance Administration. 1974. *Citizen Dispute Settlement.* Washington, D.C.: U.S. Department of Justice.

Lear, M.W. 1972. "Q. If You Rape a Woman and Steal Her TV, What Can They Get You For in New York? A. Stealing Her TV." *New York Times Sunday Magazine,* January 30.

Legal Division Bulletin. 1974. Office of the Deputy Commissioner, Legal Matters, New York City Police Department, V. 4, N. 3, 26 April.

Lemaire, L. 1946. *Legal Kastration.* Copenhagen: Munksgaard.

Levin, Y. and A. Lindesmith. 1937. "English Ecology and Criminology of the Past Century. " *Journal of Criminal Law and Criminology* 27, pp. 801-16.

LeVine, R.A. 1959. "Gusii Sex Offenses: A Study in Social Control." *American Anthropologist* 61, pp. 465-790.

Little, Arthur D. Inc. 1966. *Community Renewal Programming: A San Francisco Case Study.* New York: Praeger Special Studies in U.S. Economic and Social Development.

Lottier, S. 1938a. "Regions of Criminal Mobility: Introduction to a Detroit Study." *Journal of Criminal Law and Criminology* 28, pp. 657-73.

_____. 1938b. "Distribution of Criminal Offenses in Metropolitan Regions." *Journal of Criminal Law and Criminology* 29, pp. 37-50.

_____. 1938c. "Distributions of Criminal Offenses in Sectional Regions." *Journal of Criminal Law and Criminology* 29, pp. 329-44.

Lyman, S.M. 1970. "Red Guard on Grant Avenue." *Transaction* 7, pp. 21-34.

_____ and M.B. Scott. 1967. "Territoriality: A Neglected Sociological Dimension." *Social Problems* 15, pp. 236-49.

McClintock, F.H. 1963a. *Crimes of Violence.* London: MacMillan.

_____. 1963b. "Crimes Against Person." Manchester Statistical Society Meetings.

_____ and Gibson, E. 1961. *Robbery in London.* London: MacMillan.

MacDonald, A. 1911. "Death Penalty and Homicide." *American Journal of Sociology* 16, pp. 88-116.

MacDonald, J.M. 1961. *The Murderer and His Victim.* Springfield: Charles C. Thomas.

_____. 1971. *Rape: Offenders and Their Victims.* Springfield: Charles C. Thomas.

McKay, H.D. 1967. "A Note on Trends in Rates of Delinquency in Certain Areas in Chicago." *Task Force Report: Juvenile Delinquency and Youth Crime.* U.S. President's Commission on Law Enforcement and Administration of Justice. Washington, D.C.: Government Printing Office.

Mannheim, H. 1965. *Comparative Criminology.* New York: Houghton-Mifflin.

_____, ed. 1960. *Pioneers in Criminology.* London: Stevens and Sons.

Marat, J. et al. 1967. *Drugs in the Tenderloin.* Economic Opportunity Council Inc. of San Francisco.

Maye, J.B. 1963. "Delinquency Areas." *British Journal of Criminology* 13, pp. 216-30.

Meyer, E.L. 1974. "Rape Corroboration Held Unneeded." *The Washington Post,* January 24, p. A.1.

Morris, A. 1955. *Homicide: An Approach to the Problem of Crime.* Boston: Boston University Press.

Morris, N. and Hawkins, G. 1970. *The Honest Politician's Guide to Crime Control.* Chicago: University of Chicago Press.

Morris, T. 1957. *The Criminal Area.* London: Routledge and Kegan Paul.

_____ and L. Blom-Cooper. 1964. *A Calendar of Murder: Criminal Homicide in England Since 1957.* London: Michael Joseph.

Moses, E.R. 1947. "Differentials in Crime Rates Between Negroes and Whites, Based on Comparisons of Four Socio-Economically Related Areas." *American Sociological Review* 12, pp. 411-20.

Mulvihill, D.J. and M.M. Tumin with L.A. Curtis. 1969. *Crimes of Violence.* Task Force on Individual Acts of Violence, National Commission on the Causes and Prevention of Violence. Washington, D.C.: Government Printing Office.

Mushanga, M.T. 1970. "Criminal Homicide in Western Uganda: A Sociological Study of Violent Deaths in Ankole, Kigezi and Toro Districts of Western Uganda." Unpublished Master's Thesis, Makerere University.

National Commission on the Causes and Prevention of Violence. 1969. *Final Report: To Establish Justice, To Insure Domestic Tranquility.* Washington, D.C.: Government Printing Office.

Nelson, S. and M. Amir. 1973. "The Hitch-Hike Victim of Rape." Paper presented at First International Symposium on Victimology, Jerusalem, September 2-6.

Newton, D. and F.E. Zimring. 1969. *Firearms and Violence in American Life.* Task Force on Firearms, National Commission on the Causes and Prevention of Violence. Washington, D.C.: Government Printing Office.

Nkpa, N.K.U. 1973. "Victims of Crime in Igbo Section of Nigeria." Paper presented at the First International Symposium on Victimology, Jerusalem, Israel, September 2-6.

Normandeau, A. 1968. "Trends and Patterns in Crimes of Robbery." Unpublished Ph.D. dissertation, University of Pennsylvania.

Pacht, A.R. et al. 1962. *American Journal of Psychiatry* 118, pp. 802-8.

Palmer, S. 1960. *A Study of Murder.* New York: Thomas Crowell.

_____. 1973. "Characteristics of Homicide and Suicide Victims in 40 Non-Literate Societies." Paper presented at the First International Symposium on Victimology, Jerusalem, Israel, September 2-6.

Pecar, J. 1971. "The Role of the Victim in Homicide in Slovenia." *Review Kriminalist Kriminol* 22/4, pp. 258-65.

Peters, J. 1973. "The Philadelphia Rape Victim Study." Paper presented at First International Symposium on Victimology, Jerusalem, September 2-6.

Peterson, R., D. Pittman, and P. O'Neal. 1962. "Stabilities in Deviance: A Study of Assaultive and Non-Assaultive Offenders." *Journal of Criminal Law, Criminology and Police Science* 53, pp. 44-48.

Phillips, P.D. 1972. "A Prologue to the Geography of Crime." *Proceedings of the Association of American Geographers* 4, pp. 86-91.

Pittman, D. and W. Handy. 1964. "Patterns in Criminal Aggravated Assault." *Journal of Criminal Law, Crime and Political Science* 55, pp. 462-70.

Pokorny, A. 1965. "A Comparison of Homicides in Two Cities." *Journal of Criminal Law, Criminology and Police Science* 56, pp. 479-87.

_____ and B. Davis. 1964. "Homicide and Weather." *The American Journal of Psychiatry* 120, pp. 806-8.

Porterfield, A. and R. Talbert. 1954. *Mid-Century Crime in Our Culture.* Fort Worth: Texas Christian University Press.

Porterfield, A., R. Talbert, and H. Mundhanke. 1948. *Crime, Suicide and Social Well Being..* Fort Worth: Texas Christian University Press.

President's Commission on Crime in the District of Columbia. 1966. *Report.* Washington, D.C.: Government Printing Office.

President's Commission on Law Enforcement and Administration of Justice. 1967. *Final Report: The Challenge of Crime in a Free Society.* Washington, D.C.: Government Printing Office.

_____. 1967. *Task Force Report: Crime and Its Impact—An Assessment.* Washington, D.C.: Government Printing Office.

_____. 1967. *Task Force Report: Juvenile Delinquency and Youth Crime.* Washington, D.C.: Government Printing Office.

_____. 1967. *Task Force Report: Science and Technology.* Washington, D.C.: Government Printing Office.

Quincy, R. 1966. "Structural Characteristics, Population Areas and Crime Rates in the United States." *Journal of Criminal Law, Criminology and Police Science* 57, pp. 45-52.

Radzinowicz, L. 1945. *The Modern Approach to Criminal Law.* London: MacMillan.

_____. 1957. *Sexual Offenses.* London: MacMillan.

Rao, S.V. 1968. *Murder.* Research Division, Central Bureau of Investigation, Ministry of Home Affairs, Government of India. New Delhi: Government of India Press.

Reiss, A.J. 1966. "Place of Residence of Arrested Persons Compared with Place Where the Offense Charged in Arrest Occurred for Part I and II Offenses." Consultant's Report, President's Commission on Law Enforcement and Administration of Justice. Washington, D.C.: Government Printing Office.

_____. 1967. *Studies in Crime and Law Enforcement in Major Areas.* Field Surveys III, President's Commission on Law Enforcement and the Administration of Justice. Washington, D.C.: Government Printing Office.

Robinson, W.S. 1950. "Ecological Correlations and the Behavior of Individuals." *American Sociological Review* 40, pp. 351-7.

Rochford, R.T., Director, Research and Development Division, Chicago Police Department. 1974. Personal communication, March 19.

Rosen, L. 1970. "I Divorce Thee." *Transaction* 7, pp. 34-37.

Roy, K.K. 1973. "Feelings and Attitudes of Raped Women of Bangladesh Towards Military Personnel of Pakistan." Paper presented at the First International Symposium on Victimology, Jerusalem, Israel, September 2-6.

Royal Commission on Capital Punishment. 1953. *1949-1953 Report.* London: H.M.S.O.

Royko, M. 1971. *Boss: Richard J. Daley of Chicago.* New York: E.P. Dutton.

St. Louis Police Department. 1966. "Allocation of Patrol Manpower Resources in the St. Louis Police Department." Report conducted under OLEAA Grant #39, Washington, D.C. July.

Sawtell, R., Project Director. 1974. "Conflict Management: Analysis/Resolution." Draft report submitted by the Northeast Patrol Division Task Force, Kansas City Police Department, to the Police Foundation. Washington, D.C.

Scarf, M. 1974. "The Anatomy of Fear." *New York Times Magazine,* June 16, p. 10.

Schafer, S. 1965. "Criminal-Victim Relationships in Violent Crimes." Mimeo. Research study submitted to the Public Health Service, July.

_____. 1968. *The Victim and His Criminal.* New York: Random House.

_____ and M. Veenstra. "Changing Victims of Changing Homicide." Paper presented at the First International Symposium on Victimology, Jerusalem, Israel, September 2-6.

Scheff, T. 1967. *Being Mentally Ill.* London: Weiden and Nicholson.

Schiff, A.F. 1971. "Rape in Other Countries." *Medical Science and the Law* 11/3, pp. 139-43.

Schmid, C.F. 1937. *Social Saga of Two Cities.* Monograph, Bureau of Social Research, The Minneapolis Council of Social Agencies, Minneapolis.

_____. 1954. Manual of Graphic Presentation. New York: Ronald Press.

_____. 1960a. "Urban Crime Areas: Part I." *American Sociological Review* 25, pp. 527-42.

_____. 1960b. "Urban Crime Areas: Part II." *American Sociological Review* 25, pp. 655-78.

_____ and E.H. MacCannell. 1955. "Basic Problems, Techniques and Theory of Isopleth Mapping." *American Sociological Review* 50, pp. 220-39.

Schuessler, K. 1962. "Components of Variations in City Crime Rates." *Social Problems* 9, pp. 314-23.

Schultz, L.G. 1960a. "Interviewing the Sex Offender's Victim." *Journal of Criminal Law, Criminology and Police Science* 50, pp. 448-52.

_____. 1960b. "The Wife Assaulter." *Journal of Social Theory* 6, pp. 103-11.

_____. 1962. "Why the Negro Carries Weapons." *Journal of Criminal Law, Crime and Police Science* 53, pp. 476-83.

_____. 1969. "The Victim-Offender Relationship." *Crime and Delinquency* 14, pp. 135-41.

Seattle Law and Justice Planning Office. 1975. *Seattle Law and Justice Plan for 1975.* Seattle.

Seitz, S.T. 1972. "Firearms, Homicides and Gun Control Effectiveness." *Law and Society Review* 6/4, pp. 595-613.

Selvin, H.C. 1957. "A Critique of Tests of Significance in Survey Research." *American Sociological Review* 22, pp. 519-27.

Shah, D.K. 1971. "Women Attack Rape Justice." *National Observer* 9, October.

Shannon, L. 1954. "The Spatial Distribution of Criminal Offenses by States." *Journal of Criminal Law, Crime and Police Science* 45, pp. 264-73.

Shaw, C.R., and H.D. McKay. 1969. *Juvenile Delinquency and Urban Areas.* Chicago: University of Chicago Press.

Sherrill, R. 1973. *The Saturday Night Special.* New York: Charterhouse Books.

Shevky, E. and W. Bell. 1955. *Social Area Analysis.* Stanford: Stanford University Press.

Sills, D., ed. 1968. *International Encyclopedia of the Social Sciences.* New York: Macmillan.

Silverman, R.A. 1971. "Victims of Delinquency." Unpublished Ph.D. dissertation, University of Pennsylvania.

_____. 1973. "Victim Precipitation: An Examination of the Concept." Paper presented at the First International Symposium on Victimology, Jerusalem, Israel, September 2-6.

Simondi, M. 1970. *Dati Su Attanta Casi Di Omicidio.* Empirical Research Series No. 5. Department of Mathematics and Statistics, University of Florence, Florence, Italy.

Skolnick, J. 1966. *Justice Without Trial.* New York: Wiley.

Slovenko, R., ed. 1965. *Sexual Behavior and the Law.* Springfield: Charles C. Thomas.

Smith, D.E. et al. 1970. "The Health of Haight-Ashbury." *Transaction* 7, pp. 35-45.

Smith, L. 1963. *Killers of the Dream.* Garden City, New York: Anchor Books.

Sociological Abstracts. 1973. Supplement 38, December. Abstracts of papers presented at the First International Symposium on Victimology, Jerusalem, Israel, September 2-6.

Sornarajah, M. 1971. "The Doctrine of Continuing Provocation." *Journal of Ceylon Law* 2/1, pp. 101-17.

Strauss, J.H. and M.A. Strauss. 1953. "Suicide, Homicide and Social Structure in Ceylon." *American Journal of Sociology* 58, pp. 461-69.

Sulzberger, C.L. 1973. "Arms and the Soviet Man." *New York Times*, "News of the Week in Revieww," July 29.

Sutherland, E.H. 1937. *The Professional Thief.* Chicago: The University of Chicago Press.

_____. 1939. *Principles of Criminology.* Third Edition. Philadelphia: Lippencott.

_____. 1947. *Principles of Criminology.* Fourth Edition. Philadelphia: Lippencott.

_____ and D.R. Cressey. 1960. *Principles of Criminology.* Sixth Edition. Philadelphia: Lippencott.

Sutherland, S. and M. Scherl. 1970. "Patterns of Response Among Victims of Rape." *American Journal of Orthopsychiatry.* 40, pp. 503-11.

Svalastoga, K. 1956. "Homicide and Social Contact in Denmark." *American Journal of Sociology* 61, pp. 37-41.

_____ . 1962. "Rape and Social Structure." *Pacific Sociological Review* 5, pp. 48-53.

Tamotsu, S. 1955. "Reference Groups as Perspectives." *American Journal of Sociology* 60, pp. 562-69.

Tardiff, G. 1966. "La Criminalite De Violence." Unpublished Master's Thesis, University of Montreal.

Thomas, W.I. and F. Znaniecki. 1927. *The Polish Peasant in Europe and America.* 2 Vols. New York: Alfred A. Knopf.

Tiffany, L., D. McIntyre, and D. Rotenberg. 1967. *Detection of Crime.* Boston: Little, Brown & Co.

Time Magazine. 1973. "The Rape Wave." January 29, p. 59.

_____ . 1974. "Revolt Against Rape." July 22, p. 85.

Ting, S.K. and K.K. Tan. "Post-Mortem Survey of Homicides in Singapore (1955-1964)." *Singapore Medical Journal* 10.

Turner, S. 1969. "The Ecology of Delinquency." In T. Sellin and M. Wolfgang, eds., *Selected Studies in Delinquency.* New York: John Wiley and Sons.

Tyron, R.C. 1968. *Identification of Social Areas by Cluster Analysis.* Berkeley: University of California Press.

U.S. Department of Commerce, Bureau of the Census. 1966. *Current Population Reports*, Series P-23, No. 19, "Characteristics of Families Residing in 'Poverty Areas,' March 1966." Washington, D.C.: Government Printing Office.

_____ . 1972. *General Social and Economic Characteristics: United States Summary*, 1970 Census of Population, PC (11)-C1. Washington, D.C.: Government Printing Office.

U.S. Department of Justice, Law Enforcement Assistance Administration, National Criminal Justice Information and Statistics Service. 1974a. "Crime in the Nation's Five Largest Cities." Advance Report. Washington, D.C.: Government Printing Office.

_____ . 1974b. *Preliminary Report of the Impact Cities Survey Results*, draft.

U.S. Department of Labor, Bureau of Labor Statistics, and U.S. Department of Commerce, Bureau of the Census. 1970. *Social and Economic Statistics of Negroes in the United States.* Washington, D.C.: Government Printing Office.

Van Bemmelen, J.M. 1960. "Data on Sexual Delinquency in the Netherlands." In M. Grunhut, et al., eds., *Sexual Crime Today: A Symposium.* The Hague, Netherlands: The University of Leiden.

Verkko, V. 1951. *Homicides and Suicides in Finland and Their Dependence on National Character.* Copenhagen: G.E.C. Gad's Forlag.

Von Hentig, H. 1940. "Remarks on the Interaction of Perpetrator and Victim." *Journal of Criminal Law and Criminology* 31, pp. 303-9.

_____ . 1948. *The Criminal and His Victim.* New Haven: Yale University Press.

Voss, H.L. and J.R. Hepburn. 1968. "Patterns in Criminal Homicide in Chicago." *Journal of Criminal Law, Criminology and Police Science* 59, pp. 449-508.

Washington Post. 1968. "A Survey of Weapons and Gun Control." June 23, pp. 7, 24.

_____ . 1973. "Black Attacks Flare in Boston." October 5, p. 8.

West, D.J. 1968. "A Note on Murders in Manhattan." *Medicine, Science and the Law* 8, pp. 249-55.

White, C.R. 1932. "The Relation of Felonies to Environmental Factors in Indianapolis." *Social Forces* 10, pp. 498-509.

Wilcox, S. 1973. "The Geography of Robbery." In F. Feeney and A. Weir, eds., *The Prevention and Control of Robbery*, Vol. 3. The Center on Administration of Criminal Justice, U. of Calif., Davis.

Wilks, J.A. 1967. "Ecological Correlates of Crime and Delinquency." *Task Force Report: Crime and Its Impact—An Assessment.* U.S. President's Commission on Law Enforcement and Administration of Justice. Washington, D.C.: U.S. Government Printing Office.

Williams, O. 1962. "Some Reflections on Robbery In London." *Criminal Law Review*, pp. 6-11.

Wilson, J.V., Chief of Police, Washington, D.C. 1974. Personal communication, March 28.

Wilt, G. and J. Bannon. 1974. "A Comprehensive Analysis of Conflict Motivated Homicides and Assaults—Detroit 1972-1973." Final Report. Washington, D.C.: The Police Foundation, May.

Wolfgang, M.E. 1958. *Patterns in Criminal Homicide.* Philadelphia: University of Pennsylvania Press.

_____ .1959. "Suicide By Means of Victim Precipitated Homicide." *Quarterly Review of Psychiatry and Neurology* 20, pp. 335-49.

_____ . "Uniform Crime Reports: A Critical Appraisal." *University of Pennsylvania Law Review* 111, pp. 708-37.

_____ . "Youth and Violence." 1969a. Report submitted to the Office of Juvenile Delinquency and Youth Development, Department of Health, Education and Welfare, January.

_____ . 1969b. "Who Kills Whom." *Psychology Today* 3, pp. 7-9.

_____ and B. Cohen. 1970. *Crime and Race: Conceptions and Misconceptions.* New York: The American Jewish Committee.

_____ and Ferracuti, F. 1967. *The Subculture of Violence.* London: Social Science Paperbacks.

_____ , R. Figlio, and T. Sellin. 1972. *Delinquency in a Birth Cohort.* Chicago: University of Chicago Press.

_____ , ed. 1966. *Patterns of Violence, The Annals of the American Academy of Political and Social Science*, March.

_____ , ed. 1967. *Studies in Homicide.* New York: Harper and Row.

Wood, P.L. 1973. "The Victim in a Forcible Rape Case: A Feminist's View." *The American Criminal Law Review* 11, pp. 335-54.

Yen, C. 1929. *A Study of Crime in Peiping.* Peiping (Peking), China: Yenching University, Department of Sociology and Social Work, Series C, No. 20, December.

Zimring, F.E. 1968. "Is Gun Control Likely to Reduce Violent Killings?" *University of Chicago Law Review* 35, pp. 721-37.

_____. 1972. "The Medium is the Message: Firearm Caliber as a Determinant of Death from Assault." *Journal of Legal Studies* 1/1, pp. 97-123.

_____ and G. Hawkins. 1973. *Deterrence.* Chicago: University of Chicago Press.

Indexes

Index of Names

Index of Subjects

About the Author

Lynn A. Curtis is Research Associate at the Bureau of Social Science Research in Washington, D.C. and Director of the National Alternative Inner City Futures Project, a Delphi study concerned with domestic policy priorities and conflict resolution. He is also on a Police Foundation-financed study of rape victims and the police in New York City. Author of *Violence, Race and Culture*, the companion volume to this book, and coauthor of the *Crimes of Violence* Task Force Report of the National Commission on the Causes and Prevention of Violence, Dr. Curtis has most recently published in *Social Problems, Contemporary Sociology, The International Review of Criminal Policy*, and *Issues in Criminology*. He received the A.B. from Harvard University, the M.Sc. from the University of London, and the Ph.D. from the University of Pennsylvania in 1972.